Gandhāran School of Buddhist Paintings

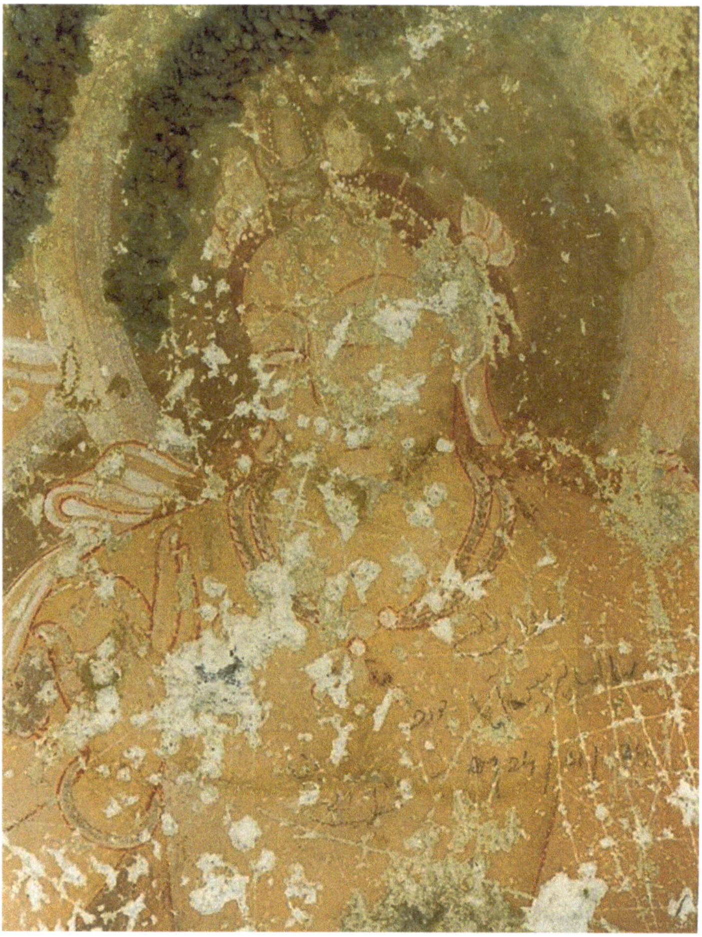

M. Nasim Khan

Gandhāran School of Buddhist Paintings

商務印書館
创于1897 The Commercial Press

Springer

M. Nasim Khan
World Arthistory Institute (WAI) at
Shanghai International Studies University
Shanghai, China

ISBN 978-981-96-9309-2 ISBN 978-981-96-9310-8 (eBook)
https://doi.org/10.1007/978-981-96-9310-8

Jointly published with The Commercial Press, Ltd.
The printed edition is not for sale in China Mainland. Customers from China Mainland please order the print book from The Commercial Press, Ltd.
ISBN of the Co-Publisher's edition: 978-7-100-25487-8

This Springer imprint is published by the registered company Springer Nature Singapore Pte Ltd.
The registered company address is: 152 Beach Road, #21-01/04 Gateway East, Singapore 189721, Singapore

Preface

In recent decades, archaeological discoveries in the Gandhāra region have multiplied, leading to increasingly refined studies of Gandhāran Buddhism—including its art, history and broader cultural significance. Among these developments, the study of Buddhist paintings has attracted particular attention, especially following the remarkable discovery of rock shelter paintings at *Paṭvano Gaṭai*. These findings have prompted scholars to acknowledge wall painting as a major medium of Gandhāran Buddhist art, standing alongside other artistic forms as a vital means of conveying the spiritual expressions and devotional sentiments of both the general populace and dedicated Buddhists.

Since then, the subject has generated substantial scholarly interest, inspiring the publication of this book, which compiles the most recent discoveries of Gandhāran paintings. Given these new findings, researchers must now revisit and reassess earlier interpretations, as updated studies may offer fresh perspectives on the broader landscape of Gandhāran Buddhist art.

This work not only revisits the paintings examined in previous research—such as those published by the author in 2000 under the title *Buddhist Paintings in Gandhāra*—but also incorporates new discoveries that deepen our understanding of this artistic tradition. Expanding beyond frescoes, the monograph includes a diverse array of painted images and inscriptions found in rock shelters, as well as on domestic and ritual objects.

Crucially, the inscriptions accompanying some of these paintings—particularly the frescoes—now provide valuable insights into the chronology of the *Gandhāran School of Buddhist Paintings*. Additionally, variations in style, colour palettes and motifs raise important questions: Was this school influenced by other contemporary painting traditions, or did it develop independently within Gandhāra? The latter possibility aligns with the region's broader artistic heritage, where a synthesis of diverse cultures—evident in Gandhāra's sculpted and moulded Buddhist art—may have similarly shaped its painted works.

Shanghai, China M. Nasim Khan

Acknowledgements

I extend my deepest gratitude to the Directorate of Archaeology and Museums, Government of Khyber Pakhtunkhwa, for granting me access to study the museum objects. I am also grateful for the Directorate's financial support, which enabled me to conduct excavations at Aziz Ḍheri during 2007–2008, where we uncovered remarkable frescoes. This support further allowed me to study antiquities previously discovered at Aziz Ḍheri and to physically examine the Yaktoot frescoes held in the Directorate's collection. My special thanks go to the late Saleh Muhammad Khan, former Director General of Archaeology, Government of Khyber Pakhtunkhwa, for his invaluable support and guidance. I would also like to thank the excavation team of the Abba Shai Cheena Buddhist site for generously sharing their experiences with me. Their insights proved invaluable to my research, particularly regarding the fresco discoveries. Subsequently, I visited the site to personally assess the significance and preservation status of these frescoes.

The other institution that assisted me in gathering data for this book was the Federal Department of Archaeology, to which I am equally indebted for providing me with photographs and other relevant information about its significant discoveries in the field of Buddhist wall paintings from Taxila. In particular, I am grateful to Dr. Fazal Dad Kakar, former Director General of Archaeology, and Dr. Abdul Ghafoor Lone, Director of the Islamabad Museum. Their collective support and generosity have been instrumental in advancing my research.

Finally, the vibrant academic atmosphere and collegial environment at Shanghai International Studies University (SISU) provided the ideal conditions for completing this book. As a token of my appreciation, I extend my deepest gratitude to my colleagues at the World Arthistory Institute (WAI), especially to Professor LaoZhu (ZHU Qingsheng), for their support and enthusiastic encouragement—both for this project and my forthcoming publications.

Contents

Chapter 1
History of Art in Pakistan

The landscape of Pakistan is formed of high mountains with cavernous and deep gorges, profound valleys, vast arid terrain and a very fertile land which the mighty Indus with its tributaries irrigate and the river is used to generate energy for the country as well (Fig. 1.1). Lying in a temperate zone, the climate of the country is as varied as its topography. Strategically, Pakistan is located at the crossroads of Asia bordered by China to the north, India to the east, and Iran and Afghanistan to the west. Apart from its sea routes used for global trade, the southern seaports are also the main trade route to the locked countries in Central Asia. The Karakorum Highway connects Pakistan to China via Gilgit-Baltistan located in northern Pakistan. Through these routes foreign invaders have come to settle while some continue on their way but have prompted the natives of the land not only to absorb and assimilate foreign cultural elements but these roads also exude wisdom for thousands of years from and to the outside world. Evidence of such cultural exchange can be found in the archaeology and art of Pakistan which has spread over the centuries.

The history of Pakistan spans over thousands of years and is traditionally divided into three main periods: prehistoric, proto-historic and historic era. The prehistoric culture is mainly known by the discovery of stone tools in the Soan Valley and the famous cave of Sanghao, the latter located in Gandhāra (Fig. 1.2). However, the Neolithic phase, which made a valuable contribution to agriculture and animal domestication, is confirmed by the evidence recovered from the site of Mehrgarh, in Baluchistan Province, and is dated to 8215 BC to 2500 BC. The proto-historic phase of Pakistan's history goes through different revolutionary stages of development such as the beginning of agriculture and settled human societies started in the early 9th millennium BC to 4th millennium BC. Therefore, the beginning of the proto-history or the urban phase of Pakistan dates back to the 2nd half of the 4th millennium BC and gives rise to the famous Indus Valley Civilization. After the fall of this great Civilization by, perhaps, the hands of the Aryan invasion in the fifteenth century BC, the post-urban phase remained limited to regional cultures and the history stayed shrouded until Gandhāra became one of the satrapies of the Achaemenid Empire

M. Nasim Khan, *Gandhāran School of Buddhist Paintings*,
https://doi.org/10.1007/978-981-96-9310-8_1

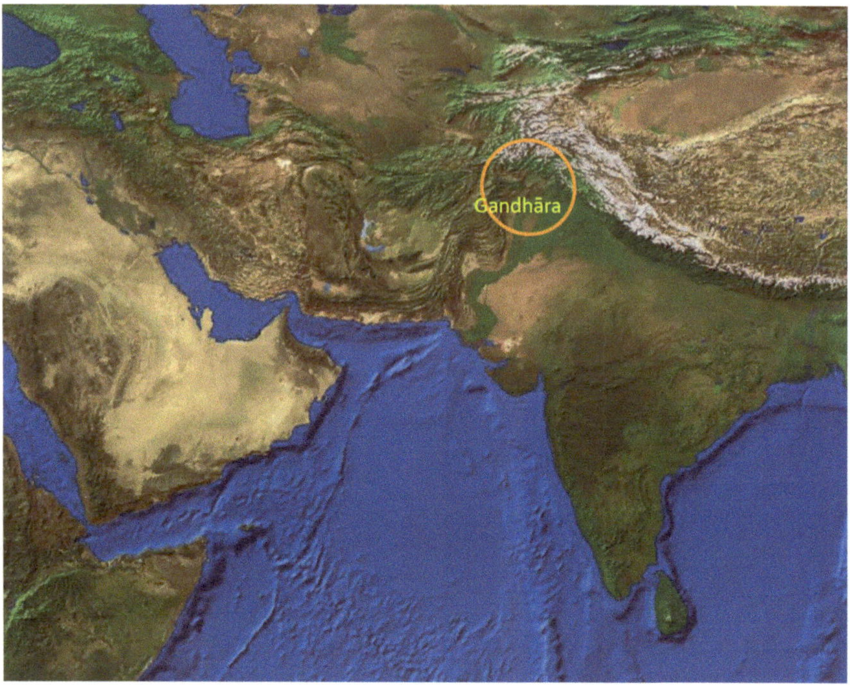

Fig. 1.1 Map showing geographical position of Gandhāra

in the sixth century BC. Even though some of region's ancient history is pieced together primarily from literary testimony, its history is largely based on archaeological evidence which are the form of inscriptions, coins, monuments and visual art, etc.

The history of Art in Pakistan goes back to the prehistoric era when men started to express their feelings and expression in visual form through their creative skill and imagination, executed initially inside rock shelters or on surface of rocks. The travel of this art continues with technical mastery and proficiency, the beauty, the emotional powers or with the divers' conceptual ideas. In its long journey from the distant past to the present, different forms of the art have developed with borrowed ideas making them more aesthetic but at the same complex.

These multifaceted visuals are to be classified under different periods—considering their age and into different mediums and techniques, pondering on their physical and religious environment. Generally, the ancient and medieval period art in Pakistan can be divided into two main groups: rock art (engravings or paintings) and sculpted or moulded art. The rock art chiselled or carved out covers a wide range of time period starting from the prehistoric time to till date. while the latter one probably started in the Neolithic period and can later be seen in the form of contemporary art.

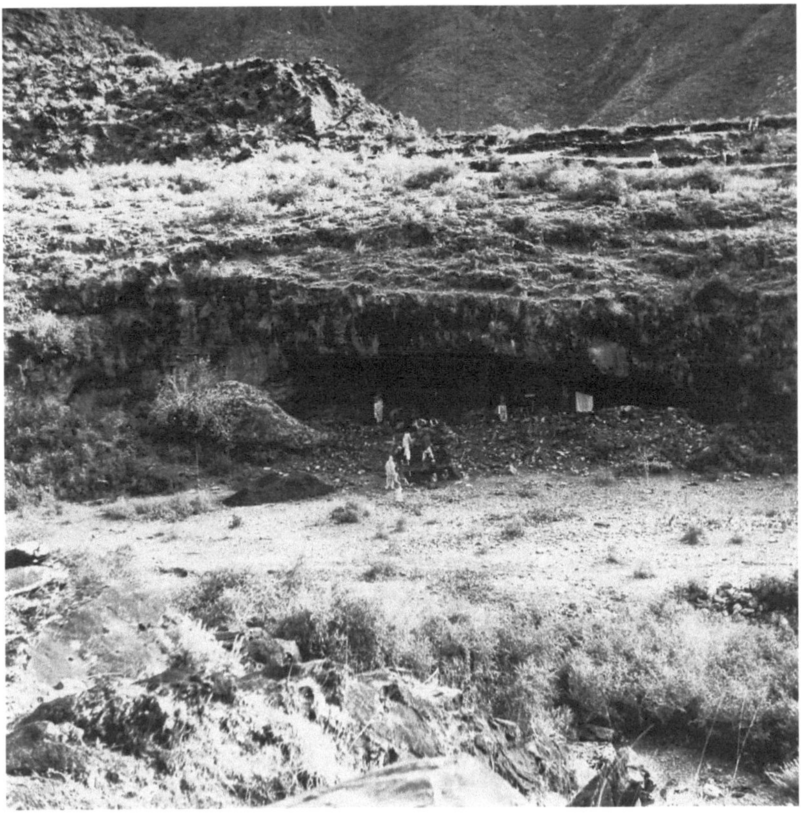

Fig. 1.2 Sanghao Cave, Mardan (Photo Sabir 1963)

The political, cultural and religious dynamics in the development of this art has been playing a significant role and on the basis of this can further be classified into different groups. With the introduction of agriculture activities in the region, the ancient art of Pakistan has been shaped into moulding techniques. TC figurines were first introduced about 7000 BC discovered in the site of Mehrgarh in Baluchistan, southwest region of Pakistan. Superb TC figurines, and some other daily used objects—painted with images (e.g. Figs. 1.3 and 1.4) and ornament—have been discovered in large number (see, e.g., Durrani 1988; Flavin et al. 1994–95) some of which are presently in the zenith of different museums in Pakistan and abroad.

Besides paintings on ceramics, cast art has continued, covering ancient periods of human evolution at least from the Neolithic period to the period of the Indus Valley Civilization. The Priest King of Mohenjo-Daro (Fig. 1.5) and the Dancer of Harappa (Fig. 1.6) are good examples of early sculptural art in Pakistan. While the earliest possible literary reference to carved art at Gandhāra comes from Rigveda, which, while referring to the original inhabitants of Dasyus—who in the later period

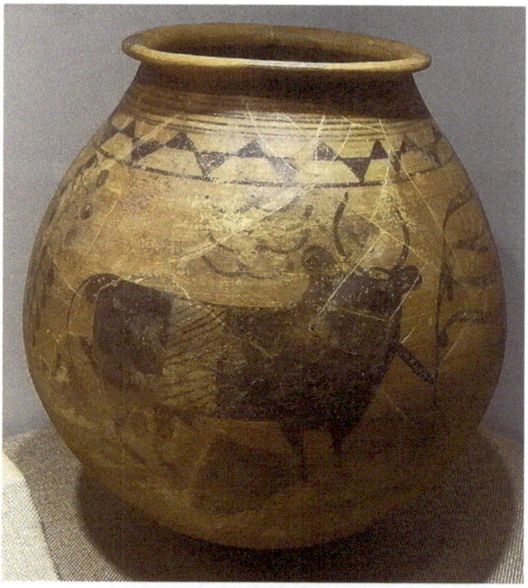

Fig. 1.3 Clay pot painted with humped bull (2700–1800 BCE) (Islamabad Museum)

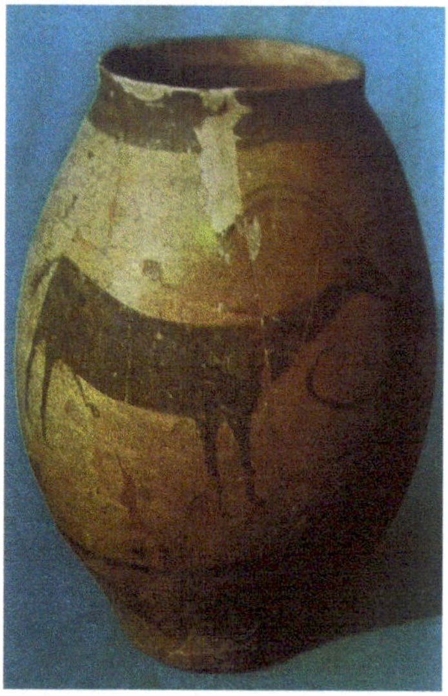

Fig. 1.4 Clay pot painted with animal figures. From Amri site in Sind Province

became the fourth caste as the Sudra, described them as worshipers of the phallus (MacDonnell 1909: 153).

Likewise, from the time between Mehrgarh to the Indus Valley (2500 BC), the art of painting on cast or moulded objects has continued. At the same time, if not earlier, figurative designs, painted and engraved, began to appear and these images

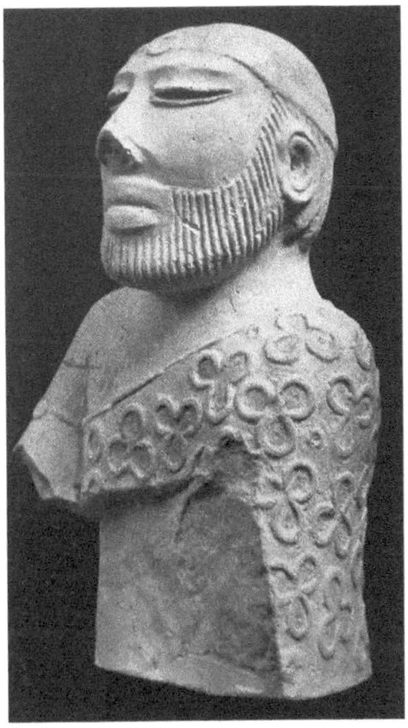

Fig. 1.5 King priest from Mohenjo-Daro (Wheeler 1960: Pl. XVI)

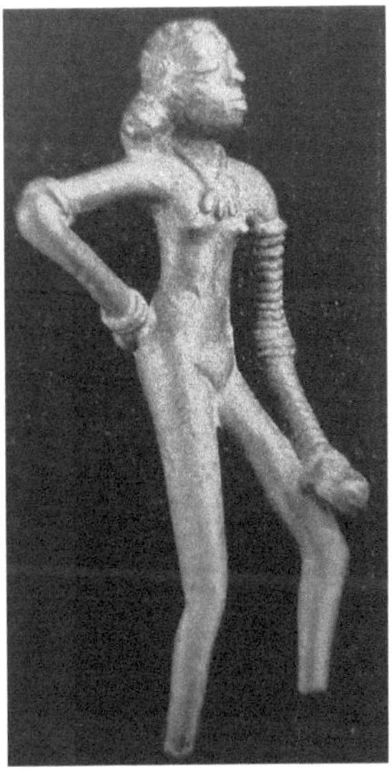

Fig. 1.6 Female figure in bronze from Harappa (Wheeler 1960: Pl. XVII.B)

were depicted on the surface of rock in open spaces (Fig. 1.7) or inside caves and rock shelters such as at Kashmir Smast (Fig. 1.8).[1]

The art of body decoration, Nepathyaprayoga in Sanskrit, is manifold and has been an important subject of art since the birth of man. To look more attractive and different from others, several methods and elements have been used by both men and women. Body decoration can be with elegant dress, flower crowns, cosmetics,

[1] Due to fire soot the paintings are damaged and are hardly visible.

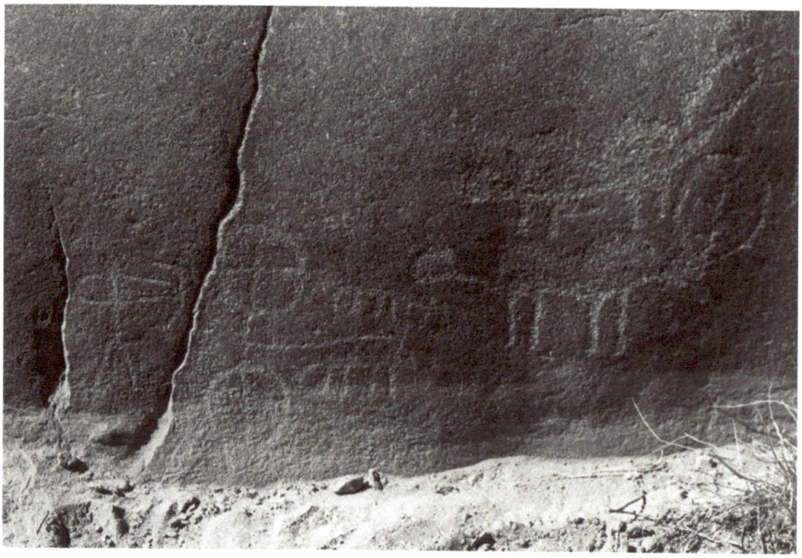

Fig. 1.7 Chariot and bulls, Khalaṭ Das (Thor North) rock carvings site, Upper Indus Valley (Nasim Khan 1995, volume 2, Figs. 100, 140)

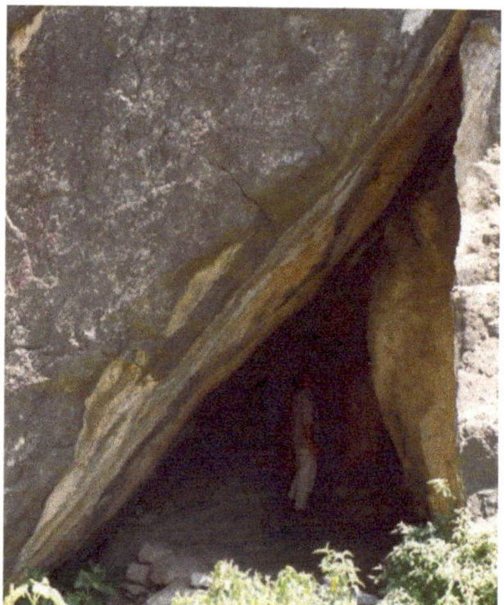

Fig. 1.8 Rock shelter at Bare Ubah, Kashmir Smast

perfumes, ornaments, paintings, etc., with many different and varied appearances. To adorn a body with ornaments and paintings and to know the art of decoration and ornamentation, this theme still remains one of the most fascinating and important research subjects in the study of ancient art. Archaeological evidence suggests that this art began at least during the Neolithic period (see above), however, literary evidence for the antiquity of the art of body decoration are few. One among the earliest of these texts would be the Natyashastra, a Sanskrit treatise on performing art composed earlier or during the first century BC/first century AD).[2] The Citrasutra of Vișhṇudharmottara Purāṇa, dated around sixth century AD, which has also received much attention from art historians, is also one of the most important ancient literary testimonies on body decoration, in particularly make-up, where its part 3 deals with the known branches, theories, methods, practices and ideals of Indian painting and deals with both its religious aspects and its secular application. Other important ancient texts that refer to body decoration, mainly with jewelleries, are the Indian epic, the Mahābhārata—written over the years from 1st to 10th AD. The epic is a very rich source of cultural material and sometimes speaks of the ornamental habits of ancient peoples. According to the Mahābhārata, gold chains and necklaces were worn by both men and women. The most complex of them was composed of gold flowers and gold lotuses. The gold collars were specially designed for elephants and horses. For the elephant, there was another thick gold chain called *graiveya*. While *mekhala* or *kañci* were worn exclusively by women—both were worn by women of the courtesan class or by *Apsaras*. Its use was typical in the female representation of the Indus Civilization until the Gupta period.

Panini in his Aṣṭādhyāyī, treatise on Sanskrit grammar, used the terms *graivaka, kancanmala, candrahāra, pralambhāra* for neck ornaments.[3] In the Jātakas, in the wonderful story of Vīśākhā, we find the description of her most valuable wedding present given by her rich father. It was an ornament when which, worn from head to toe, gave the appearance of a dancing peacock and which five hundred goldsmiths took several months to complete. Similarly, the Kautilya Arthashastra mentioned a number of neck ornaments such as *sirsaka, prakandaka* and *yaṣṭi*. The Arthasāstra gives more details about gold and goldsmiths in ancient India. Some of the gems and colours mentioned in earlier literatures are also attested by the carved, moulded and rock art of the region.

Rock Art: Even though the existence of rock art in Pakistan has a long history, research in this field is generally a recent phenomenon. The four most important regions known for rock art discoveries are the hilly areas of Karakorum-Hindu Kush in the north and northwest, Koh-e-Suleiman in the south and southwest, the Sindh plains, some carvings in the province of Punjab and evidently the region of Gandhāra. The history of this art apparently continues from prehistoric times to the present day and can be classified into two main categories: rock engravings and rock paintings. Rock carvings are executed on the surface of rocks and cliffs and are mostly found in the open, as is usually the case in the upper Indus Valley. They are normally made

[2] For use of colours in the Nāṭyaśāstra, see Kintaert (2005).

[3] Aṣṭādhyāyī of Pāṇini: IV.3.6.

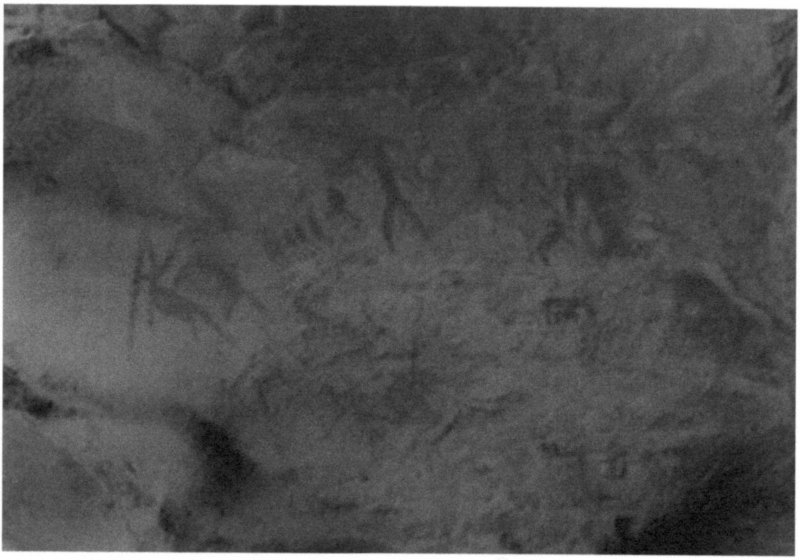

Fig. 1.9 From Musa Khel, Baluchistan (Courtesy F.D. Kakar; Kakar 2003)

with engraving, chiselling, picking and rubbing techniques using tools most likely made from stones and other sharp and strong mediums like metals. On the other hand, cave paintings are done inside rock shelters to protect them from rain due to their fragile nature and are mainly of two types, rock shelter graffiti and shelter frescoes under rock. The earliest among the cave paintings probably come from caves in the province of Baluchistan.

Baluchistan: In the southern part of the mountainous region of Suleiman range, about twenty rock shelters with paintings have been discovered in 1995–96 (Kakar 2000: 9; 2005: 22). The shelters are located 42 kms from Musa Khel, the nearest town to the sites. The total number of paintings recorded in these shelters is about 175. They are mostly human and animal figures shown in solid (e.g. Figs. 1.9 and 1.10); the animals are made with bi-triangular technique, a method well attested in the rock carvings in Gandhāra and in its adjoining areas of the Upper Indus Valley (Fig. 1.11). They are painted red, black, etc. The twenty-seven rock shelters with paintings as well as engravings were found on the northern portion of the Suleiman Range, particularly at Khostti, Lakha, Band, Dhana, Abdullahzai, etc. They are paintings mostly of human and animals, like horses, leopards, wild boar, ibex, humped bulls, etc.

Search for rock shelter sites continued in the area by others who also got involved in studying this and several other rock painting sites in the region like the Malavi Cave and the Tharia cave paintings in Pabu Mountain near Qili (village) Chatoka Bhit (mound) in the Valley of Pallimas, Tehsil Wadh, Khuzdar district (see Kingrani, date ?). These graffiti mainly depict human figures (Fig. 1.12) and animals such as wolves, horses and bulls (Fig. 1.13), etc. Humped bulls in this form are also attested in the Lower Dir areas in the Gandhāra region (Fig. 1.14). The human figures from

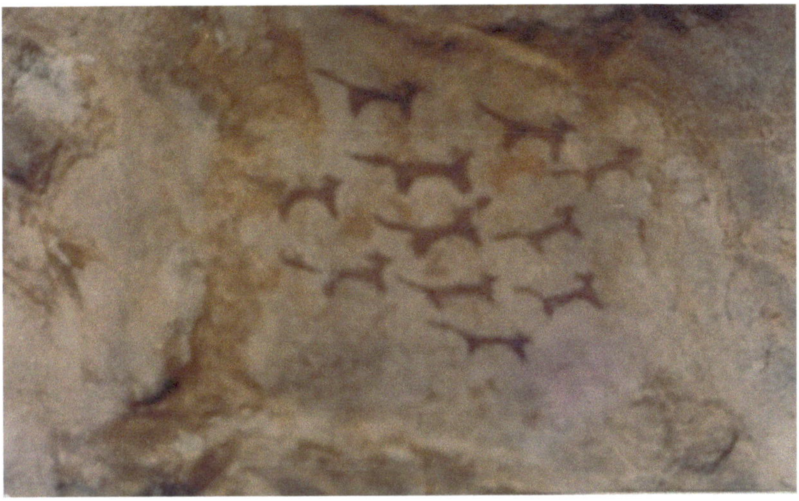

Fig. 1.10 From Musa Khel, Baluchistan (Courtesy F.D. Kakar; Kakar 2003)

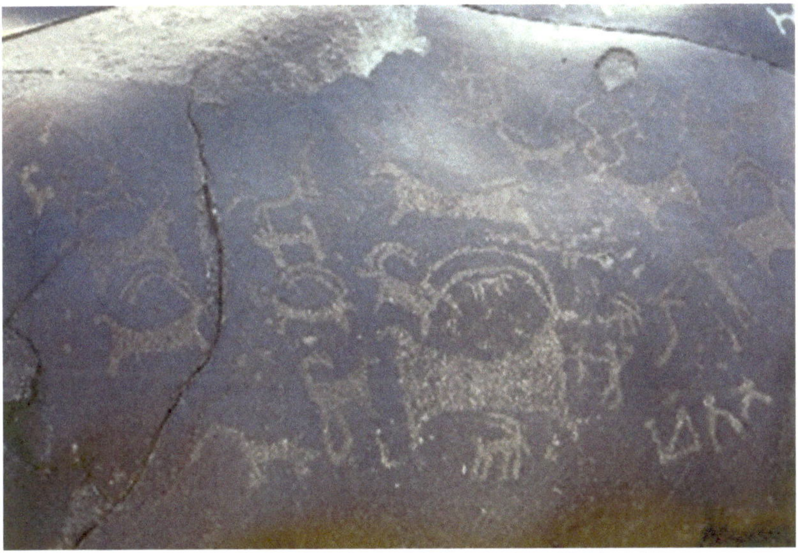

Fig. 1.11 From Khalat Das (Thor North), Upper Indus Valley (Nasim Khan 1995, volume II: Fig. 249)

Baluchistan are shown in dancing postures; the dancers hold each other's hands and form a line or circle, most probably a kind of folk dance which reminds me the group of rock paintings in Mapungubwe, Africa. The heads of the figures are very strange; possibly wearing a kind of headdress. The figures are mostly painted in brown or can be red, black and yellow. The chemical analysis will indicate the materials and their

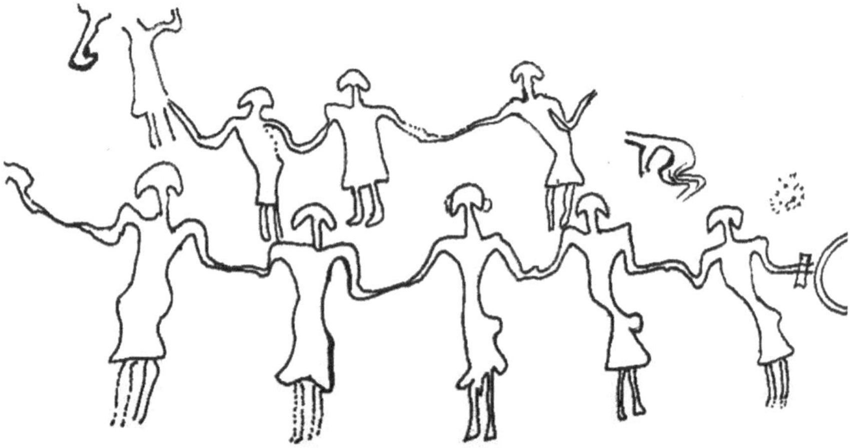

Fig. 1.12 Dancing scene; drawing of paintings found in Baluchistan

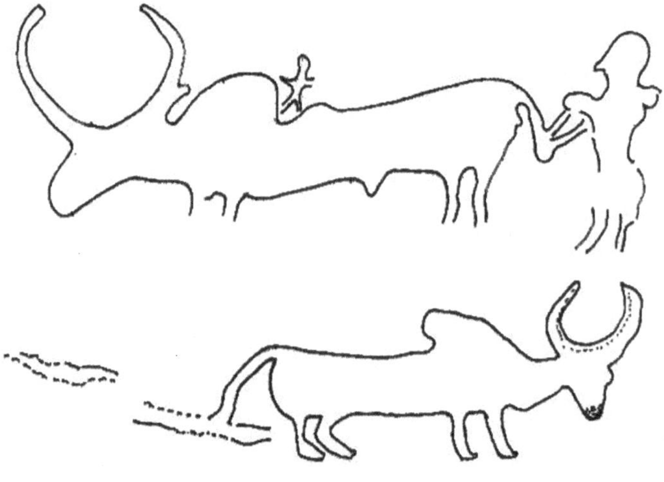

Fig. 1.13 Drawing of humped bulls in Tharia cave, Baluchistan

composition as well as determine the approximate date of the paintings. However, to my knowledge and based on circumstantial evidence, the dates of these paintings vary and the oldest of them could belong to the Neolithic period.

Sind: Cave paintings have been found at the Lahaut Rock Shelter in the Meher Valley, located 60 kms north of Karachi in the province of Sindh, but they may belong to the historic period or could also modern. The paintings are mainly human figures and geometric patterns and are presented in black, red and orange (Kalhoro 2014).

Punjab: Rock carvings/paintings are also reported at Rabwah, Cheniot, located on the right bank of Chenab River, Punjab. The significance of these rock carvings is

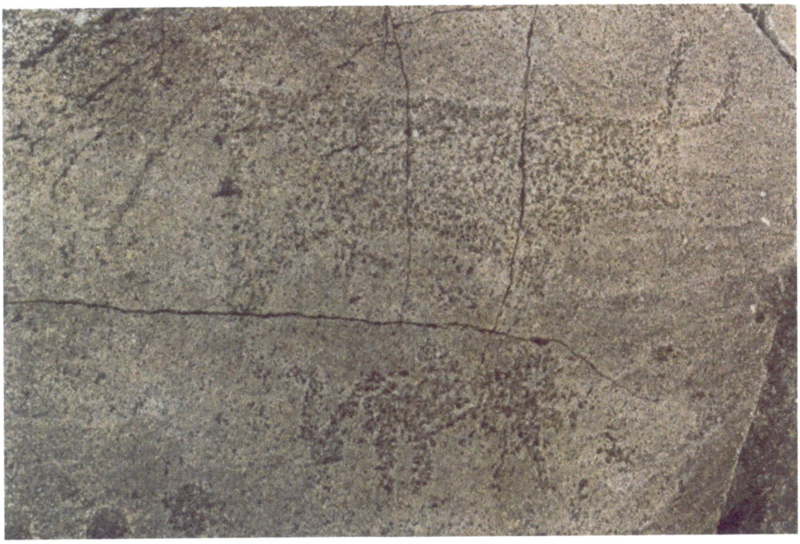

Fig. 1.14 Rock depicted with humped bulls. Talāsh, Lower Dir—Gandhāra

that some of them, carved inside a shelter, which were originally contour cut, were later made into paintings by tracing the carved contour with light brown colour. It is also possible that the addition of paint was a later work of the natives who might have scoffed at the carvings. Although the Rabwah carvings were mostly consisted of humans and animals, a drawing of a boat was also carved, and then painted, on the rock surface. It is said that the majority of the engravings area is currently being destroyed and crushed down by contractors from the Department of Mines and Minerals. The vestiges which are still there are in danger because the local people use the stone from the mountains for building roads, etc., and it is not far from the fact that in the near future nothing will be left of the carvings.

Northern Areas: The most impressive of the rock art galleries is located in the Upper Indus Valley in Pakistan. With the discovery of these rock carvings in this region, the study of rock painting in the region has also attracted the attention of scholars from national and international bodies engaged in archaeological research in the Upper Indus Valley, Northern Areas of Pakistan. Baltistan, rich in other archaeological heritages, has also produced some good specimens of Buddhist paintings. The most important are those found a few kilometres upstream from Khaplu, Ganche district, on the right bank of the Shayok River. Here, impressive Buddha images as well as numerous stūpa designs are painted in red and black on the rock surfaces.

Other significant paintings discovered in Baltistan and the Astor Valley are depictions of bodhisattvas, stūpas and other figures related to the Buddhist faith. The most important of these are those coming from Mehdi Abad, as the small village approached through the Humayun Bridge near the confluence of the Indus-Shayok River. The village is located about ten kilometres south of the bridge. The bodhisattva figure appears to be first sketched and painted red, then engraved with a pointed instrument. Another important place in the region where paintings are available is Shigar, located about 35 kms north of Skardu on the main Skardu-Ashkole road, which then leads to the famous Baltoro Glaciers and Mount K2. About two kilometres from Shigar, there are images of three Buddhas and Bodhisattvas.

But, the most significant paintings found in the Baltistan region are the Chaghdo Buddhist paintings (Figs. 1.15a and b). The site is located about 20 kms east of Skardu, on the Skardu-Khaplu road, on the right bank of the Indus, near the village called Nor or Nar village of Shigar. They were first discovered and drawn by Mr. Muhibuddin the then photographer of the Gilgit Sub-Regional Office of the Directorate of Archaeology and Museums Government of Pakistan. The paintings cover an area of $3 \times 5 \times 2$ meters and are sheltered by a small ledge. They are made on a rough surface of a rock which is cracked, broken and damaged at several places. Due to flaking from the surface, part of some of the drawings are missing. Most of the images are faded and some of them are difficult to read with the naked eye; the rest is faint but readable. The images are painted in dark red, used for line art, and red for dresses. This group of paintings is composed of three stūpas visited and worshiped by different standing and kneeling male and female (?) figures. The stūpas are added with ribbons and bells and the human figures carry different offerings in their hands such as flowers, banners,[4] lamps. Two of the figures are depicted with a halo behind their heads. Pūrṇa-ghaṭa/s and flora are visible all around. The royal or noble costumes worn by the human figures and the standing horses, each one depicted with an impressive saddle and seat, suggest that the set of figures may represent a group of royals or a royal procession visiting the sacred site. From the style and on the basis of comparison with the engravings of the region, the Chaghdo paintings appear to be of a very late date. Similar images, like the Shigar paintings, are artistically drawn on the varnished rock surfaces found in the Gilgit and Chilas regions. These engraved images are normally accompanied by Brāhmī inscriptions dated to the fourth–tenth centuries AD and based on stylistic similarity between the stūpas of both these region, the Chaghdo paintings could be of the same date or slightly of later period.

Gandhāra: During the historic period of Gandhāra, the paintings are also found in the Buddhist establishments and the paint is either applied to the images or shown in murals representing different themes from the life of the Buddha or they represent other Buddhist themes. They are made with the help of both fine and thick brushes or are rarely resulted from splashing or sprinkling painting technique which is seldomly used in the paintings on the surface of a rock.

Apart from the research on paintings presented here, the exploration in the area continues by different national and international institutions and there is a great hope for some further important discoveries in the context of the Buddhist art and archaeology in Gandhara. However, the data in hand so far available from different regions of Pakistan is enough to study the evolution of rock paintings in Pakistan. While the Buddhist rock paintings would no doubt reveal the prevalence, popularity

[4] This could also be a heraldic flag or pennon.

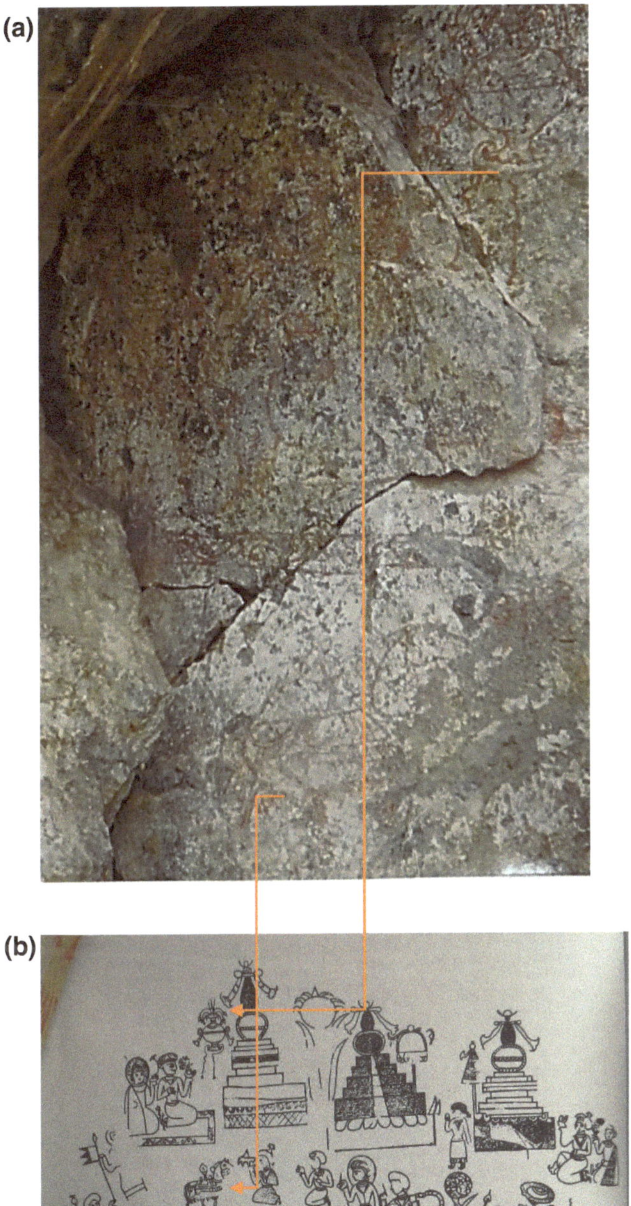

Fig. 1.15 (**a**) Buddhist rock paintings at Chaghdo, Baltistan. (**b**) stūpa worship, 7/8th century AD (After Nazir Khan)

and worship of Buddhist faith in Gandhāra and in other parts of the Northern Region of Pakistan.

Chapter 2
Gandhāra, Buddhism and the Buddhist Art

Gandhāra

The ancient geography of Gandhāra (Fig. 2.1) had different manifestations, such as political, cultural and religious, and is often discussed by scholars in their own contexts, like history, religions, art and architecture, numismatics, epigraphy, etc. Therefore, there is no need to repeat the same and to discuss the history of Gandhāra which has already been, to date, elaborated by others in the light of whatever evidence available to them. To know the extent of the work of those scholars, it suffices to read the voluminous bibliography in the different published works available on the history and archaeology of this region. However, before discussing the Buddhist paintings so far discovered in Gandhāra, for those unfamiliar with Gandhāra region, an overview or the few notes included here may be helpful in getting to know the history of this area.

Although fragile, sources for reconstructing the ancient history of Gandhāra are still various and numerous. The most important of them are the local traditions, the writings of foreign travellers and historians, and a number of archaeological evidence. The indigenous traditions are mostly recorded in native literatures, like Vedas, Upaniṣads, Sanskrit epics, Jātakas, Pāli chronicles, etc. While the writings of foreign travellers and historians mainly consist of Persian, Greek and Roman historians or envoys records, there are aslo important records from Chinese travellers such as Faxian, Sung Yun and Xuanzang (Fig. 2.2). Other significant accounts include that of the Korean Hue Chao who travelled to Gandhāra to find the truth, and the Turkish Ou-K'ong who referred to Gandhāra as "the eastern capital of Ki-pin". Gandhāra became known to the Muslim historians mainly until the region was conquered by Mahmud of Ghazni in 1021 AD. Apart from these literary records, archaeological data is the other most essential evidence that helps to reconstruct the history of the region, the nation and the power that ruled over Gandhāra.

These earlier records ultimately show the importance of Gandhāra and explain that the area was then the centre of life and home to the ancient world. All through

M. Nasim Khan, *Gandhāran School of Buddhist Paintings*,
https://doi.org/10.1007/978-981-96-9310-8_2

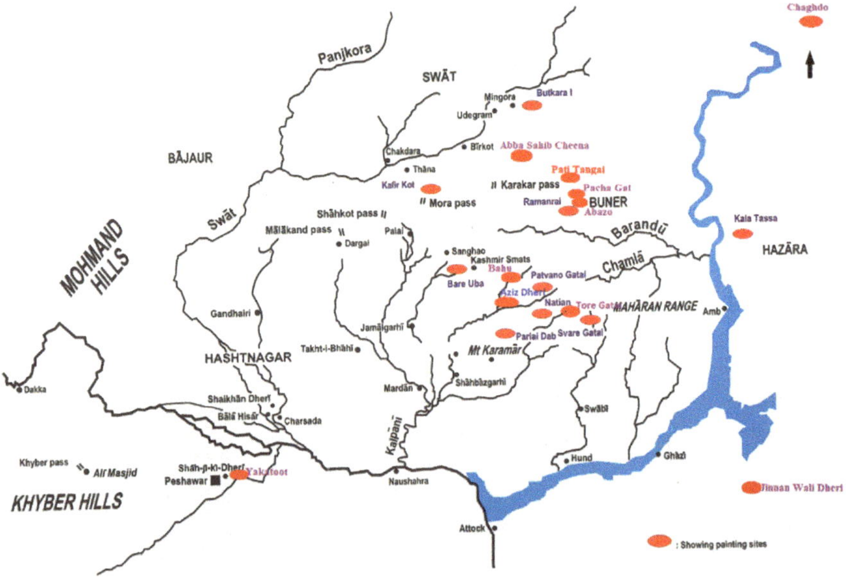

Fig. 2.1 Location map of sites containing ancient paintings. The red dots represent the approximate location of the sites. Map is not to the scale

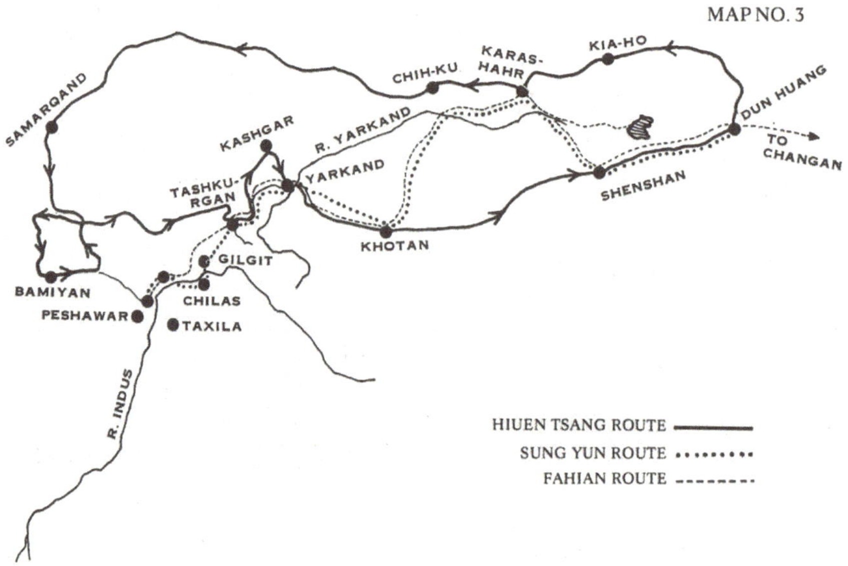

Fig. 2.2 Map showing Chinese travellers' itineraries through Gandhara (After Dani 1983)

theses centuries, the political borders have changed due to transitions to changes in the political landscape of the region. During its period of history, Gandhāra has seen many ups and downs and in this process of evolution and formation this region has never remained with a fixed geographical boundary in the world of the past as it has become somehow since the era of the British Indian Empire.

To define Gandhāra, modern historians has coined different appellations such as Gandhāra, Gandhāra region and Greater Gandhāra and delineate its borders in their own different ways. Ingholt explains Gandhāra as the area which includes the Valley of Peshawar, Swat, Buner and Bajaur (Ingholt 1957: 13), while Paul Williams extended the boundaries of Gandhāra region to Afghanistan and Kashmir (Paul Williams 1989/2009: Chapter 6, note 3). Other scholars prefer to use "Greater Gandhāra" like Salomon who, besides Gandhāra proper, also includes several neighbouring regions, especially Swat and other river valleys to the north, the region around the large city of Taxila to the east and the eastern edge of Afghanistan to the west (Solomon 1996: 3). But this term was first coined by Fussman when he used the term "le grand Gandhāra" for this region (Fussman 1994: 33). However, the first reference to the designation of "Greater Gandhara" or "Mahagandhāra" may come from Rockhill description, "Then all the Bhikshus started out for **Mahagandhāra** in the west, and it being then a time of war and trouble, the Bhiksus of India also started for Gandhāra, so that down to the Ganges there was an end of following the Dharma" (Rockhill 1884: 243–244). Nonetheless, for the purpose of this study, Gandhāra includes the areas which mainly cover Peshawar Valley, Bajaur, Dir and Swat regions, Taxila Valley and its surrounding territory.[1]

Buddhism in Gandhāra[2]

Apart from its strategic and political importance, Gandhāra is also known through its Buddhist heritage sites and the role this region has played in the development of different Buddhist sects and their expansion to the outside world. The introduction of Buddhism to Gandhāra was not an abrupt phenomenon nor perhaps a miraculous emergence, but its advent must surely have passed through different evolutionary stages like any other religion in the world before supplanting and becoming establish its roots for all the right reasons to imagine.[3]

Prince Siddhārtha—the source of Buddhism, born in Lumbini, Nepal in the middle of the first millennium BC—abandoned secular life to wander as a mendicant in search of the truth of life and suffering. After various attempts and sufferings, he attained the state of enlightenment and spent the rest of his life teaching the four noble truths of Buddhism. These noble truths which are the basic doctrines of early Buddhism are: (1) the existence of sufferings (*duhkha*), (2), suffering springs from

[1] See also Nasim Khan (2024).

[2] On more detail, see Nasim Khan (2024).

[3] For an important study on the beginning of Buddhism in Gandhāra, see Fussman (1994).

desires (*tṛṣṇa*), (3) when there is no desire, suffering ceases (*nirvāṇa*) and (4) the absence of desire is obtained by means of the Eightfold Path which are right views, right intention, right speech, right action, right livelihood, right efforts, right mindfulness and right concentration. Therefore, Buddhism is a path of practice and spiritual development that leads to insight into the true nature of reality. Two main schools of Buddhism grew out of these basic teachings of the Buddha: Theravada (the teachings of the elders) or Hīnayāna (the lesser vehicle) and Mahāyāna (the great vehicle). From the place of its birth where Buddhism emerged, it later spread to other countries in the region and became one of the main religions in some of these countries such as Gandhāra in the past.

Buddhism may have reached Gandhāra by the time of Aśoka in the third century BC, if not earlier. Aśoka's inscriptions at Shahbazgarhi (Fig. 2.3) and Mansehra and the Aramaic version of Asoka's rock edict at Taxila Museum are the earliest epigraphic evidence that can be linked to the Buddhist chronicles to date. Besides this, among the dozens of Buddhist establishments discovered in Gandhāra, some of them could also belong to the Maurya period (Fig. 2.4). Contemporary archaeological evidence and Chinese pilgrim accounts of the later period also refer to some of these monuments and associate them with Emperor Aśoka. However, after the disintegration of the powerful reign of Aśoka, the grandson of Chandragupta Maurya, Gandhāra, being part of the Maurya Empire, fell under the hands of the Greek domination which ruled over this region for about one hundred years. Regardless of the negative impact of this domination of the Greeks on the local Indian cultures, Buddhism received the support of the Greeks as evidenced by the Milindapanha, a Buddhist text which records a dialogue between the Indian Buddhist sage, Nagasena, and the Indo-Greek. King Menander, who reigns over Gandhāra in about the 150 BC.

The different ancient inscriptions, mostly in Kharoṣṭhī script, found in Gandhāra and belonging to the Indo-Greeks also suggest their support for Buddhism. The oldest among these known inscriptions is the Bajaur relic casket of Menander,[4] dated to the second century BC (Fig. 2.5; see Fussman 1989: 446, § 9.2.11). With the invasion of nomads from Central Asia through Bajaur (see Nasim Khan 2023) and other northern and north-western tracks, Gandhāra remained to enjoy the more splendid way of life, and Buddhism attained further favour and became a relatively more patronized religion. The several epigraphs written in the Kharoṣṭhī scripts refer to the establishment of numerous Buddhist establishments in the region. Buddhist texts began to appear and be composed in the form of the Kharoṣṭhī manuscripts discovered in Greater Gandhāra (Fig. 2.6; Nasim Khan 2009; Solomon 1996) which open a new window and a another horizon to the form and study of Buddhism practices in Gandhāra. Gandhāra became known not only for its fabulous Buddhist

[4] The relic casket is associated with Shinkot which is wrongly located and is placed in the Bajaur area though Shinkot is situated in the Jandul Valley, in the Lower Dir district. The actual pronunciation of the name of the place is Shahikot.

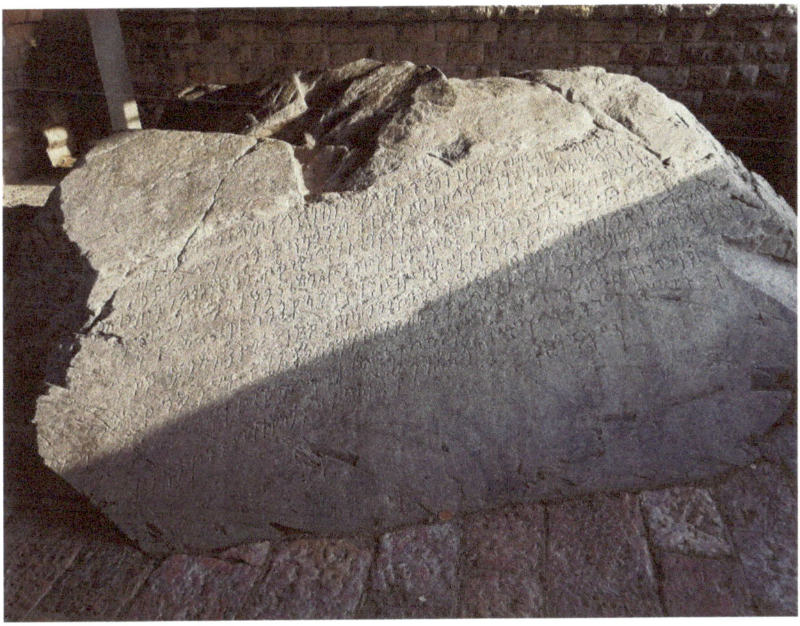

Fig. 2.3 Aśokan Rock Edicts at Shahbaz Gaṛhi

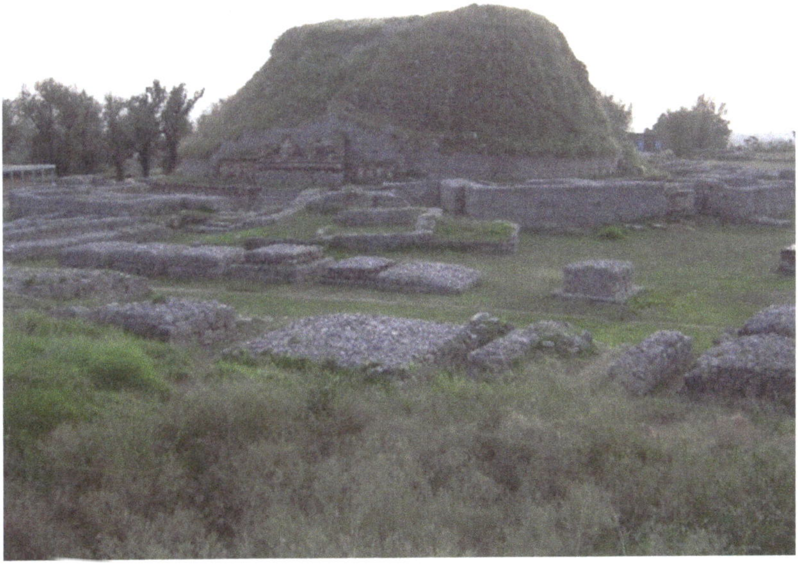

Fig. 2.4 Dharmarājika stūpa at Taxila

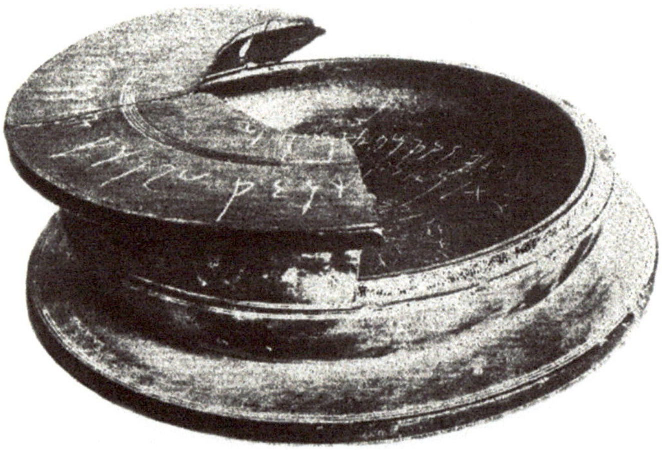

Fig. 2.5 Menander Relic Casket from Shahikot, Jandul Valley, Lower Dir

Fig. 2.6 Kharoṣṭhī manuscript from Greater Gandhāra, Probably from Jalalabad, Afghanistan. Text praising Buddha (Nasim Khan 2008: Fragment 5, pages 31–33)

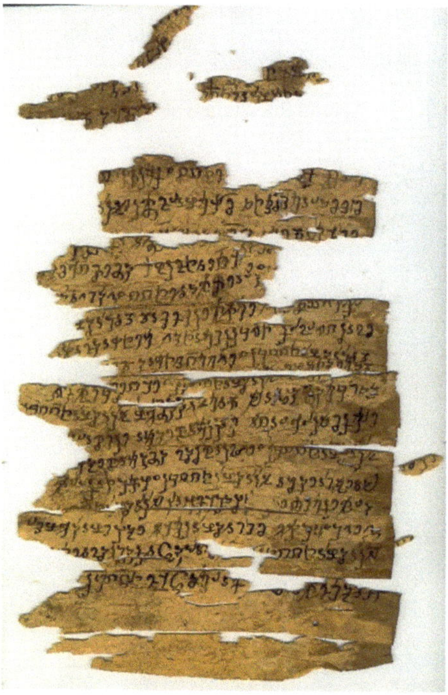

art (see infra), but this region also produced the first ever recorded documents of Mahāyāna Buddhism (Nasim Khan 2009).[5]

[5] These documents were first noticed and discovered by the author in 1996.

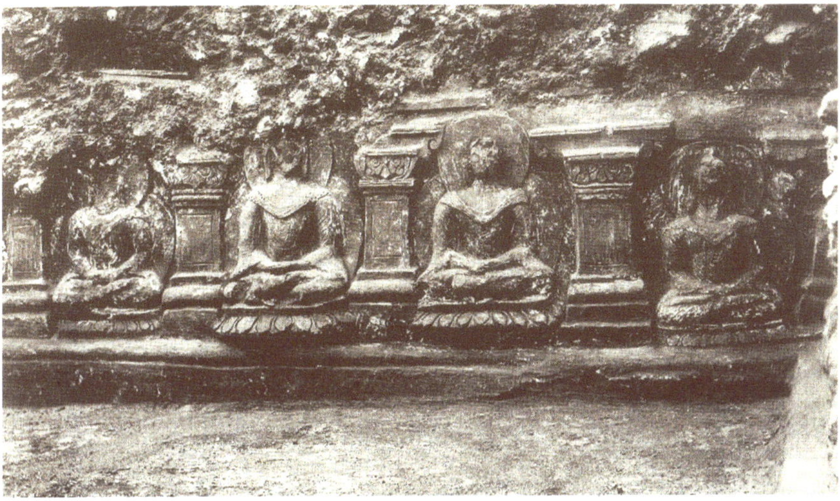

Fig. 2.7 Shahji ki Dheri stūpa (Peshawar). One of its walls shows seated Buddha figures wearing Chinese style upper garment

The Kuṣān period, especially during the reign of Kaniṣka—started in the first AD—is considered the golden age of Buddhism in Gandhāra. It was during Kaniṣka's time that the fourth Buddhist council was held in Kashmir under his patronage to systematize the texts of Sarvastivadin Abhidharma. Both literary and archaeological evidence indicates that throughout Gandhāra and beyond, a number of stūpas were built during the Kuṣān period (see, e.g., Fig. 2.7). Moreover, ancient inscriptions, found by the hundreds, and the numismatic evidence equally confirm Kuṣān's inclination towards Buddhism, as Kaniṣka coins also depict the image of the Buddha (Figs. 2.8 and 2.9) as well as other local and foreign deities. During this period, Gandhāra art has reached to its peak and different mediums were used to display and to propagate through its art style in Central Asia and China.

But the sanctity and expansion of Buddhism in Gandhāra began to shrink with the gradual decline of the Kuṣān Empire which started to fragment into semi-independent kingdoms in the third century AD when Gandhāra fell to the Sassanids and with the establishment of the Kuṣāno-Sassanian kingdom in the region. This was the period of great turbulence when the later Kuṣān and the Kuṣāno-Sassanian starting to overlap on each other that naturally disturbed and reshuffled the political boundaries inside Gandhāra. The amount of colossal sculptures and images of Buddha and bodhisattvas produced in the early Kuṣān period began to dwindle and the aesthetic sculptural beauty was lost to the coarse carvings (e.g. Fig. 2.10),[6] but, on the other hand, the moulding art has reached to its perfection (Fig. 2.11), and the beauty of the Gandhāran

[6] But it does not mean that the large-sized images of the Buddha or relief panels have ceased to exist. They were generally replaced with small-sized images as for the convenience of resources of the followers of Buddhism, due to individualism and may also be because of the loss of their faith and interest.

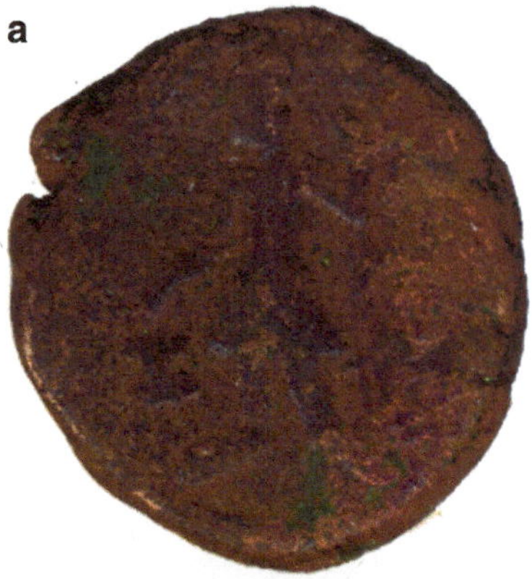

Fig. 2.8 **a** Kaniṣka coin obverse depicted with Kaniṣka figure (Nasim Khan 2007). **b** Kaniṣka coin reverse depicted with a Buddha figure

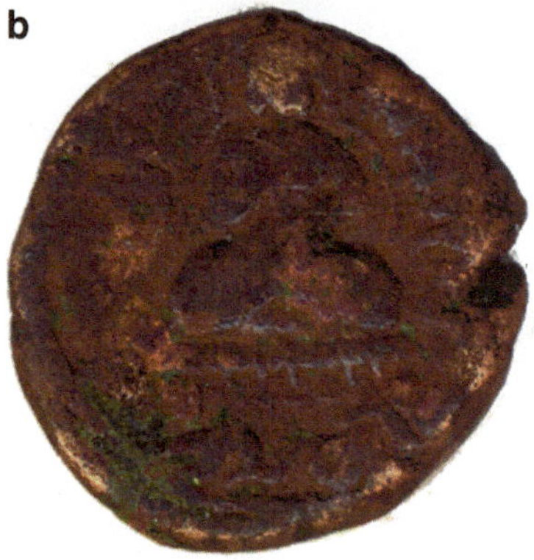

Fig. 2.8 (continued)

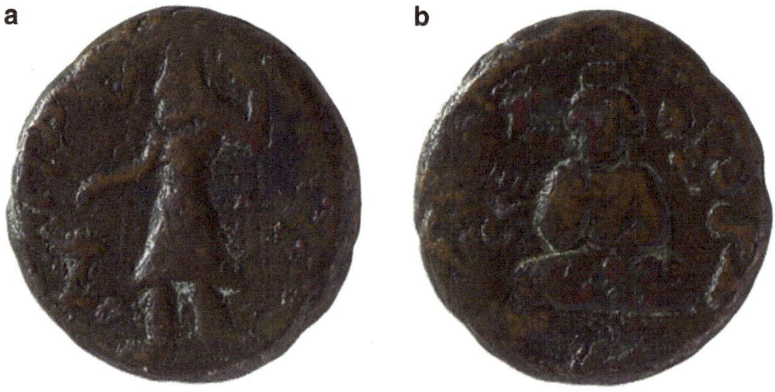

Figs. 2.9 (**a**) and (**b**) Kaniṣka Buddha coins (© BM, London)

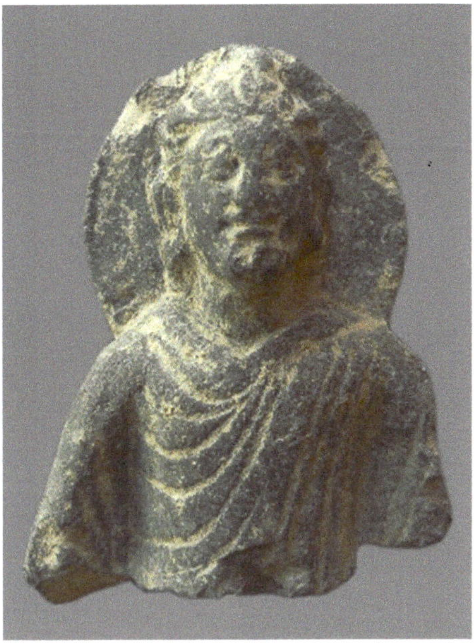

Fig. 2.10 Image measuring 7.1 × 5.23.2 cm (Nasim Khan 2010, Cat. No. 84)

Buddhist frescoes appeared and became part of the Buddhist settlements and the isolated hermits. This is a period when a shift from scholasticism to lowbrowism can be seen in the Buddhist art of Gandhāra. Despite this period of change in behaviour and the continuous change and political upsets in Gandhāra, the already established sacred sites continued to exist and be venerated and were appended by artistic and architectural development even during the occupation of Gandhāra by the Huns in the fourth/fifth century AD.

Although perhaps not on a large scale, epigraphic, numismatic and other evidence suggests that even the Huns also played their little part in the establishment or revamping of some of the Buddhist sites in Gandhāra. During this period, new Buddhist establishments were erected as well as a new form of architecture and art developed, which can be seen in the form of miniature stūpas and small-sized sculptures (Fig. 2.10).[7] But by the late fifth and early sixth centuries AD patronage of Buddhist monuments and Buddhist literature had begun to decline in the Peshawar and Taxila valleys, although in Swat and its adjacent Buner and Dir valleys, Buddhism continued to survive due to their geographical conditions and positions. The Buddhist site of Shnaisha (Fig. 2.12) and other sites in Swat are some of the good examples where one can observe the evidences of the last phase of Buddhism in Gandhāra. Swat also became a cradle of Vajrayana Buddhism which probably lasted until the tenth century AD (Fig. 2.13) when it was ruled by Hindus or went into its natural death and with the arrival of Muslims in the area.

[7] Such small stūpas were most probably used for individual worship (see Nasim Khan 2024).

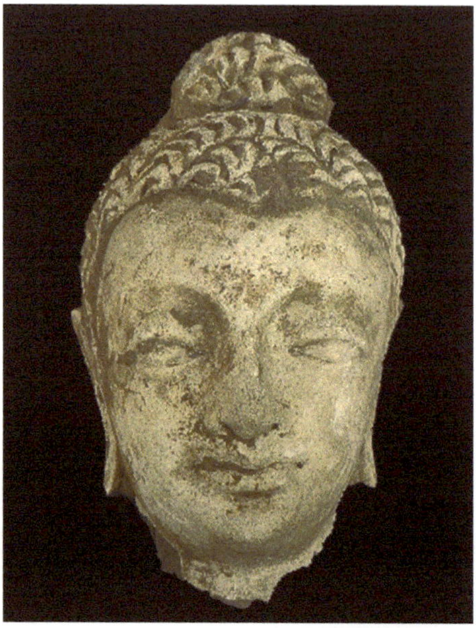

Fig. 2.11 Buddha head in Stucco (Nasim Khan 2010, Cat. No. 237)

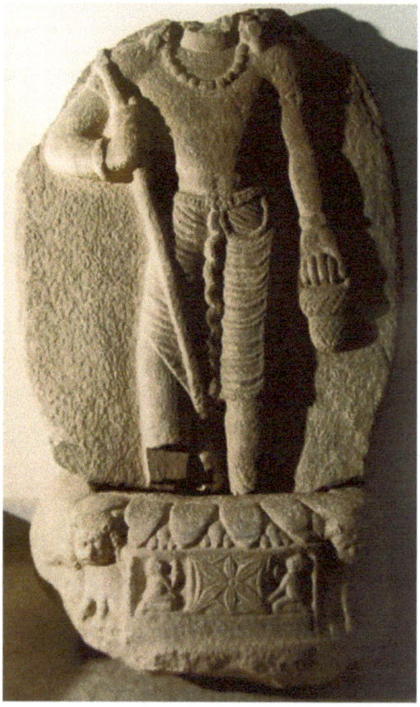

Fig. 2.12 Late Buddhist period sculpture from Shnaisha site in Swat (SSAQ Museum). Probable date fourth–sixth century AD

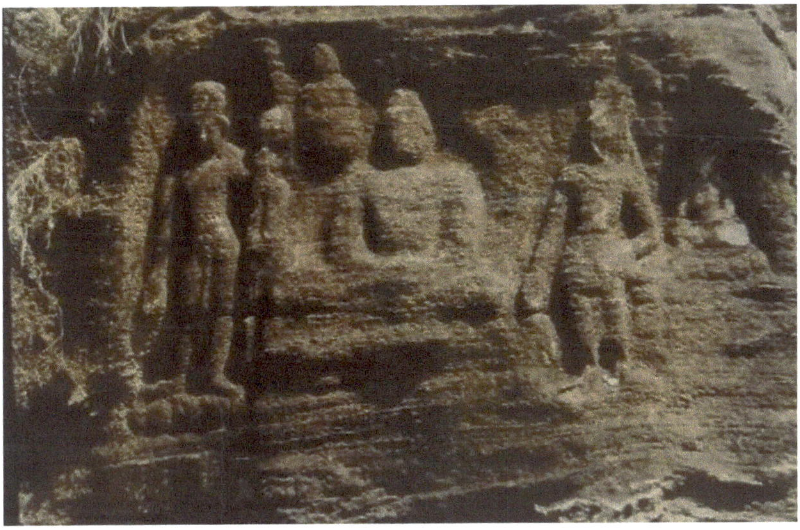

Fig. 2.13 Late Buddhist carvings at Manai Tangai, Lower Dir. Probable date sixth–tenth century AD

Gandhāran Buddhist Paintings

Gandhāra was a land where people from different walks of life met, clashed and integrated to create something new, adopt permanent life values and solid achievements. People from the West, Central, Asia, Far East and Southeast Asia came here and found a place of welcome in Gandhāra. The two oldest universities of the world, Taxila and Kashmir Smast, have opened their doors to the seekers of truth, knowledge and salvation and Hindu monasticism. They have grown weary on the way to find monastic calm for healthy discussions, to exchange ideas and to rekindle their own light, to spread and advance the message of love, knowledge, science and politics, and the hope of showing a better life for all kinds. Gandhāra, the land of Bodhisattvas, became a holy place for the followers of Buddhism, Hinduism, etc., and this land has since become known with the great Gandhāra civilization that has emerged.

Buddhism spread throughout the Indo-Pak subcontinent and from Gandhāra towards Central Asia, China and other countries of the Far East Asia. With the development of Hinduism and with the introduction of Buddhism in Gandhāra, Gandhāra art developed with a cultural syncretism. Buddhism became the most popular religion in Gandhāra and received a great royal patronage of the ruling dynasties at the time (see above).

As a result of the foreign invasions and the interactions that took place between Gandhāra and the surrounding regions, the normal process of giving and receiving also occurred in the natural process of doing. In this cultural reciprocity, Gandhāra acquired and adopted significant foreign elements which led to the creation and design of some local norms. Other forms of writing like Kharoṣṭhī and Kohī were invented, new monetary systems were developed and the science of art, immaculate local art and architecture, was shaped with new horizons. As a result of this mixing of cultures, the Buddhist art emerged in the region and within this broad spectrum of science, Gandhāra art also developed and is initially referred to as "Gandhāra Greco-Buddhist art". In this art, Buddhism and its chronicles are perfectly reflected through the ages, from its beginnings to its decline, and displayed in all sorts of mediums, from stone carvings to stucco castings and linear paintings on simple rock surfaces to advanced frescoes. This art is, therefore, important for its visual representations of the various Buddhist themes and depictions Buddha's life.

The Buddhist communities of ancient Gandhāra made good use of the region's landscape which includes both hilly and low-lying areas. Monasteries were built on the peaks, on the slopes and at the foot of the mountains as well as inside the narrow valleys and open alluvial plains. Not only could the choice of such places have been as random as is believed on earth, but also the selection of such places was certainly based on their concern for environmental changes, religious needs, and behavioural requirements. The beauty of the landscapes and the loneliness or isolation of the calms, where to establish a monastery, were not their only concerns, but the Buddhists also took into account the state of security of the time as well as the social and religious behaviour of the Buddha disciples, and so an area was then chosen to be the perfect location for their religious architectural landscape.

The two main types of environments selected for Buddhist practices in Gandhāra, where evidence is recorded, are in the form of built structures—used on a large scale, and rock shelters. In the first group of premises, hundreds of them have already been listed, and dozens of them have so far been excavated since the beginning of the nineteenth century. On the contrary, no attention has so far been given to the natural premises which Buddhists used as part of a monastic complex or were also used for secluded worship or by the wandering Buddhists.

The diverse topography of Gandhāra has provided a sensational environment for believers of different religions who have generally used all kinds of environments that can suit their needs and according to their religious beliefs. Like other topographical features, the rock caves and rock shelters scattered in the hills of Gandhāra region also helped to satisfy believers in their religious practices, as did Kashmir Smast for Hindus and Rani Gat for Buddhists. The three main rock shelters with well-defined Buddhist elements are the Kala Tassa in the Mansehra region, the Abazo rock shelter in the Buner district and the Paṭvano Gaṭai in the Swabi region. The latter shows frescoes while the others are painted with linear or brush paints directly applied to the rough surface of the ceilings of the shelters. Built architectures like Aziz Ḍheri monastery in the Peshawar Valley, But Kara I and Abba Sahib Cheena in Swat and Jinnan Wali Ḍheri monastery in Taxila were also provided with frescoes. Besides, shrines and sculptures were gold washed and painted to show utmost affiliation of their users to the Buddhist faith.

Chapter 3
Paintings in Rock Shelters

The Gandhāra region is rich in rock carving and painting sites and is mainly found in the hilly areas located in the Peshawar Valley which is bounded by hills on all sides. The hills located to the north and northeast are Sakra, Rama, Karamar and Ambela and Buner. Several rock shelters, some with paintings, are found at the foot and on the slopes of the hills which separate Buner district from Mardan and Swabi districts. These paintings include both simple line drawings and frescoes as well as inscriptions written in both Kharoṣṭhī and Brāhmī; the latter can help situate these paintings in a certain period. Though it is not the purpose here to discuss all of them in the current context, however some of them are included here for comparative study, such as the rock shelter sites of Naṭian, Tore Gate and Svare Gaṭai located in Khanpur Shikaoli, Mardan district and Swabi region.

Gandhāra rock paintings are scattered throughout the hilly region of the province, and beyond, alongside rock carvings which are found in greater numbers, especially in the area of the upper Indus Valley. These rock carvings are mostly found in open areas and are exposed to the weather. While cave paintings are executed inside rock shelters due to their fragility and are somehow preserved. These two categories of rock art are usually found along trails that connect regions in its limited or greater uses. Some of them may have been used for both political and religious purposes, e.g. the Shahbaz Gaṛhi rock edicts, while others were performed with religious zeal like the rock paintings of Paṭvano Gaṭai, while the rest may be the result of passing time and unfamiliar feelings.

The cave paintings are executed on the rough surfaces of the rocks with the exception of Paṭvano Gaṭai, and may be the Abazo paintings (see below), which are painted on a dressed surface of the shelter. With rare exceptions, these paintings are mainly animal and human figures represented in various themes but especially hunting scenes. For lack of scientific studies and epigraphic evidence, they are difficult to date. It was assumed that some of them were prehistoric in nature (Nasim Khan 2000), but this present study suggests that they may not belong to such an early date but they are seeming historical and should be termed or classified under

M. Nasim Khan, *Gandhāran School of Buddhist Paintings*,
https://doi.org/10.1007/978-981-96-9310-8_3

the category of non-Buddhist paintings. The few important sites in this category are the paintings of Naṭian, Svarai Gaṭai and Parlai Ḍab. The other group of rock paintings are certainly Buddhist, judging from their content and associated inscriptions. The iconographic study and the epigraphic analysis make it possible to date some of these paintings to the Buddhist period.

Naṭian, Mardan

The site of Naṭian (Fig. 3.1) is located about four kilometres to the east from the town of Rustam. It is on the right and about 200 m from the main Rustam Buner road and is situated south-southeast of Naṭian Police Station on the right side of the path, a shortcut to the village of Shawa (Śiva)—Swabi. The shelter opens to the north and northeast. The total surface of the painted area is 2.45 × 175 cm while its opening height is 88 cm.

The majority of these paintings are of human and animal figures and are usually very faded and one can only guess their nature from the available traces of these figures. Human figures are depicted with outstretched arms, sometimes mounted on horses. Most of these characters, coloured in red, are represented in hunting or combat scenes. Most of them are illustrated with a single line depiction technique except in few cases where the outline is used for a representative figure. The opening of the shelters is so narrow and confined that it is difficult to enter and take photographs of the paintings.

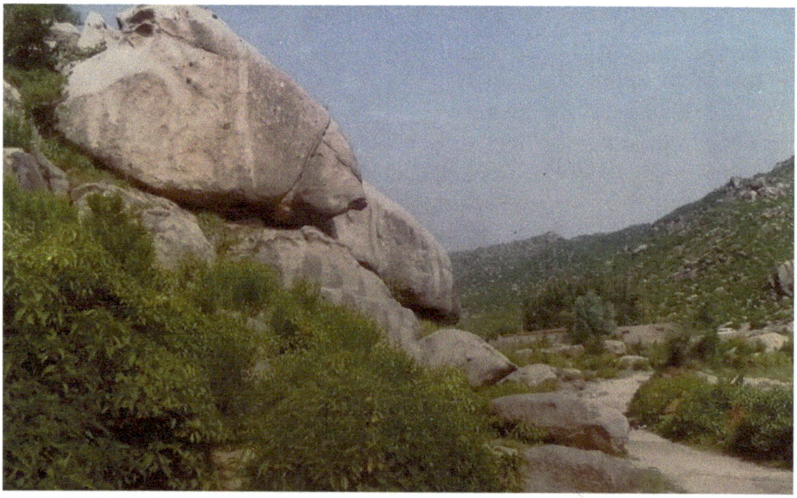

Fig. 3.1 Naṭian Rock Shelter, Mardan

Tore Gaṭai, Swabi

The site, named after the colour of the stones "Black Stone", is located slightly up the slope of the mountain separating Khanpur from Bagh and Suwarai located between the village of Shikaoli and the painting site of Svarai Gaṭai. Most of the paintings depict animals and humans showing hunting and combat scenes. The colour used for the paints is usually red except for a few which are painted black. A god numbers of them are represented by single bold lines. In some cases, they are depicted in outlines, sometimes filled with colour.

Svarai Gaṭai, Swabi

The other important site in this region where rock paintings are discovered is the shelter called Svarai Gaṭai meaning "Mounted Stones". The site is located approximately four kilometres from Naṭian to the north and northeast. To get to the shelter, one has to drive for about 2 kms from Naṭian in the direction of Buner, then walk for about an hour and a half towards the east. The site is located at a distance of about one-hour walk southeast of the village of Khanpur Shikaoli.[1] To approach the shelter, which is about 60 m above the ground, a narrow passage passes between two large rocks forming a deep and steep path which leads to the approach of the paintings (Fig. 3.2). The shelter opens to the west. The total area is 490 (NS) × 270 (EW) cm. The height of the opening is 170 cm from its maximum and 110 cm from its minimum in the centre (Fig. 3.3).

These paintings can be classified into three groups. The first group of them are simple linear representations of human and animal figures. The second shows the outline with horizontal or vertical lines. In this group, the contours are filled with colours. The last group, less represented, only shows the outline. Three types of animals have been depicted, but the majority of them are horses. In the second category are included the humped bulls. The last includes a unique depiction of a bison (Fig. 3.8) that bears great similarity in style to the one discovered at Altamira in Spain (Vialou 1998: 8).

The images are painted on the undressed surface with dark red pigment, except in one case where light red is used for the drawing of an animal most likely a horse shown in outline (Fig. 3.4). The characteristic feature of the paintings is that all human figures are depicted riding animals, may be horses, and moving in the same direction, that is to the right. Another group, possibly cavalry coming from another direction, from the right, meets them near a large tree, might be a halting or resting place (Fig. 3.5).

[1] On the way to Svarai Gaṭai, many other scattered and fragmented paintings were found in small shelters. The majority of these paints were red in colour.

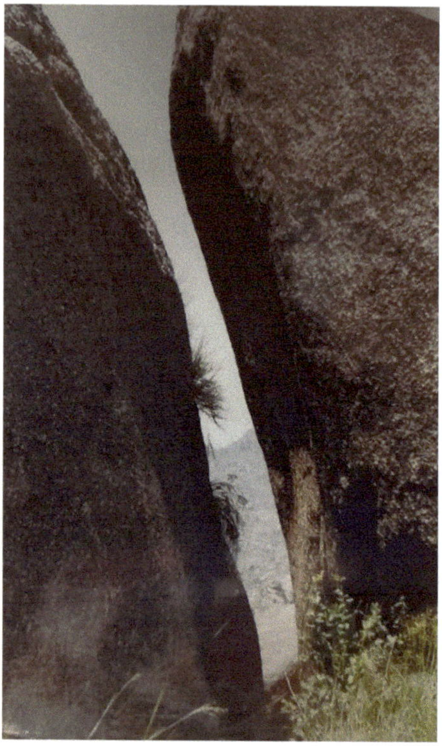

Fig. 3.2 A narrow passage to the Svarai Gaṭai paintings

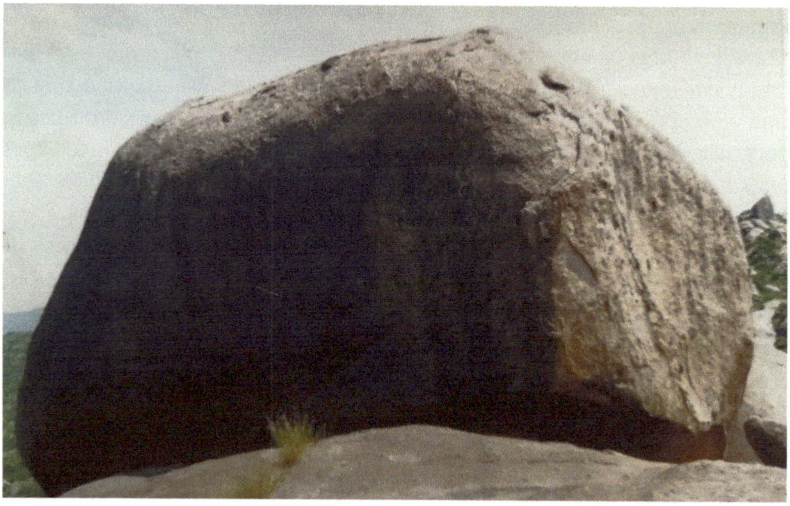

Fig. 3.3 Svarai Gaṭai (overlapping stones)

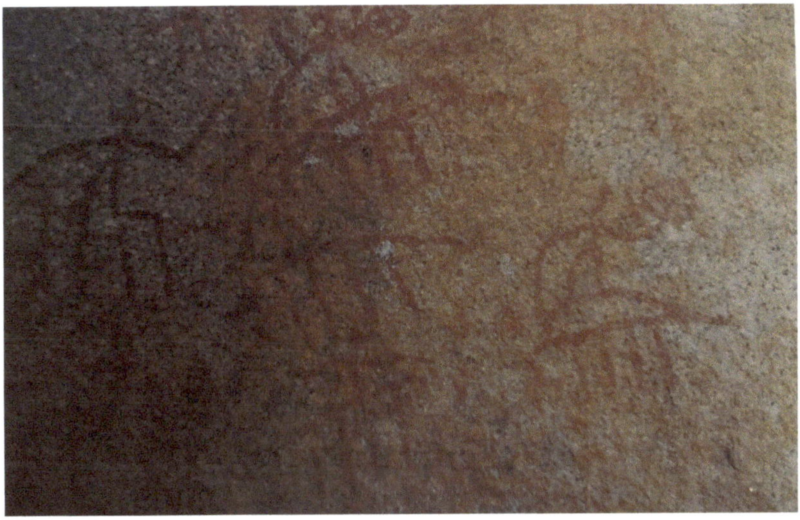

Fig. 3.4 Men riding horses drawn in contour

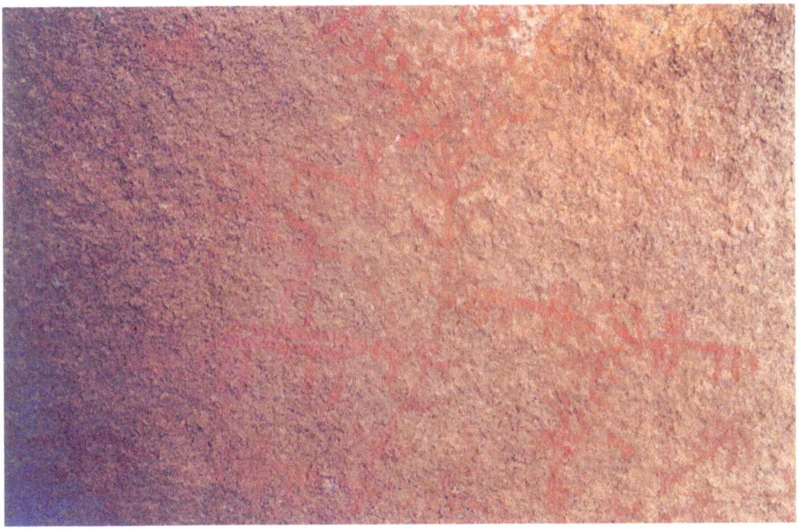

Fig. 3.5 Animals standing in the shadow of a tall tree

One thing that is unclear to me is that most runners coming from the right are holding flowers or streamers in their hands. They can also hold some sort of arm, like a bow, etc. if so, then this is definitely a scene of war between two rival groups.

On the left side, a large circle is displayed. A line is drawn from the circle. The circle can represent a village or a town because all the riders and animals seem to go in or out of the circle (Fig. 3.6); it could also a pen or cattle corral. It is possible that a caravan is leaving the village towards the tree where it encounters another group, which is coming from the right side. It starts from the left and all the animals go to the right. Another important point to note here is that all runners are in a standing position. A group among the characters on the left side moving to the left; it is a chariot pulled by four horses (Fig. 3.7).

Fig. 3.6 A circle probably representing an enclosure in the wilderness

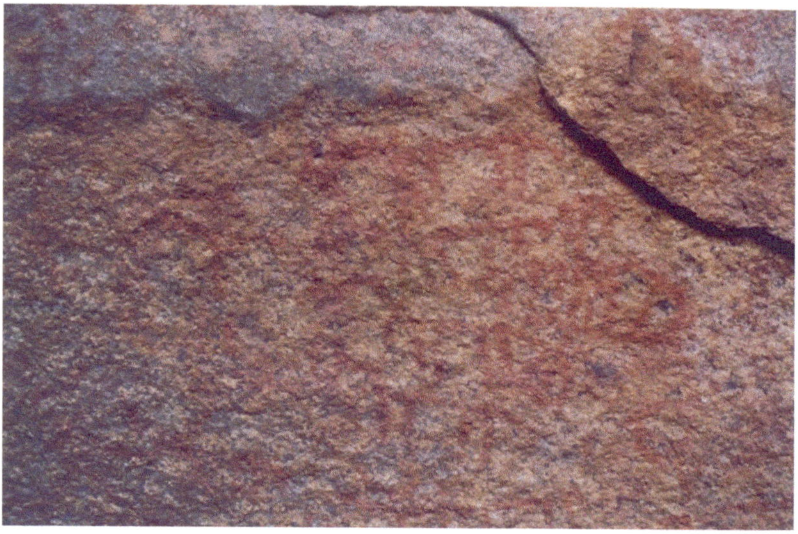

Fig. 3.7 Chariot drawn by four horses

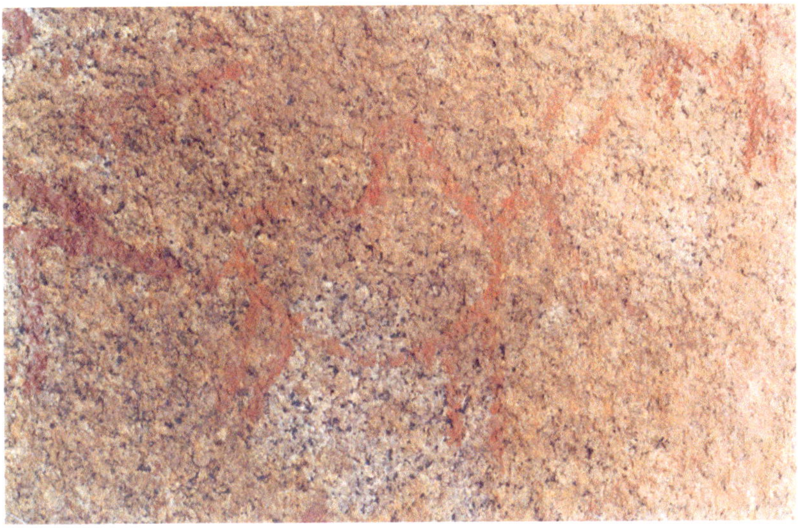

Fig. 3.8 Bison or may be a humped bull because of the long horns

At the right end of the surface is a strange drawing isolated from the rest of the paintings. It is probably a quadruped with long antlers (?) and a long tail (Fig. 3.9). The animal is moving towards the tree (Figs. 3.9, 3.10).

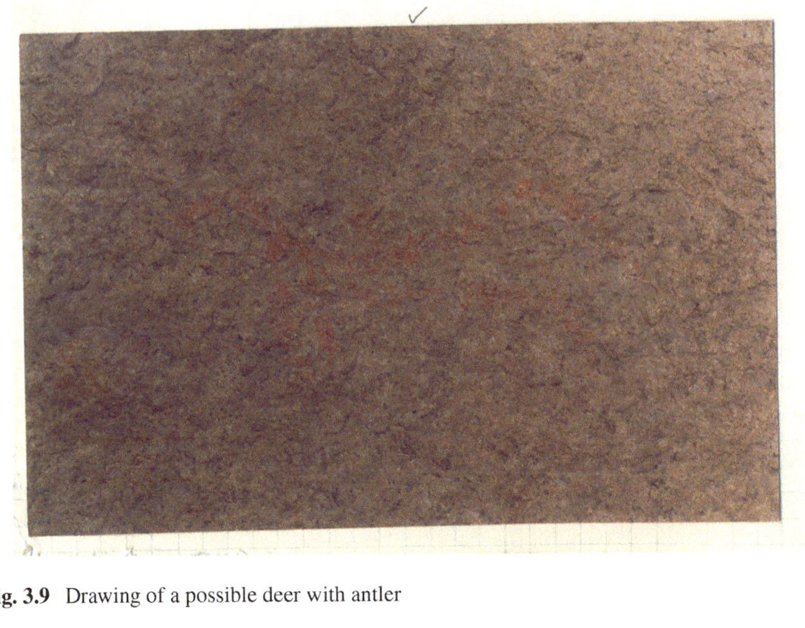

Fig. 3.9 Drawing of a possible deer with antler

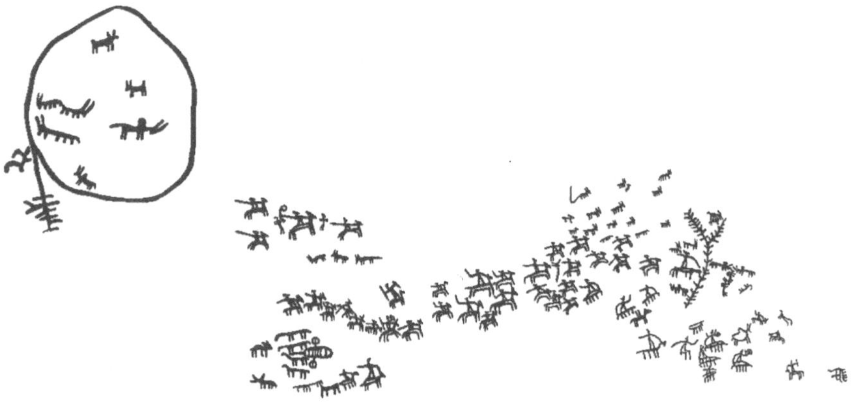

Fig. 3.10 Drawing of the paintings inside Svarai Gaṭai

Parlai Ḍab, Swabi

Several rock shelters with painted inscriptions, animal and other designs or sometimes bearing both categories of designs have been explored in the Mardan-Swabi region of the Peshawar Valley. Those with only figurative designs were previously attributed to a pre-Buddhist period (Nasim Khan 2000), but according to recent research, this may not be the case for most of them. The most important rock shelters or caves among them were found at Parlai Ḍab, Khanpur Shikaoli area and Natian—a boundary between Mardan and Swabi districts (see above).

Parlai Ḍab or Parlay Dab is located on the northwest flank of the mountain range called "Karamar" (Fig. 3.11). The area of Parlai Ḍab is situated about 3 kms northwest of the village of Gidaṛi and about 6 kms northwest of the village of Shewa (Śiva). In this region, multiple paintings have been discovered inside rock shelters to be found on either side of the valley. They were explored in 1993 by Professor Shah Nazar Khan and his team when they were surveying Swabi District to prepare a list of archaeological sites located in the area. Later in 1995 and then in 2003 the area was re-explored by a team of archaeologists from the Federal Department of Archaeology and Museums, Government of Pakistan (Khan et al. 2003: ii, iii, 82). After discovery of the shelters, Professor S.N. Khan invited me to visit the area to help him identify some of the rock shelters paintings in Parali Dab which he could not understand, especially the inscriptions.

We visited the area together and studied in detail the rock shelters bearing different paintings which include figurative and geometric designs as well as inscriptions. One of these shelters was discovered in the Jalal area and the other two in Parlai Ḍab. The Jaral rock shelter and one of the Parali Dab shelters are located on the left side of the path while the third shelter is situated higher up and in the middle of the valley and on the left side of the path. The first two shelters bear two inscriptions, one in each shelter. Jalal's rock shelter inscription, here called Rock Shelter C, is written in Brāhmī script, however, Rock Shelter B, is painted with Kharoṣṭhī inscription.

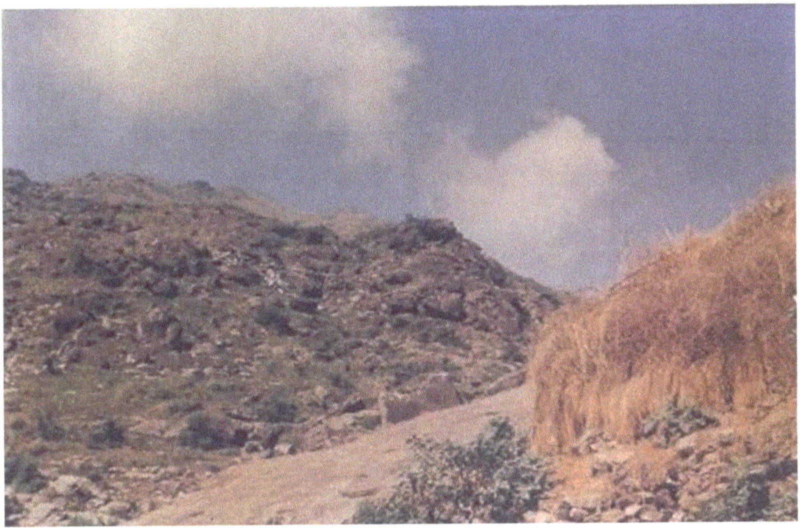

Fig. 3.11 General view of the Parlai Ḍab area

Three of the shelters wherein the paintings are somehow legible are named here Rock-Shelters, A, B, and C.

Rock Shelter A (Fig. 3.12): This shallow shelter is located on the left side just after entering the valley and near the village of Jalal. The only painting found inside the shelter is a short inscription consisting of a few characters. It is very faint but one can imagine through the preserved part of the letter that it is written in Gupta Brāhmī script. It is an inscription of less than seven letters of which five of the signs can be deciphered. The inscription reads: …yanana[sa] "of …yanana". It may represent a proper name written in the genitive case. The tripartite letter "ya" and the shape of the two letters "na" suggest a date somewhere between the second and fourth century AD. Most likely, the same name is also written inside Rock Shelter B and Rock Shelter C. The inscription is written with red paint.

Rock Shelter B (Figs. 3.13 and 3.14): This refuge for the present-day shepherds is located in the middle and on the left side of the valley and is on the steep clip of the mountain and proves difficult to access. The painted area of the shelter is low in height and sitting and painting inside the cave was hardly possible. Therefore, once entering the cave after climbing the slippery surface of the cave entrance, one could only rest right just in the entrance and on the slippery rock of the cave.

This is most likely the same cave once visited by C. Maxwell, R.E. of the British 10th Company of Sappers and Miners in April 1882. In his report, he produced a description of the inscription and the shelter with a sketch with a note from General A Cunningham who says "I am afraid that the cave paintings are not writing at all, but only boyish sketching of animals, a sort of Afghan Noali's ark".[2] Probably,

[2] Maxwell 1882, secondary reference.

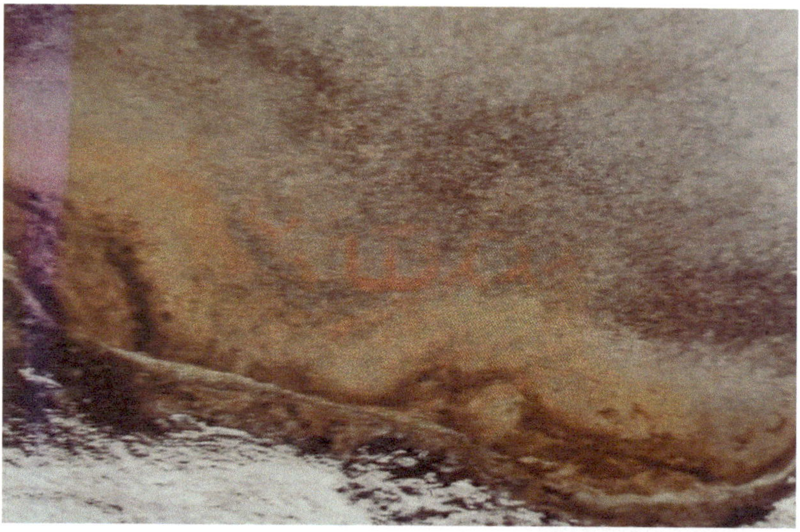

Fig. 3.12 Parlai Ḍab-Jalal, Rock Shelter A

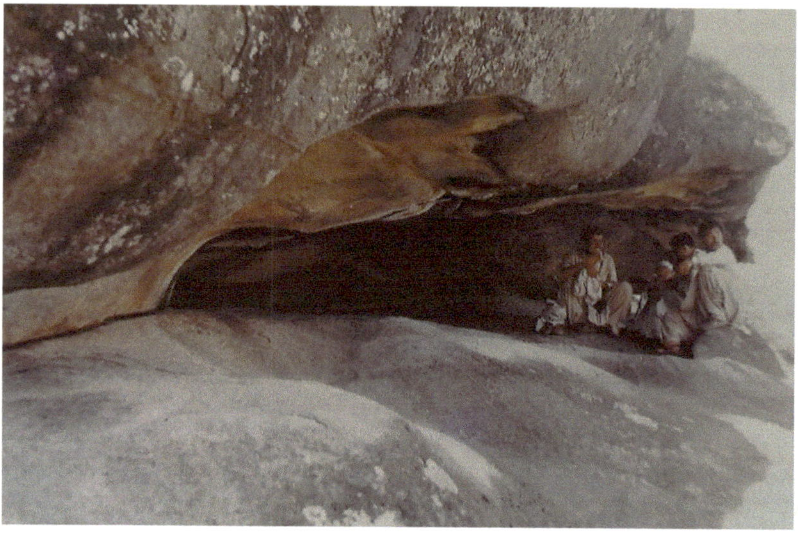

Fig. 3.13 Parlai Ḍab, Rock Shelter B

referring to this Kharoṣṭhī inscription, Maxwell also described how difficult it was to gain access to the shelter and how one could achieve it. Maxwell mentioned that the inscription is written in a script closer to Hindi and dated it to a period after the Buddhist period but before the Muslim period. He says, "I went to see one of the inscriptions near the foot of the hill and two at the top of the hill. This is an important

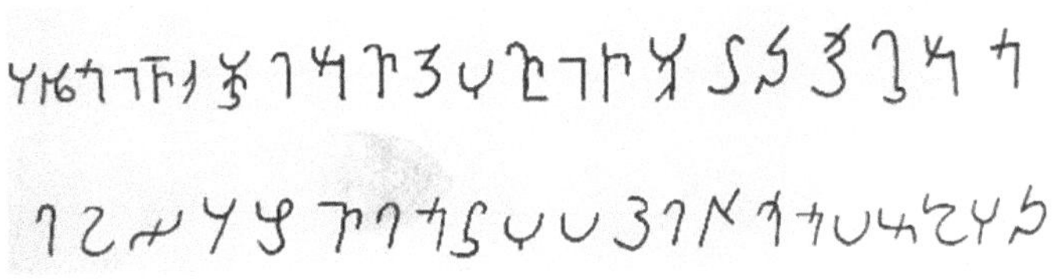

Fig. 3.14 Drawing of Kharoṣṭhī inscription of Rock Shelter B

one. There are three altogether-one at the foot and two at the top of the hill. The writing is not carved, but painted on the face of the rock. Advantage is always taken of the conformation of the rock to shelter the writing from the weather. In every case this style of writing has been found in a small cave or grotto in which the ascetic or holy man probably lived. These red paint inscriptions or rather writings appear to me not be in the Pali character, but more like Hindi; they may possibly be of a late date than the Buddhist period, and be the handwork of the Brahmans who followed them....One of them is easily got at, and though much defaced, a copy was made of it, and it is to be hoped that it may be partly decipherable. The third inscription is extremely difficult to get at. It is painted on the inner and upper side of recess in the face of cliff or large boulder. Access obtained by creeping round the edge of the cliff....How any one could have sat on it and written on the roof, is a mystery...." (Maxwell Report 1882).

The cave ceiling is probably decorated with various designs; however, I could only trace out a two-line Kharoṣṭhī inscription which is painted in red and is directly written on the rough surface of the cave. The transliteration was later published by me in an investigative report by Mr. Shah Nazar Khan (Khan 1995: 110–112). The preliminary reading, I proposed was:

viriaṃdhisa dacu pavakramo (or maṃ) cakariachu (or chaṃ) + bhavavi+kṣa

(dra or tra)mavi ine adhamamaṃ naṃ (or nu)vi akaguja (ti) haa

"Of Viriamdhi, this Pavakra, the Cakaria, the governor to be ....

The inscription belongs to 1st century BC–1st century AD.

Rock Shelter C (Figs. 3.15 and 3.16): This rock shelter is located almost at the end and on the right side of the valley. Its interior surface is decorated with several different types of paintings among which also includes a Brāhmī inscription that is written in Gupta characters and is painted with red ochre (Fig. 3.15 (1)). Above, there are traces on the right side of the inscription but it is not clear if these are the traces of the remaining part of the inscription or if they represent something else. The inscription is very faint but is readable: *oṃ varase [na] sya* "Om, from Varasena". The inscription refers either to the person who made it or to the individual to whom the shelter belonged or by whom the cave was occupied.

Further to the right there is a wavy design with high curves and is painted red (Fig. 3.16 (2)). Under Fig. 3.16 (1), there is another Brāhmī inscription but unfortunately only two letters are visible: ...*yana*.... (Fig. 3.16 (3)). The tripartite "ya" and the shape of the letter "na" are similar to that of the inscription found in Rock

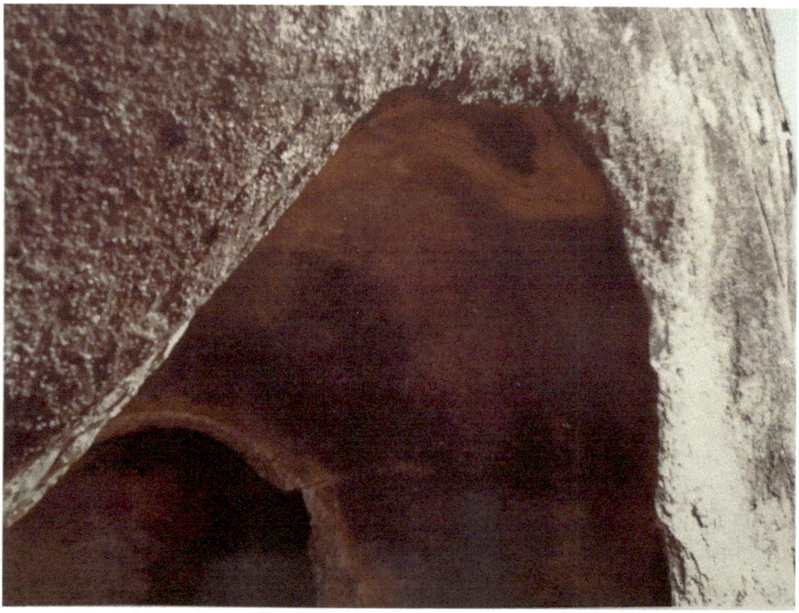

Fig. 3.15 Parlai Ḍab, Rock Shelter C

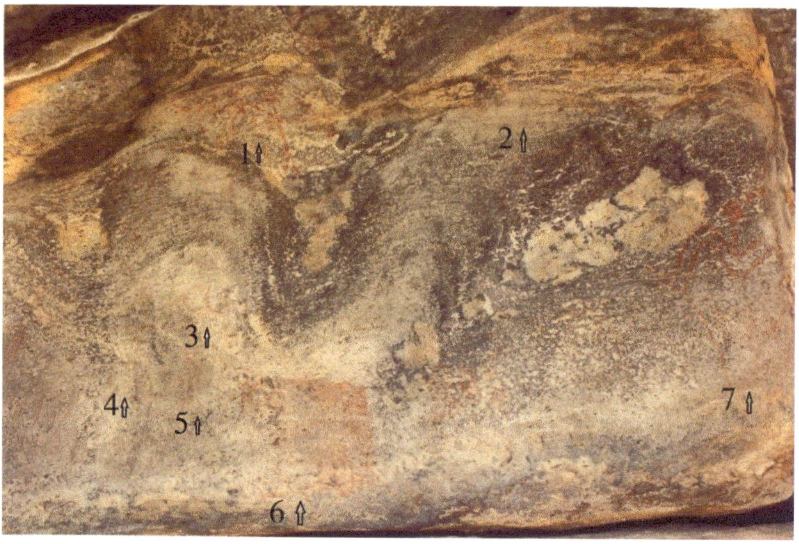

Fig. 3.16 Rock Shelter C, Parlai Ḍab

Shelter A. It is possible that both inscriptions belong to the same person and, therefore, this inscription could also be placed between the third and fourth centuries AD. Apparently, there are two other designs below the second inscription, one of them is a square structure divided into four compartments (Fig. 3.16 (4)) and the other is an arrowhead-shaped design painted in outline between the other two structures (Fig. 3.16 (5)). On the left side, there is a square design which is mostly solid and painted in red ochre (Fig. 3.16 (6)). Apparently, this drawing represents the base of a stūpa whose upper part has disappeared or it could also be an incomplete drawing of a stūpa or could also represent something else. Further to the right and a little above the square solid structure, there is drawing of a large bird painted in red on the far right of this face of the rock surface. The bird, with upstroke swings, has an extended long neck, a round head and a long beak (Fig. 3.16 (3)). The wings are shown in outline and the rest of the body is not clearly visible. Should we think of a mountain landscape, represented by the undulated drawing, where the bird flies?

There are several other types of designs that are painted inside the shelter (e.g. Fig. 3.16 (6)). They are figurative mostly include animals and humans, *cakras*, geometric designs, most likely architectural depictions, and other unidentified figures. All these are painted red on the stripped surfaces of the shelters. Most of the paintings are weathered or covered in smoke from the fire used by local herders when they occupy the majority of the shelters. Most of the shelters in the area were also used by the natives as fodder for their animals.

* * *

The rock paintings recorded in the Parlai Ḍab region, Swabi, are accompanied by inscriptions written in Kharoṣṭhī or Brāhmī, and all are painted with red ochre. The inscriptions and the figurative designs of Rock Shelter C are most likely made by the same person or a group of individuals at around the same time or at a time that cannot be earlier than the second century AD as the palaeography of the inscriptions suggests. To base our dating of the paintings on palaeographic ground, the Parlai Ḍab paintings can be placed between the first century BC and the fourth century AD. Most of these figurative, geometric and other designs recorded in the region were previously characterized as prehistoric or pre-Buddhist paintings, which may not be the case, as the present study suggests. In fact, they are not Buddhist in nature, but they certainly belong to the Hindu-Buddhist period of Gandhāra region.

Kala Tassa, Baṭagram (Hazara)

Like other areas of Mahāgandhāra, the Baṭagram and Mansehra Districts of Hazara Division are also rich in archaeological sites and the area has been under investigation for archaeological research since very early period carrying by both national and international organizations. Other archaeological sites found in this area include the famous Aśokan Rock Edicts, Oghi Inscription and so many other inscriptions which are recorded and published in different reports and monographs (e.g. Hultzsch 1925). The sites of the Hindu era are numerous but very little attention has been paid to this period. On the other hand, sites from the Buddhist period are the main focus of scholars, which has resulted in the discovery of a number of stūpa sites, like Zar Ḍheri, Bedadi, etc., in the region some of which have been excavated but only a few of them have yet been published. The most important of them is the Buddhist complex of Zar Ḍheri which was excavated and has been published by a team of archaeologists from the National Museum in Tokyo, Japan (see bib. Zar Ḍheri). Apart from the stūpa and monastery sites, rock carvings from the Buddhist period have also been reported in this region, but they are unfortunately not yet properly recorded and studied by the scholars who are engaged in this region.

Most notable among the paintings from the Buddhist period are those discovered at Kala Tassa, located in the Batagram District of Mansehra in Khyber Pakhtunkhwa (Fig. 3.17). Near this cave, locally called Kala Tassa or Qila aur Tassa and located near the hamlet of Peshawṛi or Peshoṛa between Mansehra and Thakot, remains from the Buddhist period have also been found. The site is southeast of the Indus River and about 300–400 m above the Karakorum Highway, now the Hazara Motorway, inside a narrow valley above the village from Peshawṛi (Peshoṛa) (Fig. 3.18). The small rivulet joins the Nandihar stream which falls into the Indus at Thahkot in the Upper Indus Valley. The paintings belong to the first century AD. The famous gold adornment of the Indo-Scythian period which weighed 24 kg was also found in the same region, i.e., in the village of Pattan located north of Peshawṛi (see Nasim Khan 1998).

The total area covered by the paintings is approximately 3 × 1 m. The cave is about 10 m wide and 2.5 m long. With the exception of two horses painted white (Fig. 3.19), all the other characters are painted red. Antiquarians who attempted to remove the painted area from the surface are said to have destroyed the majority of the paintings and, at present, nothing of significance remains in the cave. These paintings are among the oldest of this genre where epigraphic, iconographic and architectural elements come together. About 55 figures are painted which form different groups representing different themes and events, such as stūpa worship, building complexes, a possible story of Jātaka, battle scenes, etc. (Fig. 3.19). Therefore, for the historian of Buddhist religion and architecture, art and iconography, they are very important and may therefore require special attention.

The Kala Tassa group of paintings appear to represent two main groups, Buddhists and non-Buddhists, but if analysed closely they are done with the same brush and are painted with the same type of colour except for two horses that are painted white. Apparently, there are possible traces of other paints which seem white in colour but they are either covered by the red-painted figures or they have faded or discoloured due to oxidation but their traces are still visible. Despite all these complexities, judging by the two paintings of white-coloured horses, they are part of the same canvas as the other paintings and the set may therefore represent the same event, painted by the same person, probably a devotee, a soldier or layman who lived or stayed here for a certain period of time.

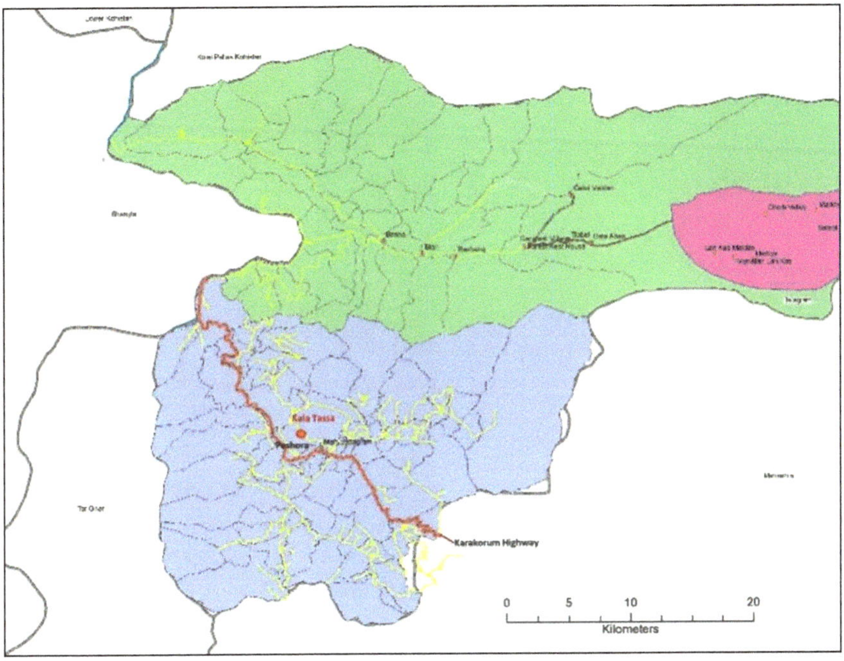

Fig. 3.17 Location map of Kala Tassa, Peshoṛa, Baṭagram

For better explanation, the figures are described here both in groups and individually. The paintings start at the left end, read left to right. The first group shows two warriors, a mounted archer and a foot archer (Fig. 3.19). Apparently, the two characters are the aggressors, with vibrant gestures, who have entered a hamlet where three humans and two animals are in front of or near their house. The rider has a bow and arrows and is ready to attack. The way the horse stands in a canter position suggests that the horse suddenly stops, so that the horse's legs are close together. The foot archer stands astride long and points his arrow at the humans and animals standing in front of him. Both attackers wear a frock like as their upper garment.

The inhabitants are traumatized and seem submissive to the attackers. The person in the left field, who appears between the warriors, standing akimbo—looking back but moving to the right—is shocked by this visit from strangers. He could also be a comrade (?) of the warriors. He wears the same type of Central Asian type of clothing as the warriors. On the far left of the surface is the drawing of an animal with four legs and a long drooping tail with a long neck and a snout like an anteater. The animal is painted white (Fig. 3.20) and turned to the left. A red line, partially visible, encircles the animal. Inside there are traces of unclear drawings painted in red.

Behind Fig. 3.20, there is another quadruped still painted white (Fig. 3.21). The body of the animal is represented solid. It is in a standing position facing left and has a long tail and a bulky head with a fleshy snout. The large eye is marked with

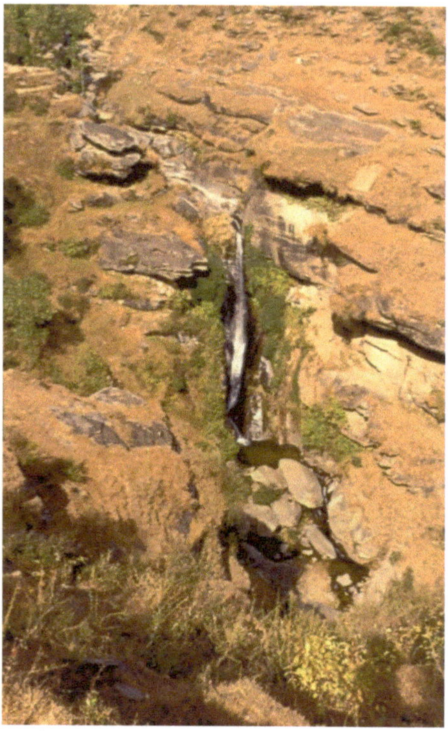

Fig. 3.18 Stream to climb to reach Kala Tassa rock shelter

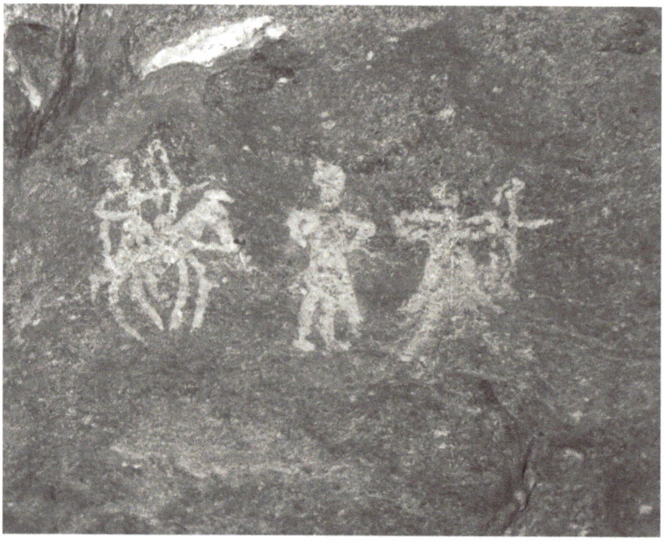

Fig. 3.19 Men with arrow and bow

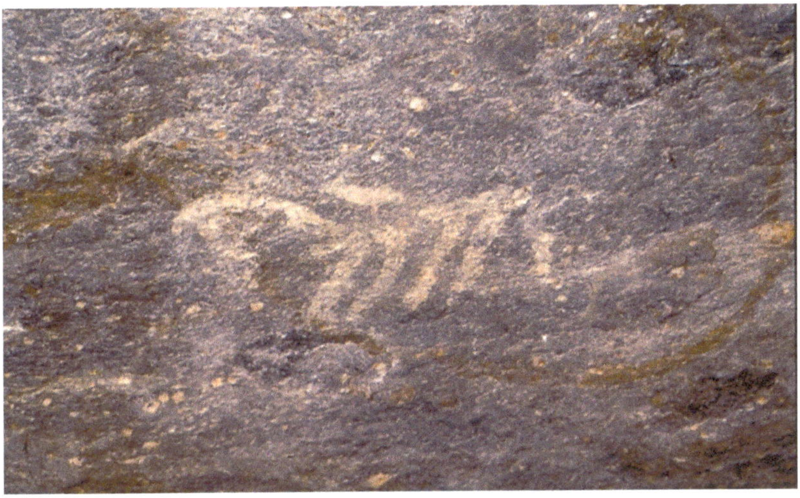

Fig. 3.20 Animal, with long muzzle, painted in white colour

a circle-shaped pattern. A thin line draws a semi-circle on the animal's shoulder that looks like a bump. Below and on its front there are unclear designs painted in red. Behind the animal there is almost a square building of at least two floors with a sloping roof inside the square. It looks like the top horizontal line of the square doesn't touch the left vertical line or extend to the left. The probably white paint above may suggest other illegible designs.

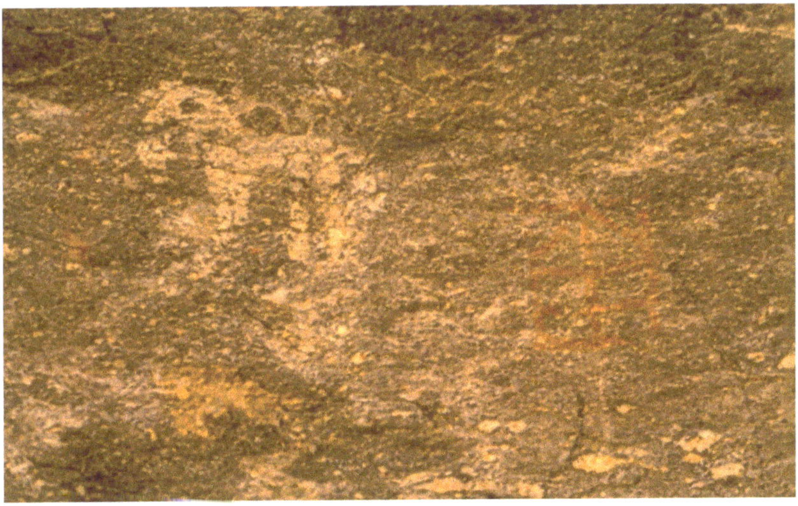

Fig. 3.21 Animal painted in white colour

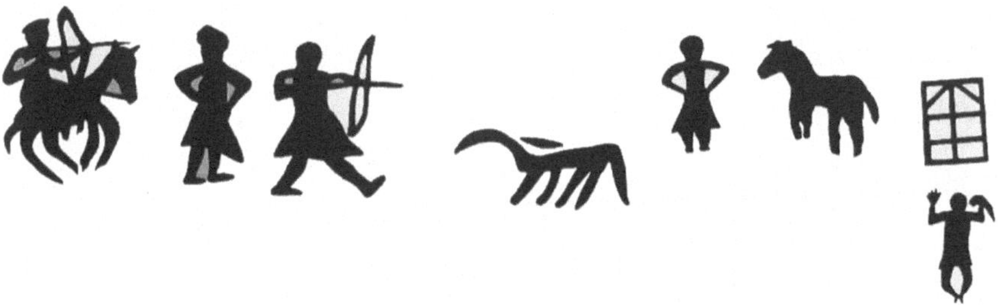

Fig. 3.22 Assault scene

To the right of this drawing is a person standing facing but with heels close together. Both his hands are up; in his left he holds an animal, probably a falcon while his raised right hand is depicted with sprawling figures (Fig. 3.22). The structure above is a multi-story building with different compartments, and its roof is both flat and pointed.

The next group consists of several drawings including human and animal figures, structures, a tree and an unclear design. The human figure at the left end is standing and facing left with its right hand against the chest while the other is in akimbo pose (Fig. 3.23). The figure most likely represents a woman who wears a long dress like a frock that reaches her knees. Behind her there is a quadruped standing on the left having a long tail and a long snout (Figs. 3.23 and 3.24); it may be the same type of animal as the one already discussed above. The animal above the women is a horse moving to the left. Its body is spotted with three circles, one on its shoulder and two on its rump or thigh (Fig. 3.25). Above and to the right, another woman (?) drawing, standing in front of a building; her head turns to the right. She has a long, fleshy, pointed nose, and her hands are placed on her hips. She is also depicted with a long tassel (?) of hair that falls over her back. Above and to the right is a structure with different compartments. The four corners are marked with circles representing the four bastions. The whole structure can represent a castle. A large strange design is seen above and to the left. It looks like a Central Asian pointed cap.[3]

Beside and to the right of this set of paintings is a group of animals with bowed heads that seem to be busy eating. Animals include a rabbit (Fig. 3.23c), two birds (Fig. 3.23b, e), a rhino (Fig. 3.23d), a chicken (Fig. 3.23f), a monkey (Fig. 3.23g), a deer (Fig. 3.23h) and a pig (?) (Fig. 3.23i). A man (Fig. 3.23a) near and above the animals seems to be feeding them. Below, a rider stopped by a person, as if to conclude with the gesture of the horse, with his right hand, the other in akimbo pose. The rider can be a messenger from another kingdom or destination and is received by the guard. Two unclear animals are drawn to the right of this scene; the top animal faces right and the bottom animal faces left. Further to the right, a plant probably planted in a large vase with a flat bottom and an angular receptacle; the front of the base is marked with a rectangular design. On the right side a man, probably a king

[3] A head preserved in the Metropolitan Museum of art, shows the same type of cap. On skull cap see also Yunusova (1997: 1–27).

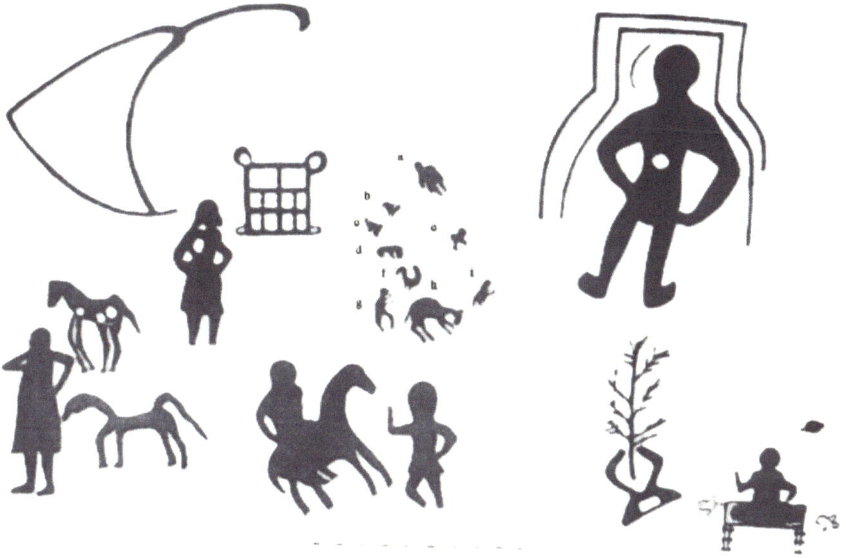

Fig. 3.23 Drawing of figures on the left side of the stūpa area

Fig. 3.24 Showing different drawing in red paint

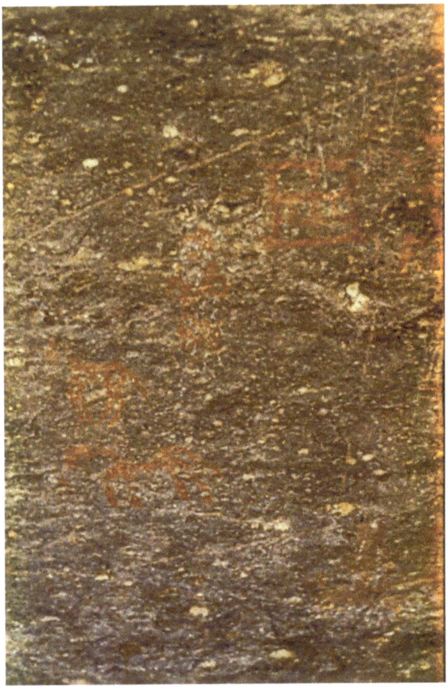

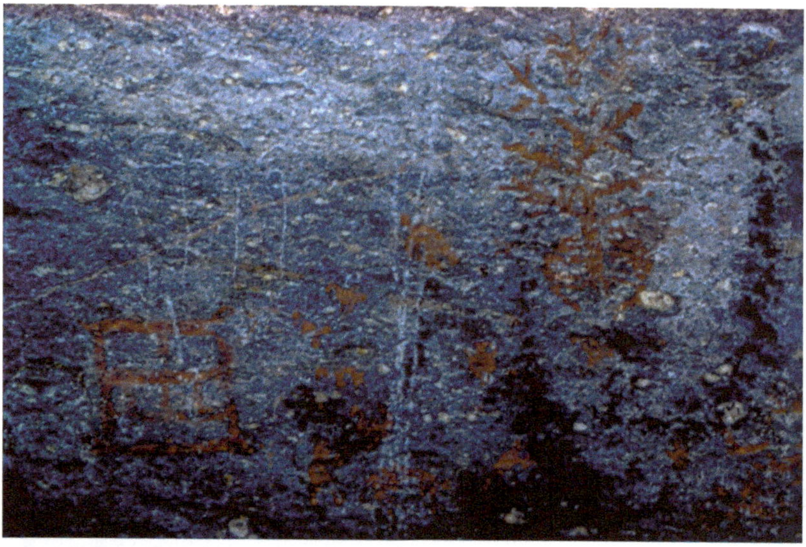

Fig. 3.25 Animals, structure and a vase drawing. Probably representing Titriya Jātaka

or lord of the village, is seated on his throne with his right hand raised and the left on his hips. Two floral motifs are represented, one on each side of the throne. Above and at the top of the tree, a man, probably a guard, stands on his haunches inside an arch or could be an entrance door to a flat-roofed palace. The large-sized image of the figure also suggests it to be some of a supernatural power like a god standing in arch. The whole scene probably represents a communal life with chief. It is also possible that the scene represents a Jātaka story such as Tittira or Titriya Jātaka.

Further to the top right, there is a Kharoṣṭhī inscription. It is partly defaced and the whole can be difficult to read. It was first published R. Salomon who read and translate it as: *[sa]vacare sataviśa-vaṣa-sa(ti)me* ?? "In the one hundred twenty seven year".[4] My reading and translation of the inscription would be: …ava budhara[ti]śa aśra[ma] "..hermitage of Buddharatiśa". On the right side, some degraded paintings of human and animal figures as well as other structural paintings. A man, hands on hips, stands in front of the building. A few other degraded paintings of two small square structures and a circle to observe at the top right of the structure with a man (see infra). Below is a defaced inscription while only three letters are visible and could be read as "budha aro…" (Fig. 3.26).

The next group of paintings of considerable importance consists of figures painted below and to the right of the painted surface of the shelter. Most important are the depictions of three stūpas with several monasteries-like structures between and above some of which have already been discussed above (Fig. 3.23). The stūpa on the left side is depicted with a drum where a seated Buddha in meditation is depicted. The

[4] Salomon (1995: 127–128). The information about the locality of the inscription given to Prof. Salomon is wrong.

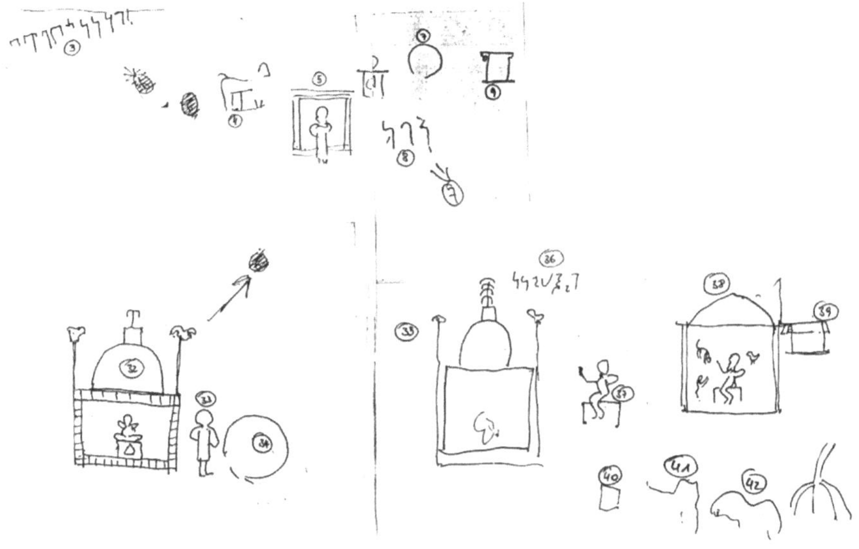

Fig. 3.26 Sketch drawing of the paintings at Kala Tassa (not to the scale)

balustrade around the stūpa is marked with horizontal and vertical beams supported by short horizontal and vertical bars. The dome, filled with red colour, shows a *harmikā* supporting a *yaṣṭi* with a single umbrella (Fig. 3.27). On either side of the stūpa is a column with a lion capital as seen in the carvings of Sanchi and Shing Nala (Fig. 3.28) in the Upper Indus Valley; columns with lion capitals are also attested in the Buddhist art of Gandhāra (Fig. 3.29). The lions sit on their hind legs and face the stūpa.

At the top right, there are possibly three monasteries or other structures and a chapel. The monastery in the upper left is a structure, with two bastions, of seven chambers, with a possible courtyard and a corridor. On the right another monastery with courtyard, three rooms and veranda or corridor. Below and between these two monasteries, a chapel where a man, probably Buddha or bodhisattva, is represented in a standing position (Fig. 3.30). The character could also be other than a Buddha or a bodhisattva and who seems represented in *añjalimudrā*. To the left of the stūpa, the painting of a monastery with a bastion at each corner is demonstrated. The monastery has sixteen rooms. On the right and left side of the monastery probably two men are depicted. The one close to the stūpa is faded but he seems standing with hands on his hips. On the right side of the monastery, a man is depicted in standing position with his hands behind or near to his chest probably portraying *añjalimudrā*. To his right there is an unclear design in form of a circle (Fig. 3.31).

The other most important building of the same group is a stūpa which shows the same style as the previous except for some minor differences and additions, e.g. the front lower balustrade is not shown here, but this stūpa is added with more umbrellas than the previous one. The stūpa shows two columns, topped with lion

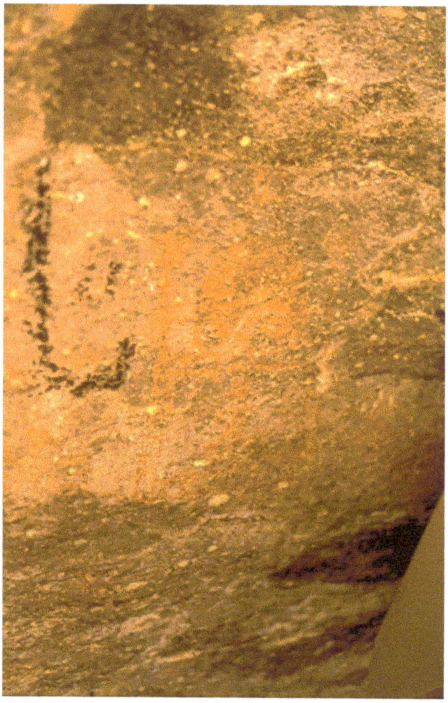

Fig. 3.27 Drawing of a stūpa

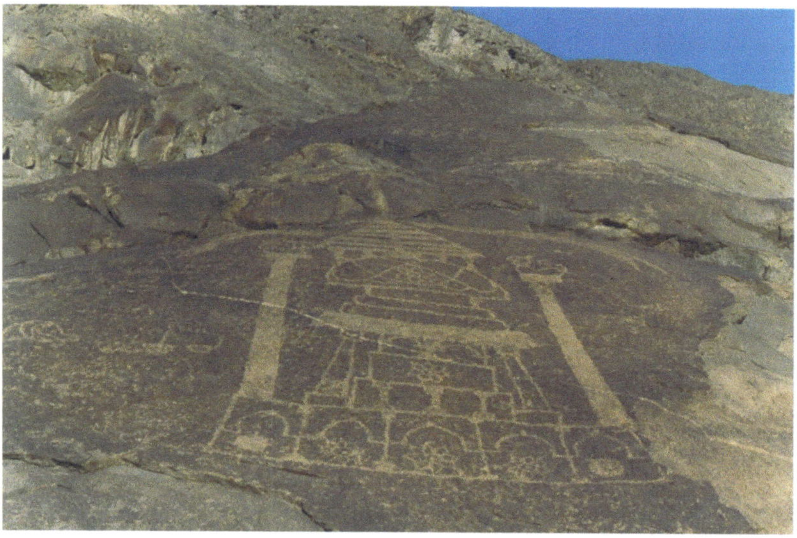

Fig. 3.28 Stūpa drawing in Shing Nāla, Northern Areas of Pakistan

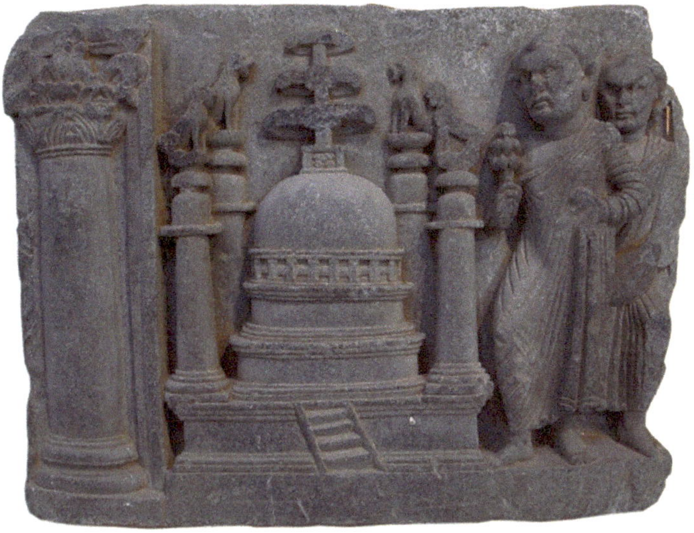

Fig. 3.29 Relief panel from But Kara III site in Swat

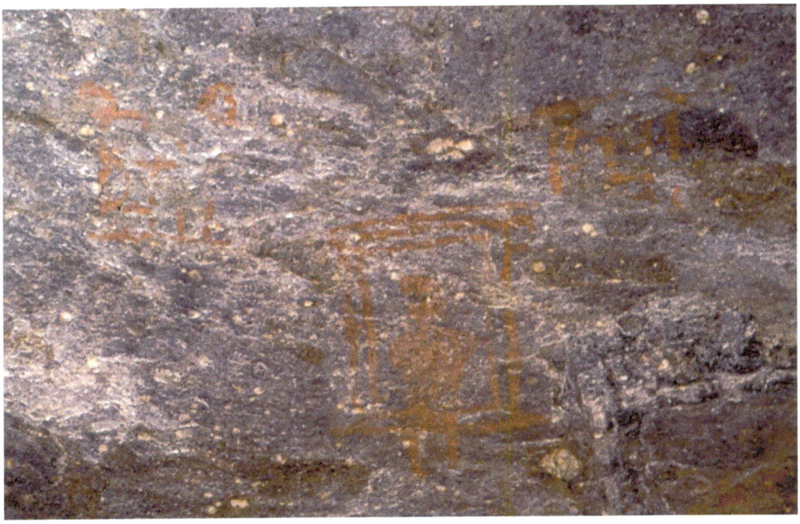

Fig. 3.30 Drawing of different structures

capitals, and a balustrade. The lions are seated and facing the same direction as in the previous example. The dome, which is not filled with colour, is rounded. Despite only one *chattra*, noticed in the other example, here four umbrellas are added to the *yaṣṭi*. At the entrance of the building, two persons are depicted paying homage to the stūpa, both seem to represent *añjalimudrā*. To the right of the dome,

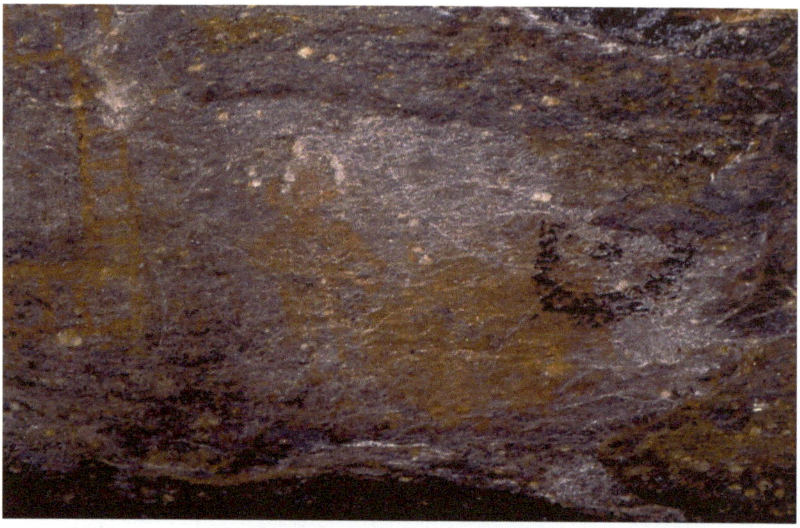

Fig. 3.31 Drawing of a stūpa and other figures

a floral motif and, at the top right, probably human figures. A beautifully and clearly written Kharoṣṭhī inscription is added to the stūpa which continues on both sides of the chattra (Fig. 3.31). The inscription reads and translates; *kaniṣka maharajasa viharo* meaning "(this) vihāra (is) of Mahārāja Kaniṣka". This inscription is good contemporary epigraphic evidence not only to show that all these paintings belong to the first century CE, but it also mentions that the Vihāra, the stūpa, belongs to Mahārāja Kaniṣka. Moreover, as the context and the iconography show, one of the figures paying homage to the stūpa could be Kaniṣka himself. Both figures wear the Central Asian dress of the Kuṣāṇa period (Fig. 3.32).

At the top right of this stūpa and at the right end of the painted surface, there is still a square structure with bastions. Below probably a seated man with outstretched arms. Further below and on the left side of the stūpa, there is a man seated on a throne with his right hand extended towards the stūpa and probably holding a flora. His left hand is on his hips. At the back of the seated figure there is a square domed structure, most likely another stūpa while the *harmikā*, *yaṣṭi* and *chattra* are missing. The lion capitals are also missing for part of the right pillar. Most likely a man is seated on his throne placed against the drum of the stūpa. His left hand is on his hips while the other is outstretched and probably holding something in his hand. The figure in question could be a seated Buddha who probably sat cross-legged and in meditation pose. There are unclear designs on its right and left sides. Below are three unclear character designs (Fig. 3.33).

In addition to the figures identified above, there are multiple traces that may belong to other similar figures either degraded or disappeared due to oxidation but their traces are still there.

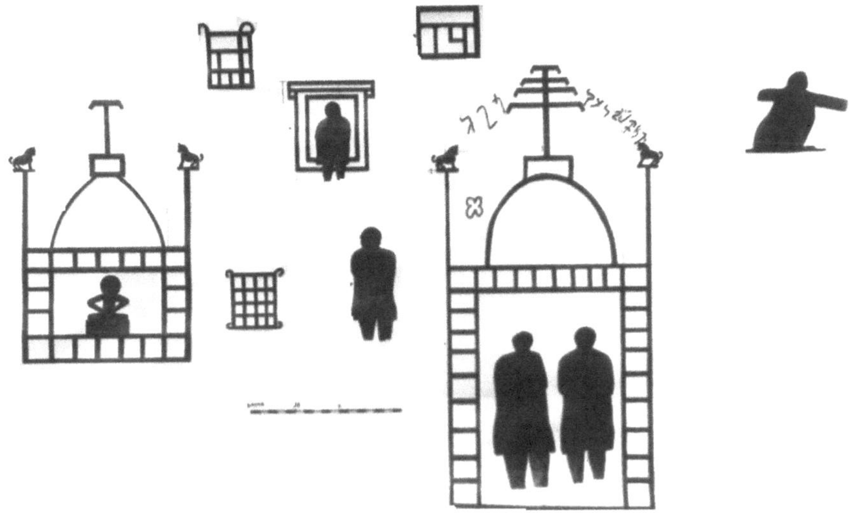

Fig. 3.32 Drawing showing two figures paying homage to Kaniṣka stūpa

Kafir Koṭ, Lower Swat Valley

Research into Buddhist rock art in the Swat Valley has a long history and the presence of this art was probably first mentioned by Faxian, in the fourth century AD, (Legge 1998: 29) and later by Xuanzang (Watters 1904–1905: 231),[5] in the seventh century AD, who, while visiting Uḍḍiyana, referred to a large flat stone depicted with the footprints of Buddha. But the documentation and study of these engravings is a recent phenomenon. Most of them have been recorded by Pakistani and Italian researchers and have been published in different reports (e.g. Tucci 1958), monographs (e.g. Sardar 2005) and articles which are published in different national and international journals (e.g. Dani 1968–1968; Olivieri 1998). Despite all these efforts, the study of the art of Buddhist paintings in the Swat region has received little attention and research in this field is still in its infancy compared to the study of the Buddhist rock carvings in this region. Since the early twenties, several rock shelters have been reported with paintings in the lower Swat Valley, especially in the Thana region, such as the paintings of Kafir Koṭ, Shamo, Marano Tangai and Hinduano Gaṭai, which have been found near Morah Sar which separates the valley of Koṭah from that of Thana. However, Buddhist cave paintings are rarely attested in this area. The few paintings found are those of the Kafirkot or Nokkono Ghwand cave graffiti located on the crest of the Mohra Pass and in the left southern part of the Swat Valley near the town of Thana (Nazir Khan et al. 1995).[6] These graffiti mainly include stūpas, human figures,

[5] The stone with footprints of the Buddha is preserved in the Swat Museum, which is also inscribed with a Kharoṣṭhī inscription which says: budhasa śakamunisa padani "footprints of the Buddha Śākyamuni". The site was visited by Stein in 1926 (Stein 1929: 86, 88, Fig. 47).

[6] Nazir Khan et al. (1995).

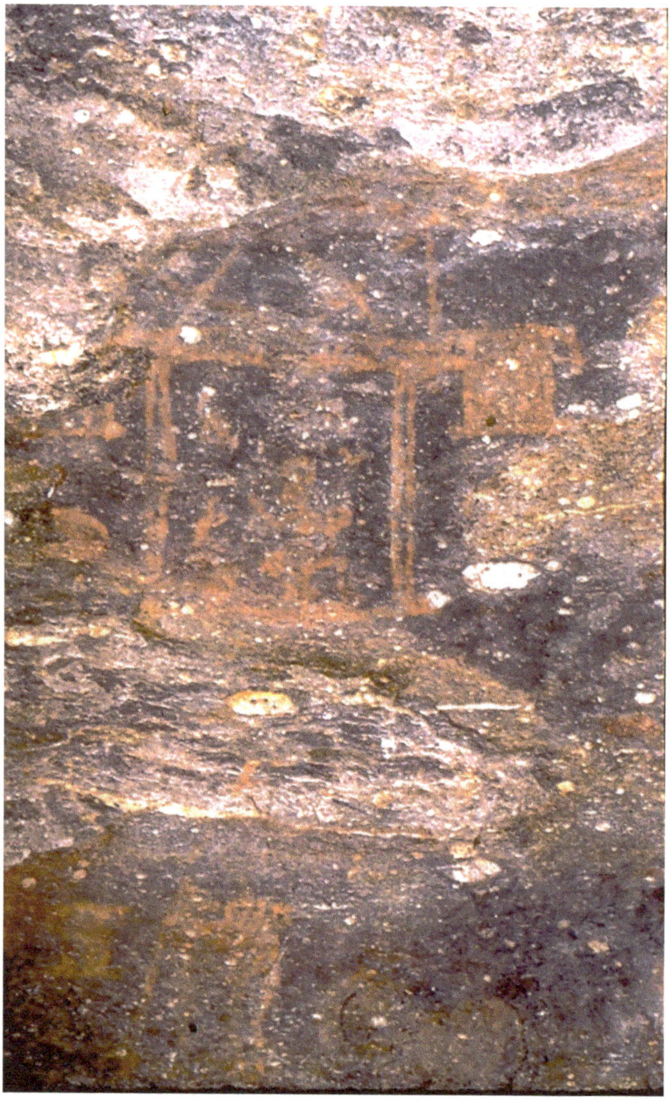

Fig. 3.33 Drawing of a structure at the extreme right end of the painted surface

horsemen, warriors, birds and some unclear drawings. The subject is probably an assault on Buddhist monuments and their supporters. About seventeen stūpas are drawn, usually depicted with a drum, *harmikā* dome with *yaṣṭi* and *chattras*. Three warriors on foot and one on horseback are shown with bows and are depicted in action. They are located in different places in the area of the stūpa complex. The warrior on horseback even touches one of the stūpa, in right field, and probably tries to damage it. The two human figures, hands on hips, seem to let them go. An unclear drawing to see in the right field.

Red, orange-red and yellow pigments are used in paint applied directly to the uncoated surfaces of the shelters. The probable date suggested for these paintings is between the first and fourth centuries AD; I presume they belong to a late date.

Abazo, Buner

Buner district is bounded by Swat and Shangla in the north, Hazara in the east, Malakand branch and Mardan district in the west and Swabi district in Swat. The current administrative division may not correspond to the cultural area in which Buner was placed in antiquity. However, based on its artistic style, it might be more related to the Swat regions than the Peshawar and Taxila valleys. Needless to discuss the exact ancient geography of Buner and its cultural connection with other parts of the region, Buner is known for its extremely rich Buddhist heritage sites and is visited and passed through by travellers and invaders at different periods of the history. Different archaeological expeditions have carried out surveys in the area as some of them are already available and are the main sources of information on the sites, some of which still exist while others are simply compiled in files.

In 2014–2015, a survey in the Buner area was conducted by the Directorate of Archaeology and Museums by a team of archaeologists led by Mr. Zafar Hayat Khan, one of my Ph.D. students. Among other ancient remains, the team also explored four rock shelter sites with paintings which are: Bakro Maidān, Paṭitañgai (Ghāṛ), Pāchā Gaṭ and Abāzo stūpa, published in Volume 11 of the Journal, Gandhāran Studies (Khan, Z.H. 2017). But this report does not mention that the shelters have already been explored in 1994 and 1995 (see Khattak 1997). These newly discovered paintings include hunting scenes and Buddhist figures. They are roughly attributed to the pre-Buddhist and Buddhist periods. These are depicted on the rough surface inside the ceiling of a rock shelter called Abazo (Fig. 3.34) (see Khan, H.Y. 2017: 82). The refuge is located on Topyala hill about 6 kms south of Kalpani village of Tehsil Gagra in Buner district. The shelter appears to be part of the Abazo stūpa complex which lies at a distance of 300 m. The rock shelter is ten meters long and 6 m high).

On the surface of the rock, inside the Abazo Rock Shelter, there are traces of orange and black paint. The majority of them are signs of blurred images, probably of human figures, and animal figures (Area C), especially in areas A and B. The only three human figures that are certain are the three seated figures, arranged in a row, located at the extreme left of the shelter, read from left to right, as shown in area A (Fig. 3.35). For some of them only the milky outlines, resulting from the oxidation of the paint, are imaginable. For the rest of the images, nothing can be said with certainty, but the context and the circumstantial evidence, such as the plastered background—particularly in area B, suggest that they are the remains of human figures. Area B is more covered than area A and the supposed lime plaster could

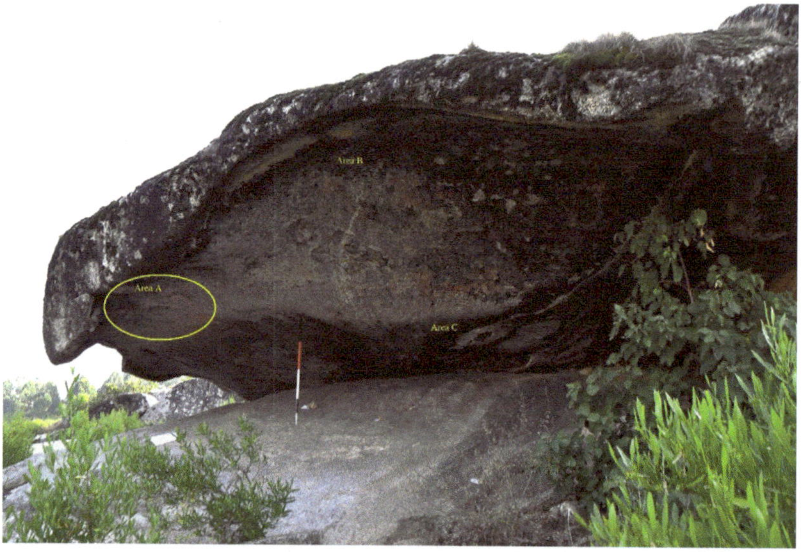

Fig. 3.34 Abazo Rock shelter

also be the remnants of a thick patina which is flaking mainly for different reasons suggesting a thick section of the supposed plaster. Conservation and material analysis should be done, by the concerned department, of the surface in particular and of the rock shelter as a whole (Fig. 3.36).

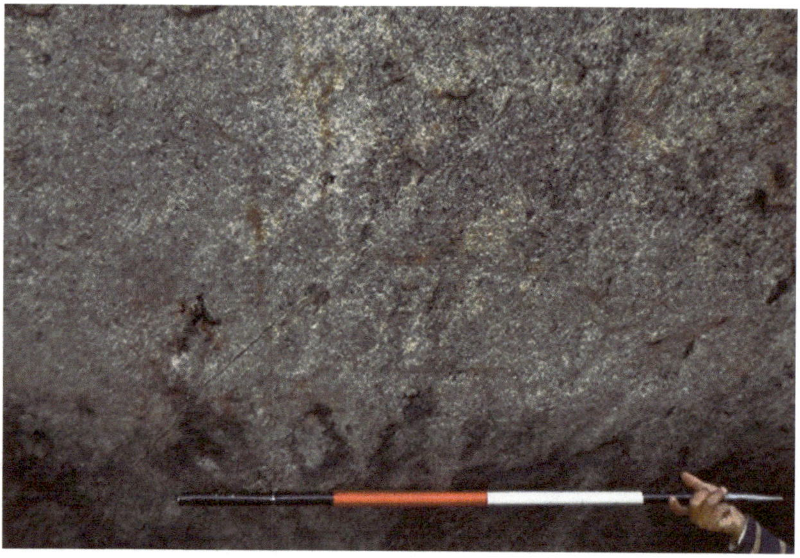

Fig. 3.35 Unidentified paintings

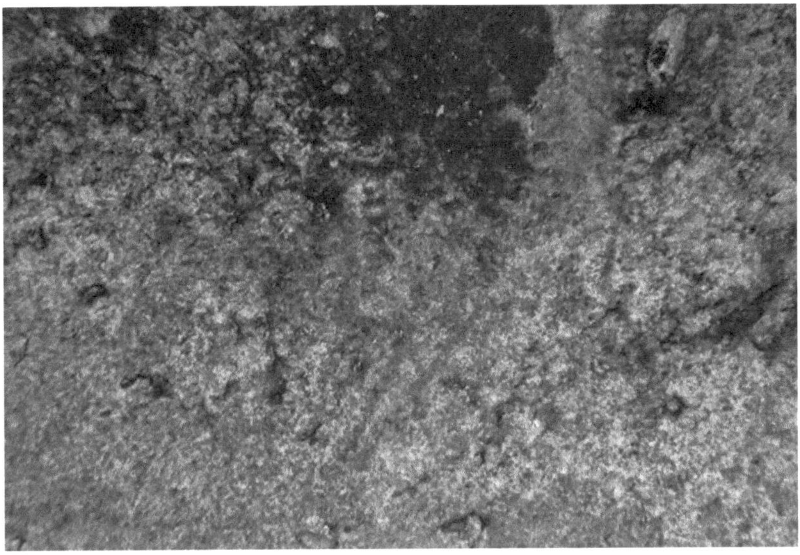

Fig. 3.36 Unidentified paintings

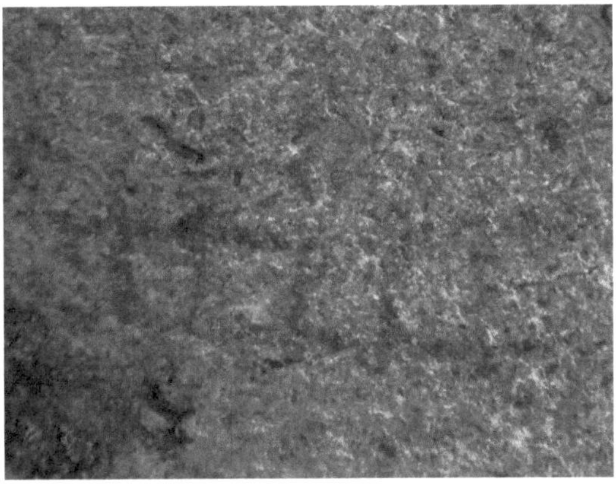

Fig. 3.37 Unidentified paintings

Inside the shelter, the entire surface is painted with pictures, some of which are still visible while others can be recognized by their traces, while a third group of paintings are completely washed out due to weathering or other reasons. The somehow preserved paintings are located on the far left of the shelter. This group is made up of three Buddhist images (Fig. 3.40), most likely representing the Buddhist triad. The seated Buddha figure in the centre sits cross-legged and in meditation poses or he could also form *dharmacakramudrā*. The lower part of the body and the throne on which he sat are heavily weathered and blackened by weathering. Buddha is represented from the front but his head is slightly turned to his right. The contour of the parts of the face is marked by linear drawings of orange colour. The hair and

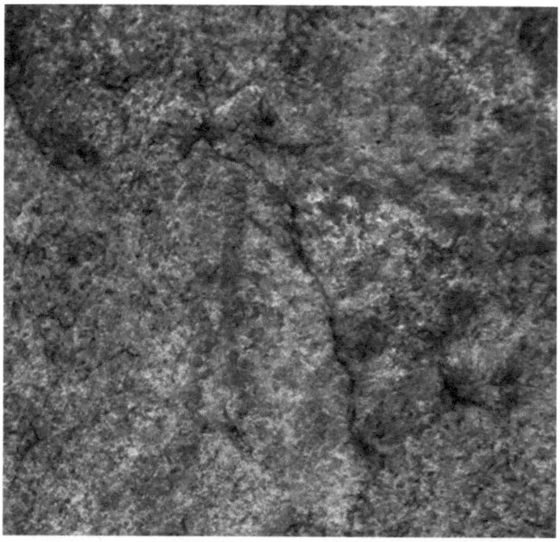

Fig. 3.38 Unidentified paintings

Fig. 3.39 Unidentified paintings

the *uṣṇīṣa* are painted black. He is depicted with open eyes which show orange-painted eyebrows and eyelids. The mouth and nose are barely visible. His right ear is degraded while the left is clearly visible and the contour lines are shown in red colour. He wears a dark orange-coloured garment and probably covers both of his shoulders. Due to the patina on the surface of the rock, the folded hands and legs have become blackish, dark black and dark brown. It may also be due to soot from the fire since the shelters are used by herders as well as visited by the natives. Behind the

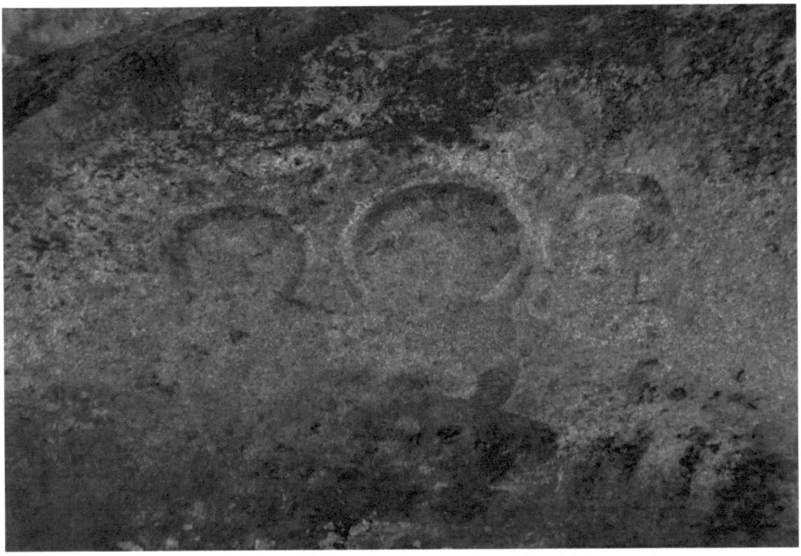

Fig. 3.40 Rock shelter shows three Buddhist images painted in orange, black and white ochre

head of Buddha there is a large round halo-painted black or white with a dark border tint with an orange-coloured margin but it has become whitish due to weathering or oxidation. The halo colour has faded and turned whitish in some places, possibly due to weathering (Figs. 3.37, 3.38, and 3.39).

The figure to the right of Buddha is also seated cross-legged with an unclear gesture of the hands. His right hand is directed towards his knees[7] while his hand is degraded and the position is unclear. He is seated almost facing forward but his head is turned ¾ to his right. The face area is delimited by an orange outline. Most part of the face is washed out except for his left eye where the sclera is white in colour and the iris and pupil are painted with black ochre. The iris is not in the middle of the eye but is moved to its right corner suggesting that it is looking to its right. The hair is originally shown with black colour but currently it has turned milky due to oxidation or could be due to other reasons as well. He wears a garment that covers his right shoulder but the left one seems to be left bare. The hue of the garment and the body is the same orange ochre except that the colour of the dress is darker than the paint on its body. The figure is added with the same type of halo, in terms of design and colours, behind the head as the previous figure. There is a limited gap between this image and the previous one and both are sitting close to each other. The unidentified object he probably holds in his left hand is extended towards the figure in the centre and crosses his right arm. The object in question is like a wide strip of ribbon or any other similar object (Fig. 3.40).

[7] If it was the case, this figure may represent the figure of the Buddha Śākyamuni displaying the *Bhūmīsparṣamudrā*.

The figure seated on the left side of the Buddha is faded, damaged and is also covered by recent writings. The whole body of the image is washed out. Only the head and some traces of the chest are visible. Apparently, the image is seated facing forward with the head turned towards the image in the centre. The hair on the head has turned light black. The face is painted with orange colour. The eyes are overlapped by modern script while the nose and rest of the face are chipped or defaced due to weather conditions. The halo behind the head is displayed in white colour with a black tint at the margin which was originally bounded by an orange line, but is currently displayed mostly in white line as it is the case in the previous two examples. A little above and also to the left of the three figures, there are traces of orange paint, some of which have turned white. Though the exact nature of these drawings is difficult to recognize still the outlines shows that these traces belong to two seated figures.

Zone B, which formed the model of an almond-shaped eye, retains traces of multiple patterns probably applied to a thin layer of lime plaster or a thick layer of patina on the surface of the shelter. The rest of the rock shelter is optionally covered with a thin layer of lime to make a floor for the murals. Unfortunately, for some reason the plaster has peeled off in many places causing damage and loss to the paintings. The other reason that has harmed the paints may be due to chemical reaction or weathering. There are several other paintings on this side of the rock shelter but they are mostly oxidized leaving a milky appearance on the rock surface or have exposed the original rock surface suggesting traces of the wall paintings. The few reconstructions made here are therefore with a certain margin of error.

The central figure is probably that of Buddha who is seated cross-legged and facing forward. The body is depicted in light orange while dark orange or maroon colour may represent its drapery. Its head is almost clear and stands out from a halo of which very little is preserved. Hair is shown in black. The folded legs are partially preserved. On his right and on his left, there are multiple traces of paintings in orange and black colours but nothing can be said with certainty about these traces of drawings. The complete canvas of images is explained by the previous author as, "As far as the Buddhist paintings are concerned, they illustrate three figures of Bodhisattva[8] (Fig. 3.24) painted in the left field of the shelter and four in the right field. All these seven are depicted in meditational poses. A red pigment is used in both the contour lines and in filling the body of the figures, whereas the hallo behind them is filled in blackish colour. The left field of Abāzo shelter is adorned with one large size seated Bodhisattva in the centre, which is flanked by one standing and one seated Bodhisattva on either side. The central figure is roughly measured about 118 cm high and 65 cm wide. Hands of the central figure are resting in the lap, whereas the gesture of other figures cannot be identified. The standing figure on the left is 150 cm high and 46 cm wide. The small seated figure at the right is 70 cm high and 45 cm wide. A long band of circles is provided above this series of Bodhisattvas, whereas several dots are painted inside the circles. This decoration is further flanked by a long band of lotus flowers while chakra symbols are also adorned at both the

[8] In some aspects, that is the subject matter of the painting, the Buddhist figures of Abāzo can be related to Paṭvano Gaṭai paintings (see below).

ends of the band. In the right field of the rock similar seated type figures are depicted at different places. These are mostly defaced by the rainwater and the stain of rock surface" (Khan, Z.H. 2017: 82). The other areas (C and D) are probably painted with drawings of animals and the like.

The date of the paintings is difficult to determine because no other contemporary datable evidence is found. The nearby Buddhist establishment to which this evidence may be associated is thought to be dated to the second to fourth centuries AD. The other possibility of dating these paintings is to use an absolute dating method such as radiocarbon dating, provided that organic material was added during the preparation of the painting.

Ramanṛai, Buner

Apart from the Buddhist paintings, evidence of rock paintings has also been recorded in the Buner Valley. Here several rock shelters have been reported, some of which have been found painted with different designs, either applied to the rough surface of the rock or plastered over to create a floor for the frescoes. The paintings have been reported from different areas of Buner; some of them were discovered during an archaeological survey of the valley conducted in 1994 and 1995 by the Federal Department of Archaeology and Museums, Government of Pakistan (Khattak 1997: i). during this extensive survey work in the area, paintings were noticed inside the Ramanṛai rock shelter and another located in the Naro Ubo Tange area. Unfortunately, no photographs are provided of the shelters or their paintings. The few liner notes that explained the paintings are, "Further to the southeast of Bangosar on the way to Bai Kale through a narrow track going down, is a rock shelter on the left side at considerable height. The rock shelter contains images, five in all. These images have also been badly treated, and coloured with charcoal. It took us considerable to clean these paintings, but could not fully succeeded in our efforts. These images are of various sizes and the huge rock has provided them complete shelter from rain and direct sun rays, but alas! That they could not survive the cruel hand of man" (Khattak 1997: 72). The other shelter where paintings have been noticed is the Ramanṛai rock shelter. The rock shelter is located near a stūpa site. The author described the paintings in the following words, "To the north-east, north-west of the above stūpa is a big complex hardly 100 m away. A solid rock in the north-western portion of the complex has a big rock shelter and apparently used as a room, the rock shelter has serving as a roof, the ceiling of which has been lime plastered. Motifs of plants, flowers and images of animals in different colours are still visible on the intact portions of the thick lime plaster" (Khattak 1997: 76). Apart from the description above, there are no further details on the exact nature and technique used for these paintings.

Paṭvano Gaṭai, Mardan

Among all the discoveries of rock paintings made in Gandhāra, the most significant and unique painting are those called Paṭvano Gaṭai means "pictures bearing stones". The shelter is located in the mountain range separating Suddham Valley from that of Buner (Fig. 3.41). The paintings are situated few meters to the west of Tanur, a small village in the slope of the mountains. The site is accessible from Ambela police station situated on the main Buner and Suddham road. For arriving the paintings, one has to climb the mountains and walk towards the North West for about 30 min from Ambela Police station.

The area is popular for their big boulders (Fig. 3.42). One among these massive gneiss granitic rocks, approximately 400 × 350 × 900 cm, bears paintings on its south and south eastern part of its shelter (Fig. 3.43). The painted surface of the shelter, opening east, is 185 cm high from ground on its maximum and 105 cm on its minimum.

According to the information, initially collected during survey and documentation, only few years back these images were very clear and intact but, unfortunately, when I visited the site on 2nd of October 1999, major part of the painting was destroyed by the locals and antique dealer. The image on the south side is even tried to flak off by the antiquity dealer resulting in that the lower part of the body is totally damaged

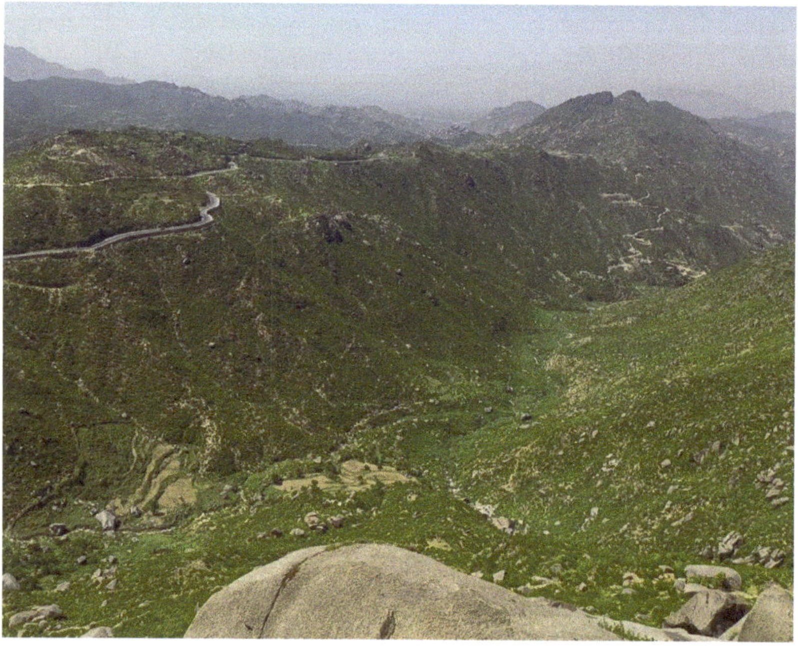

Fig. 3.41 Valley separating the Suddham area from the slope of the mountain located between Districts Mardan and Swabi which separates them from Buner

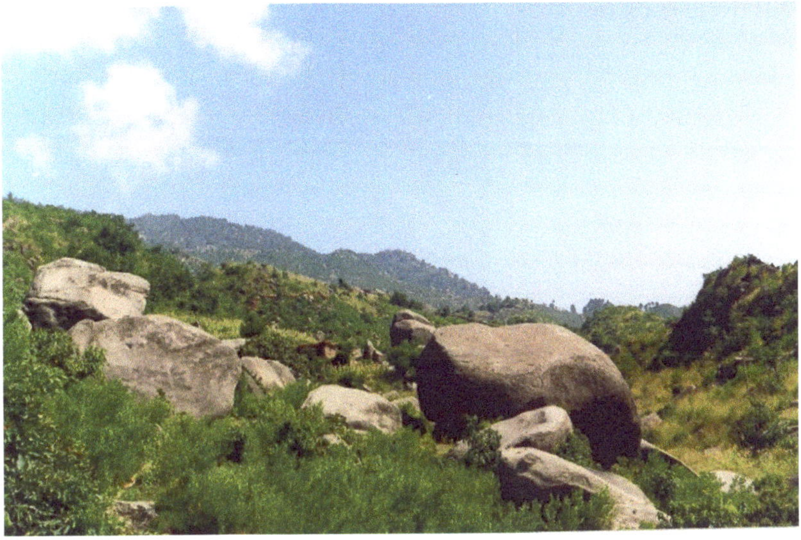

Fig. 3.42 General view of the Paṭvano Gaṭai area

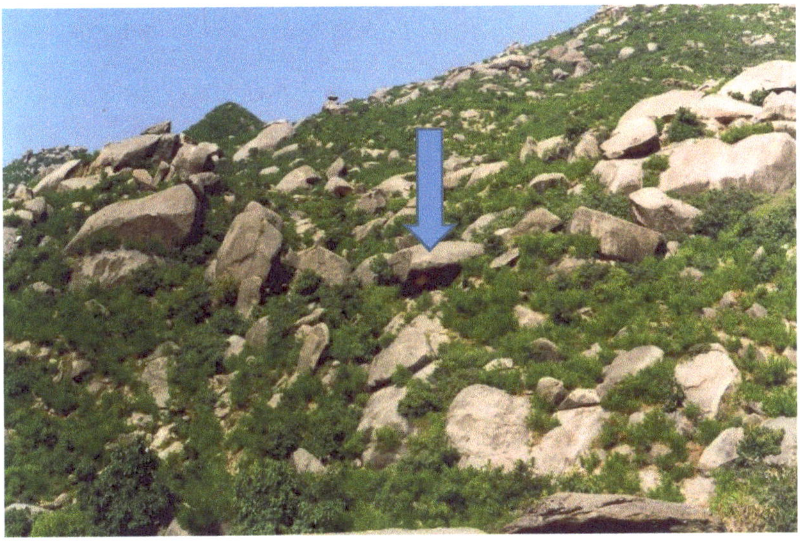

Fig. 3.43 Another view of the Painting area

and missing. It was observed that the local people, either by their curiosities or by a fanatic view, had tried to damage the paintings, especially the faces. According to

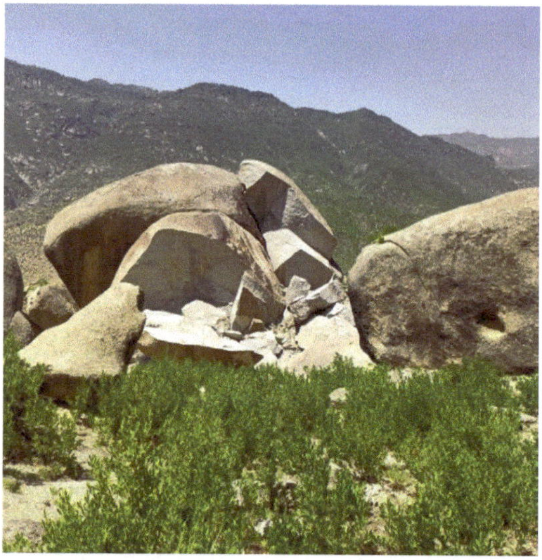

Fig. 3.44 Fragments of the rock shelter after blast

recent information, the rock shelter is blasted with dynamites by the antique seekers who were believing that a treasure was lying underneath the rock (Fig. 3.44).[9]

Paṭvano Gaṭai paintings were perhaps the most conspicuous surviving monuments of art in Gandhara executed probably during fourth/fifth century AD. These paintings were very important not only due to their aesthetic merit and because of their unique characters but also for the reason that these were the only fresco Buddhist paintings discovered in this part of the subcontinent. The theme of the Paṭvano Gaṭai paintings was a religious in tone.

The Paṭvano Gaṭai paintings were originally a group of three images: a seated figure of a Buddha in meditation flanked by two bodhisattvas (?); they were found in a more developed style (Fig. 3.45).

Image 1 (Figs. 3.46, 3.47): The figure on the right side of the Buddha was badly damaged and the lower body was completely missing and only the bust was found preserved. Major part of the face was equally damaged making the identification difficult. The size of the preserved portion of the figure at that time was 42 × 50 cm.

The head of the figure was inclining to the right where Buddha was sitting in mediation pose (*dhyānasāna*). I observed in this figure sensuous fullness of bodily form. The preserved half-opened eye was elongated and was showing almond-shaped form. I did do not confirm the position and gesture of his left hand. The moment of the upper arm towards the chest, however, was showing that the hand might been close to the chest. The right arm was totally damaged and nothing could be said about its position and gesture. The figure was shown crowned and bejewelled. The head-dress was quite interesting seemingly decorated with flowers and other various devices.

[9] I am very thankful to Dr. Ghayyur Shahab, Curator Mardan Museum and in charge of the sites in the area, who sent one of his assistant to the Paṭvano Gaṭai site to inform me about the present condition of the paintings. But, unfortunately, according to him, they no more exist.

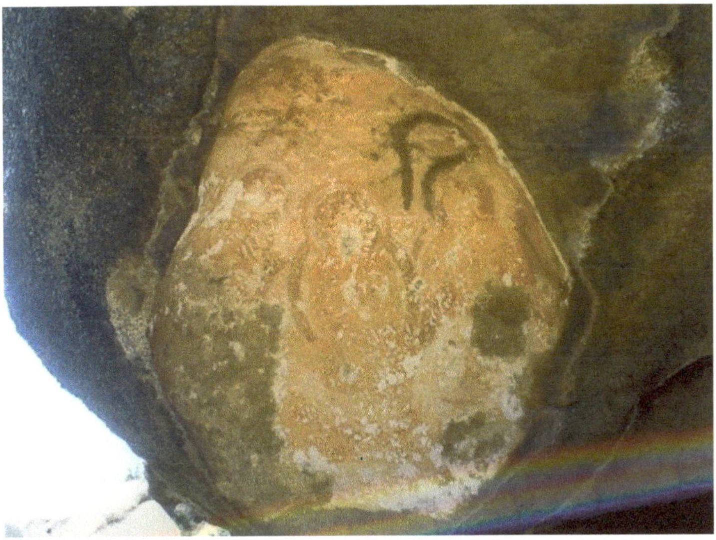

Fig. 3.45 Painted surface of the rock shelter

The ribbon which were visible behind the shoulders were seemingly attached to the hair. The figure was also wearing two rows necklace of pearls.

Nothing could be said about the ear ornaments because the ears were damaged especially that of the right ear. The figure was shown clad with a monk rob covering both his shoulders.

The figure is painted with chocolate colour contoured in red. The hair dress or the crown was shown in whitish contoured in red colour. Part of the headdress was falling on his shoulder. The drapery was shown in dark brown while the body was in light brown or light yellow colour. White strips were shown on the arm dress, probably sleeves.

Nimbus, having no sign of any decoration, was shown behind the head. The margin of the glory was showing different bands painted in whitish and light brown colour; the rest was demonstrating with dark brown pigment. The background was shown in light brown with white circle.

Image 2 (Figs. 3.48 and 3.49): As compared to the other two figures, the central figure was comparatively well preserved except the face. The size of the image was 50 × 90 cm. Buddha was shown seated (*dhyānasāna*) with crossed legs and the hands were in *dhyānacakra* pose.

He was dressed with a monastic rob covering both the shoulders. The feet were covered with drapery, while folds in the drapery were shown with red thin lines.

The hair was marked with a dark brown colour, with a mixture of red pigment, while the body was showing chocolate or light brown colour. The dresses were in brown ochre. The face was damaged but part of the right eye was found preserved. The ears with long lobs were contoured in red.

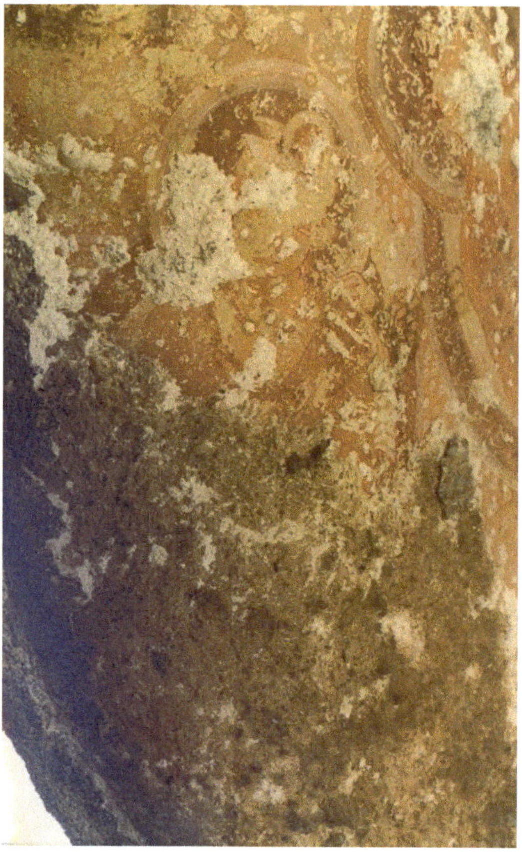

Fig. 3.46 Bodhisattva on the left side of the Buddha

The nimbus was showing three colours. The two bands on margin were painted in light brown and whitish, respectively, while the rest was with dark brown colour. The extreme margin of the nimbus was marked with a narrow white line. Besides the nimbus, an aureole was shown behind the body. In contrast to the nimbus, here the margin strips were in whitish and in dark brown colours while the rest was painted with whitish colour.

The throne or the seat was demonstrating whitish colour but the upper margin of the seat was decorated with dots and the lower one with a thin red line. The white dots on the upper margin gave the impression of a certain jewellery.

Image 3 (Figs. 3.50, 3.51, and 3.52): On the right side, a figure with the upper body partly preserved but the lower one completely damaged was seemingly also to be in sitting position as figures 1 and 2. The figure measured 42 × 80 cm including the seat. Its head was inclining to the left and its face was turning little towards the Buddha sitting to its right.

The upper body was probably nude since no distinction was apparently made in between the colours of its body and dresses as we had in the other two cases. The

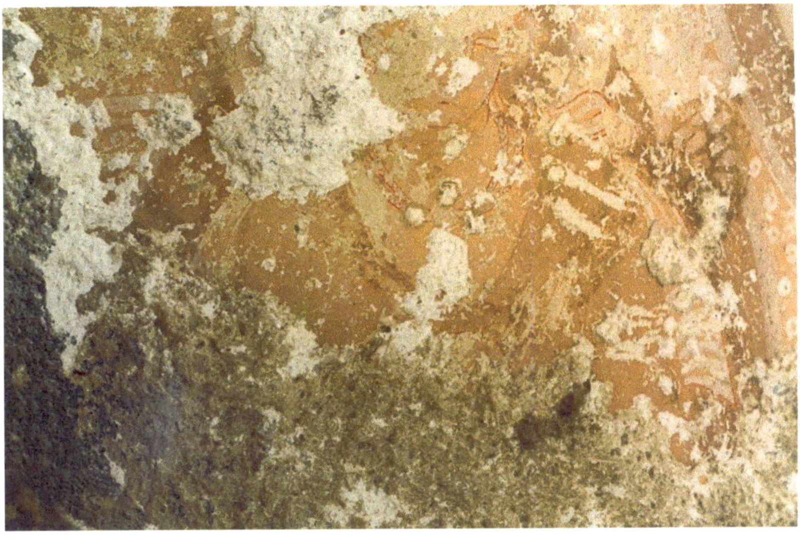

Fig. 3.47 Another view of image 1

folds of its dress on both sides might indicate that the back of the shoulders was covered and the chest was left exposed. Possibly, the figure was cladded with Indian *dhoti* and also with a stylish scarp while the upper body was left bared.

The right hand was raising against the right shoulder; the open palm was turning backward in *vismaya* (surprise pride) gesture. The little finger and the thumb were coming closer and presenting a gesture-like *vitarakamudrā* (gesture of arguing).

Such a gesture, as far as, I know, is never shown in the Buddhist art of Gandhāra. One of the few examples that we have in the Indian Buddhist art is that coming from central Asia.[10] The figure was showing half-opened narrow eyes, crescent eyebrows and prominent nose. The lips were tight. The ears lobs were very elongated, the form which is common in the Chinese Buddhist art. These parts were contoured with red colour to become more prominent.

The ornament that adorned the dead were of particular significance. The figure was provided a crown and some customary ornaments. A chain of pearls, shown in white contoured in the red passes through the hair, shown in dark brown with a mixture of a red. Above the forehead, a barrel-shaped gem was encircling with a chain of pearl and was place in the centre of a crescent.

Floral designs were also added to the headdress of the figure. The most beautiful example was the representation of a fully blown lotus flower displayed on the right side above the ear. The lotus flower was apparently tightened with pearls string that the passing through the hair of the figure. The flower was shown with white colour contoured in red. Ribbons were shown attached to the crown.

---

[10] Bussagli (1978: 30).

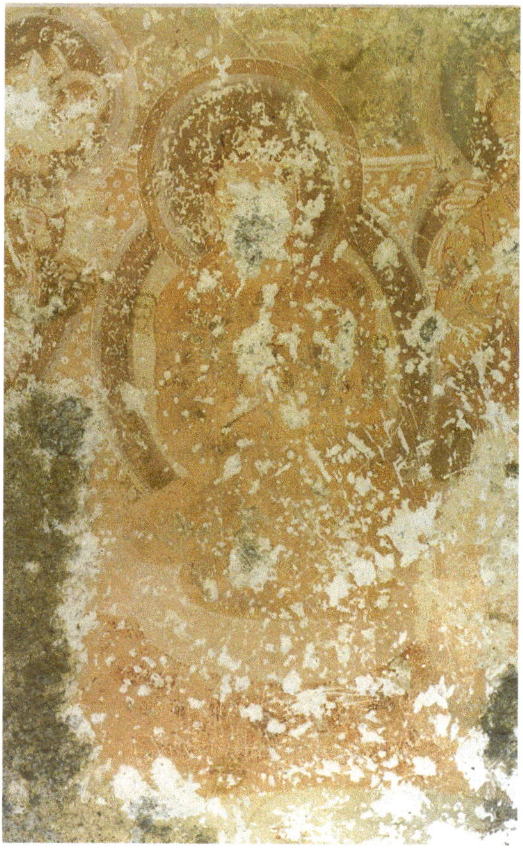

Fig. 3.48 Buddha seated in *dhyānamudrā*

The figure was lavishly adorned with pearl necklace of two rows, similar to image 1, and a pearl string for the decoration of hair. Both ends of the necklace were coalescing into each other end and was added with a white pearl. From the right left side end and additional pearl in oval shape could have been observed. The nimbus of the figure was showing different bands painted in white and light brown colour as it was the case with image 1.

As a whole, the figure was revealing a delicate physical type, depicting a well proportional form and accomplishment in treatments. From aesthetic point of view the figure presented a refine and subtler form and was a work of artistic mastery that the author has ever known in this field. Is this a figure of female bodhisattva?

Decoration in the background and on the border (Figs. 3.53 and 3.54): In the background, a white-coloured strip in horizontal was going behind the heads of the figures. Another parallel line in white, thinner than the first one, was equally added with a space between the two; the space was filled in light brown colour. The area shown in light brown, below the strips, was decorated with designs in white circles.

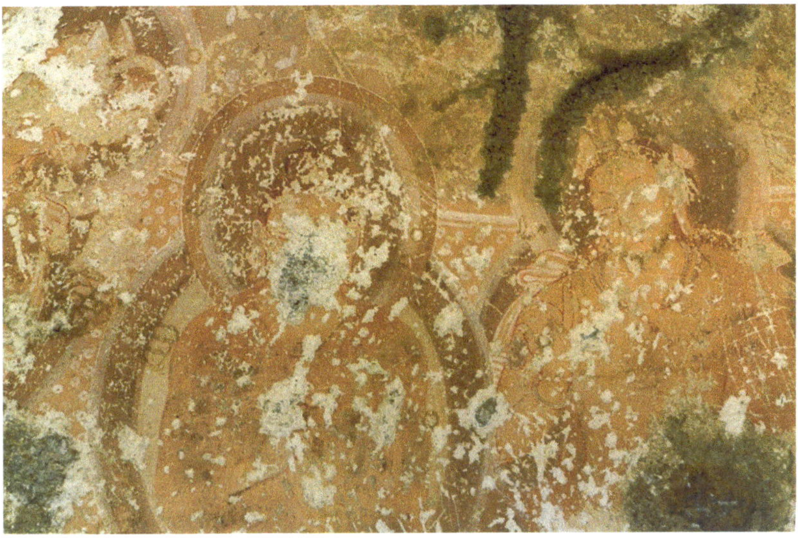

Fig. 3.49 Close view of the Buddha and the figure to his left

The margin of the background was decorated with lotus flowers in red. The average size of these flowers was 5 × 5 cm. The border was also showing hollow triangles in black colour; the average size was 4 × 7 cm.

Techniques and colours: The techniques and colours in the preparation of the above painting were of special interest. The surface of the shelter was first dressed, then coated with a thick layer of mud plaster and lastly lime plaster has been used for levelling and evenness the field. For further smoothness of the ground and as background, a small amount of the light brown ochre was applied. After the ground was ready, the following colures were used as finishing coat.

A red pigment was applied for making contours/borders of the body parts, hair dress, jewellery and floral designs displayed on the border of the plastered area. Dark paint, obtained probably from carbon or soot (Sanskrit Kajjala), was only used in the hollow triangle exhibited on the border of the plastered area. While shady brown with mixture of red was used especially for the hair and the central part or margin of the halo, chocolate or brown colour had got an important role and was applied for the body of the figures; light chocolate was used for the background.

White was applied in drawing the eyes, nails, parts of the aureoles or halo, in the hair dress, in the background, etc.

Date: In the absence of any datable material associated material to the paintings, the exact date of the paintings would be difficult to determine. However, the circumstantial evidence and the iconography suggest that the Paṭvano Gaṭai paintings may belong to a period between the second–fourth/fifth centuries AD. This is the period when the Aziz Ḍheri and Kashmir Smast paintings in valley were executed (see below).

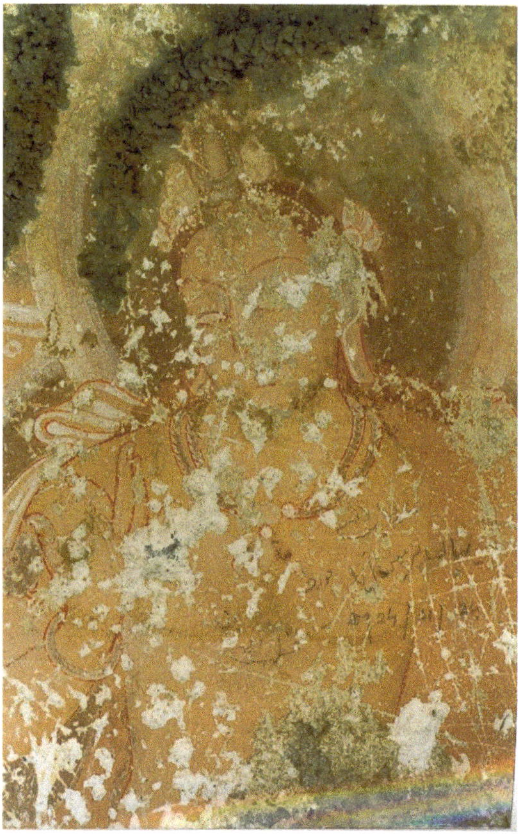

Fig. 3.50 Bodhisattva sitting to Buddha's left side

* * *

The discovery of Paṭvano Gaṭai paintings is of particular value since they are completely different, in character and subject matter, from other Buddhist period paintings, so far, discovered in Gandhāra. In the case of the Paṭvano Gaṭai paintings, the first thing that would impress the art historians is the quality of art presented there which show how the art of paintings has attained its degree of currency and excellence almost equal to that of stone carvings in Mahāgandhāra. From these evidences, it is also clear that how the mechanical skill of the artist in the region of Gandhāra reached its height which might have been started during the Kuṣān and has to be continued even during the Huns period fourth–fifth century AD, the presumed date of the Paṭvano Gaṭai paintings.

Moreover, the mixture of Indian—theme and facial features, and central Asian—colour scheme and combination, influence in these paintings confirms that the region of Gandhāra not only geographically but also historically and culturally also knitted together by caravan routes and trade relations. Furthermore, the existence of these and other paintings has shown that it is far from the truth that in the region of Gandhāra,

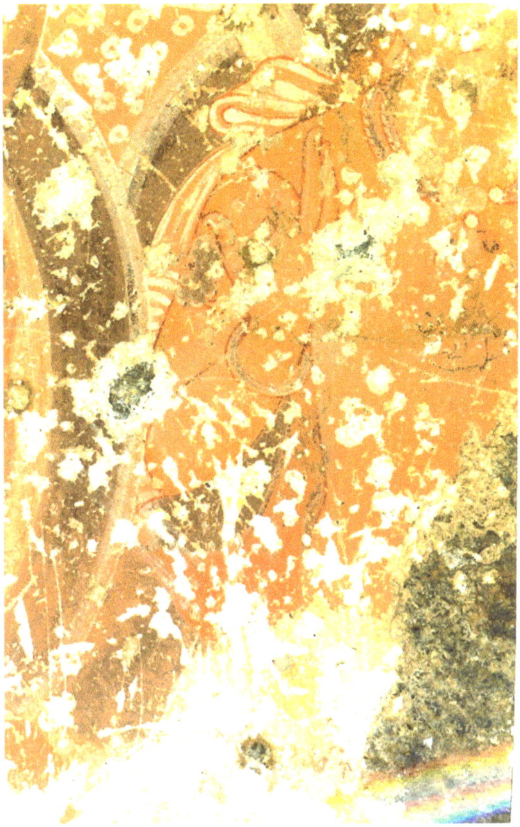

Fig. 3.51 Close up of the hand gesture

frescoes could not survive due to its climate condition. The Paṭvano Gaṭai paintings have proved that the moisture and expose to the air did not affect the paintings but, in fact, the damages are only and solely due to human hazards.

Kashmir Smast, Mardan

The site of Kashmir Smast (Fig. 3.55), the earlier seat of Hindu learning, is located in the Sakra Mountain range which separates the Peshawar Valley from the Buner district and also not very far from the Paṭvano Gaṭai area. The site was visited by the Chinese pilgrim Xuanzang and mentioned its importance as a pilgrimage centre visited by people from different regions. This is also confirmed by the archaeological evidence documented and excavated by the present author (Nasim Khan 2006: 199, Fig. 185: 1,2; 2008: 222; 2018: 307–308). The site of Kashmir Smast is located in the same mountain range where Paṭvano Gaṭai paintings were found. It is a remote area and can only be reached on foot, either through the village of Pirsai situated to the

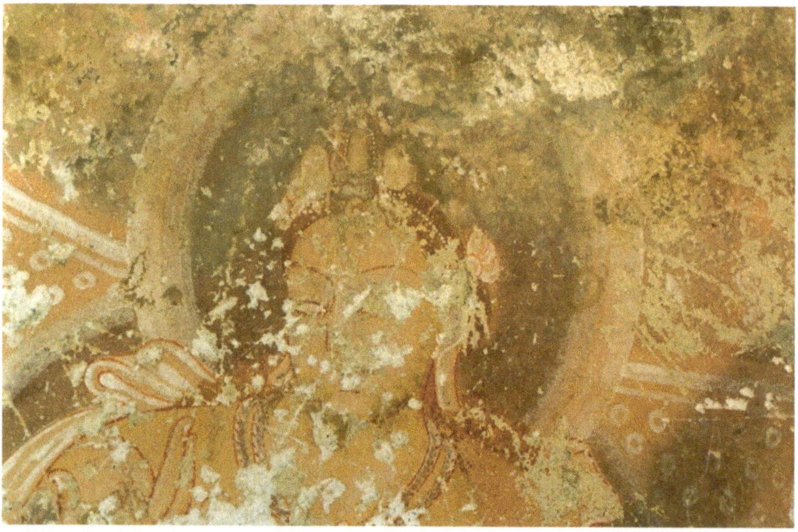

Fig. 3.52 Details of the upper body

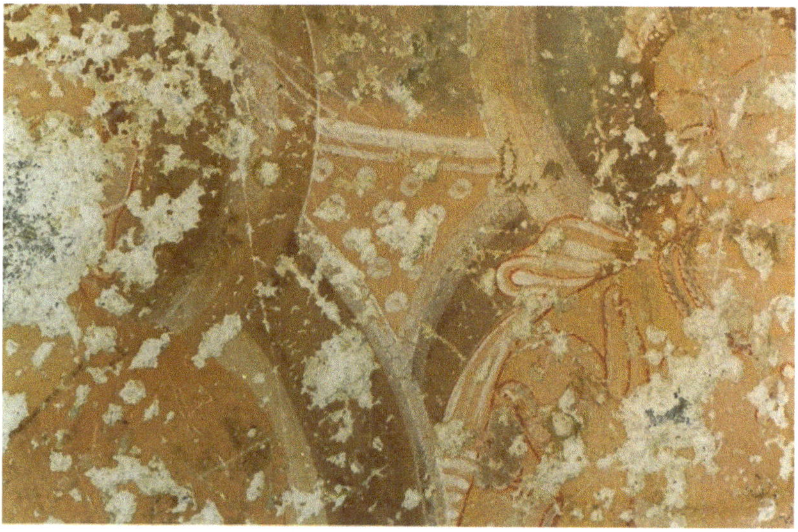

Fig. 3.53 Details of decoration of the field between two figures

east or through the village of Babuzai located to the west of the site. From both sides, one needs to walk and climb the mountain for two to three hours to reach the site. Inside the valley that connects the village of Babuzai to the site, there are several rock shelters on either side of the tracks leading to the Hindu Shrine of Kashmir Smast. Three of these shelters retain Brāhmī inscriptions from the fourth/fifth century AD

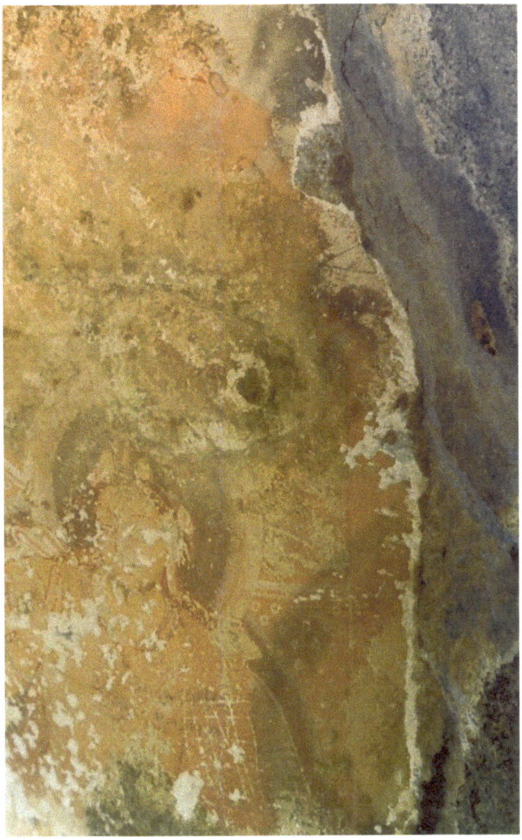

Fig. 3.54 Decoration on the right border of the painted surface

(Nasim Khan 2009). They are written on the rough surfaces of the shelters with black and red ochre. However, the only colour used for the inscriptions in the main shelter, called the Sacred Rock (Fig. 3.56), is black (Fig. 3.57). The total number of painted inscriptions discovered in this particular and limited area is sixty-five. They could be Buddhist or Hindu. Fragments of Buddhist sculptures were recovered from the site, named Bare Ubah, located nearby. Despite the discovery of a large number of ancient, engraved and painted inscriptions, no frescoes Buddhist image has yet been found in this area.

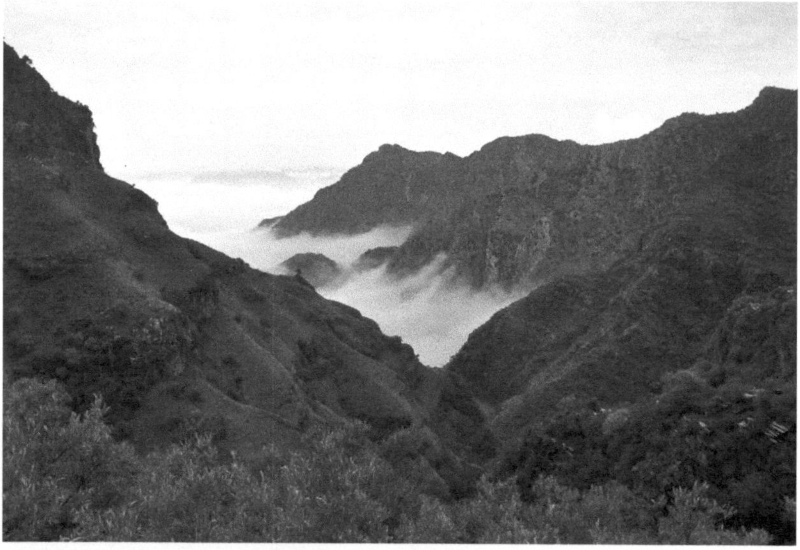

Fig. 3.55 The Valley of Sita Mahā Kandara; view from the Kashmir Smast site

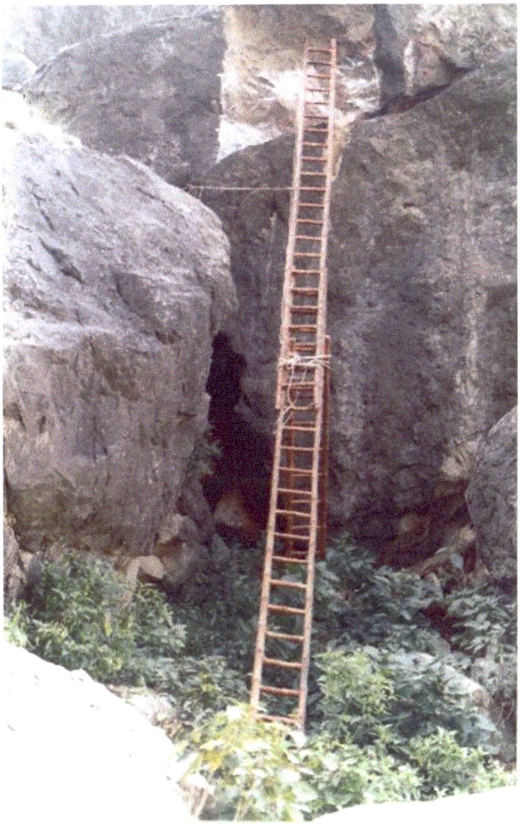

Fig. 3.56 View of the Sacred Rock at Bare Uba. Documentation of the inscriptions by the author is in progress

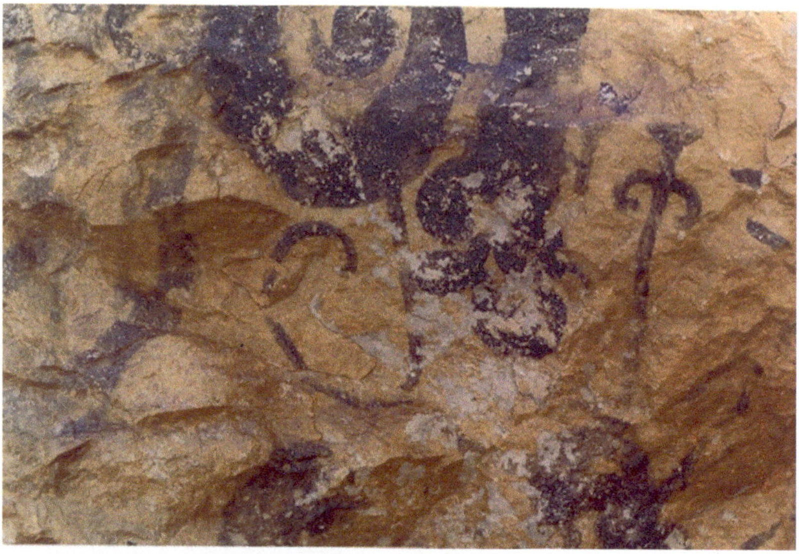

Fig. 3.57 Close view of some of the inscriptions written in Gupta Brāhmī

Chapter 4
Murals in Buddhist Shrines, Built Structures

Material evidence shows that the Buddhist stūpas and monasteries of Gandhāra were richly decorated with carvings mostly in stone and stucco. Some stone carvings also show that they have been washed with gold while those in stucco have been painted, mostly with orange, red and black colours. There are indications which also confirm that when and wherever possible stūpas were also washed with gold and walls of monasteries were added with beautiful murals and the images were painted in different colours. This form of offerings and devotion to the stūpa could continue throughout the history of Buddhist worship in Gandhāra. In Buddhist texts, such an act of offering to a stūpa is considered meritorious as well as beneficial for the Buddhists. About the construction of a stūpa and its offerings, the Dīgha Nikāya says, "But, Lord, what are we to do with the Tathāgata's remains?" "Ānanda, they should be dealt with like the remains of a wheel-turning monarch". "And how is that, Lord?" "Ānanda, the remains of a wheel-turning monarch are wrapped in a new linen-cloth". This they wrap in teased cotton wool, and this in a [142] new cloth. Having done this five hundred times each, they enclose the king's body in an oil-vat of which is covered with another iron pot. Then having made a funeral-pyre of all manner of perfumes, they cremate the king's body, and they raise a stūpa at a crossroads. That, Ānanda is what they do with "the remains of a wheel-turning monarch, and they should deal with the Tathāgata's body in the same way. A stūpa should be erected at the crossroads for the Tathāgata. And whoever lays wreaths or puts sweet perfumes and colours there with a devout heart, will reap benefit and happiness for a long time" (DN ii, 141–143). Similarly, in late Buddhist texts, the act of offering to a stūpa is also considered a deed deserving much merit. For example, in the instructions of Padmasambhava (eighth century AD), a member of the Yogācāra sect of Tantric Buddhism, a long list of offerings to stūpas comes with many benefits that can be derived from it. Therefore, the land of Gandhāra which originally housed a number of stūpas and monasteries must have also received such offerings throughout the centuries when this land was nurturing and nourishing the souls of the Buddhists, both locally and across many countries.

M. Nasim Khan, *Gandhāran School of Buddhist Paintings*,
https://doi.org/10.1007/978-981-96-9310-8_4

Gandhāra has produced numerous stūpas some of which have been excavated and preserved while others have collapsed and disappeared due to many reasons. But those that have been excavated and then preserved in one way or another indicate that they were richly decorated, according to accessibility, with all kinds of precious materials and bright colours available at the time. Fragmentary evidence of frescoes or simple varnish paintings on carvings is also available for the majority of Gandhāran stūpa sites, however, there are very few sites where the presence of frescoes and paintings is more prominent and significant due to the parts preserved from these paintings.

The earliest reference to fresco paintings from the Buddhist period, which have been found at the various monastery sites in Gandhāra, was made by Marshall when referring to the paintings noted at the site of Sirkap and Mohra Moradu (Marshall 1951: Vol. 1, 171, 360).[1] The next discovery was at the Buddhist site of Butkara I (Swat) where, among other paintings, a beautiful fresco depicting a princely figure was recorded (Faccena 1981: Part 5.1, col. pl. I). The discovery of wall paintings inside Buddhist monasteries continues and to this list can be added four more important Buddhist sites in Gandhāra, such as Aziz Ḍheri , Abba Sahib Cheen, Jinnan Wali Ḍheri and the Yakatoot frescoes.[2]

Aziz Ḍheri, Swabi

Among all the archaeological remains that we know of, so far, in the Swabi region, Aziz Ḍheri (Fig. 4.1) is considered to be one of the largest archaeological mounds in the region with a rich assemblage of cultural artefacts and a well-organized settlement history. The site of Aziz Ḍheri (N.34.24958; E 72.39449; altitude 350.8 m, 1151') is located about three kilometres west of the village of Ganghu Ḍher which itself is positioned almost eight kilometres north of the Jrando Bridge, a viaduct built over a canal on the main Mardan-Swabi road. The Buddhist site of Ranigaṭ is situated 7 km in the same direction. The other famous Buddhist site is the stūpa of Bahu recently excavated by the Provincial Directorate of Archaeology and Museums of the Government of Khyber Pakhtunkhwa.[3] Excavations at Aziz Ḍheri site (Fig. 4.2) began in 1993 and since then they have continued, on stop basis, and have, so far, revealed significant finds of antiquities and structures of great importance. Among these discoveries are the murals of the area designated DVIII-8. In this part of the site, a small square structure was unearthed, located south of the main stūpa, at a depth of about 8 m below the datum point. The structure is surrounded by walls on

[1] Traces of paintings have also been noticed inside a shrine located at the Buddhist site of Takht-i-Bhai. The structure is termed *Vihār* by Cunningham (Cunningham 1875: 28).

[2] The Yakatoot paintings have not been found in situ, so I have not yet been able to confirm if they were originally recovered from a Yakatoot site or if they were removed from any other site in the Gandhāra or its beyond. In any case, they must belong to a stūpa or a monastery.

[3] Traces of Murals have also been reported from this site (Fig. 4.1). Excavation report of the site by Dr. Fawad Khan is in progress.

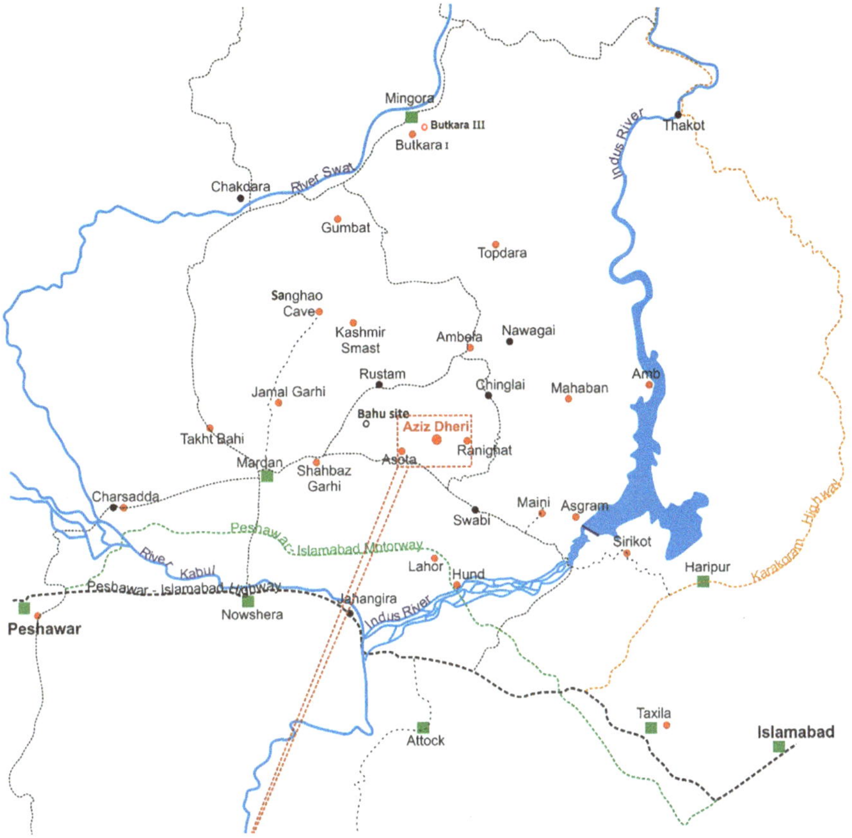

Fig. 4.1 Location map of Aziz Ḍheri

all sides. There is no direct access to the hall except for the steps which are added on the inner side of the north wall, which would have meant first climbing the wall by any means and then taking the steps to the north to descend into the room where the square structure still exists.

Different construction phases of dissimilar types of stones were also observed. A personal communication involved in the excavations of Aziz Ḍheri indicates that many sculptures were found dumped in the corridor located against and to the east of this room (Figs. 4.3, 4.4, and 4.5).[4] The main objective of the excavation in this particular area was to understand the reason why the stūpa was built inside the room and also the reason for the difficulty of accessing to this structure. We also searched for the ground level of the stūpa and for any evidence that could help to date the stūpa itself and the structures around it. Finally, we were keen to investigate below the ground level of the stūpa and find out if it was built on natural ground or if cultural

[4] In his previous research, the author mistakenly mentioned that the sculptures were found inside the room (see Nasim Khan 2010, volume 1: 68) which was, in fact, not the case.

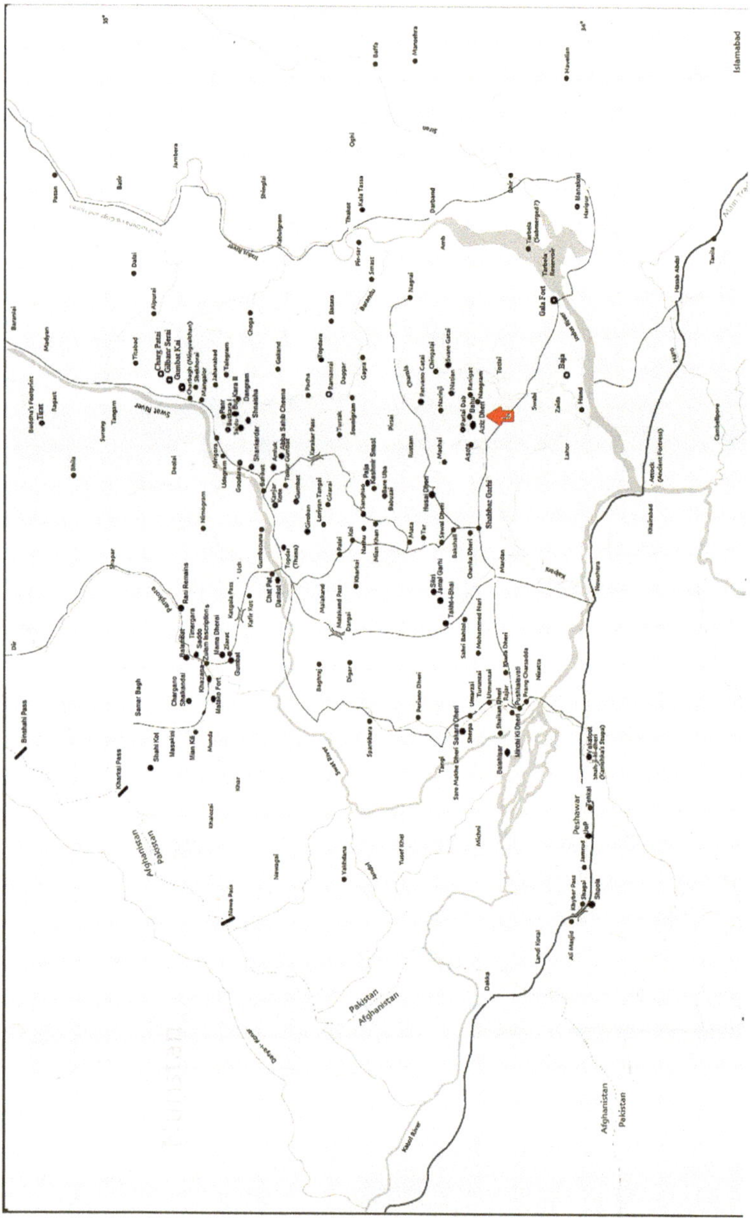

Fig. 4.2 Location map of Aziz Ḍheri Buddhist site Gandhāra

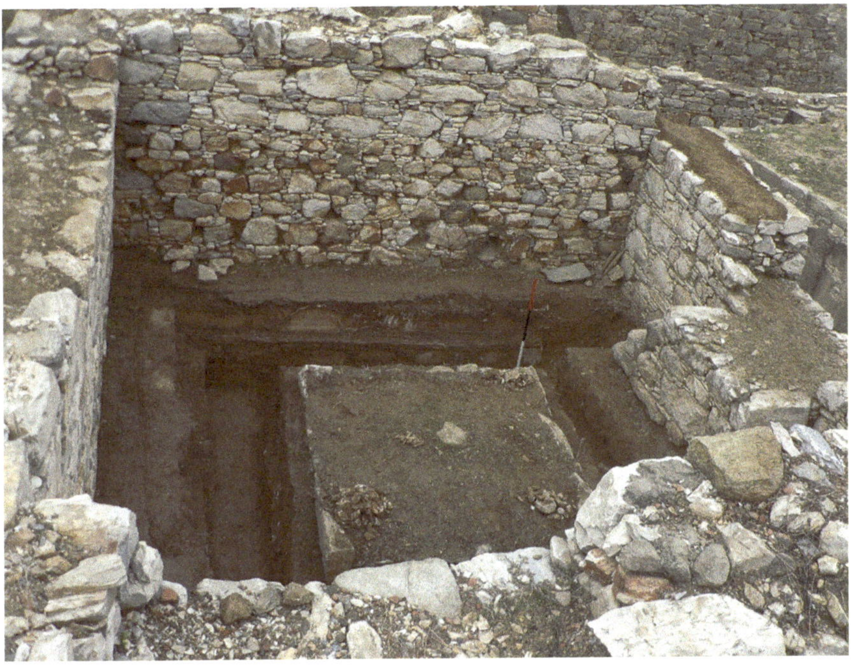

Fig. 4.3 Shrine with paintings located to the south of the main Stūpa at Aziz Ḍheri

activities were taking place before the construction of the stūpa and the hall. Due to lack of evidence, we could not confirm whether the stūpa was originally covered or not, however, the presence of the murals has suggested that this structure was originally sheltered. If it was the case, this would give special meaning to the whole structure in this zone.

Besides other important findings at DVIII-8, the most exciting discovery was of course the unearthing of fresco paintings that were applied to the plinth and mouldings of the platform, at least on its three directions, west, south and east. As mentioned in one of the reports (Naeem Qazi 1993: 77), these paintings were first exposed in 1993, but the condition of the paintings shows that they were treated mercilessly and badly damaged during that time. The lime clods found on the upper level come from these earlier excavations. As the condition of the platform itself explained that the lime plasters had been haphazardly excavated, which caused great loss to most of the paintings (Figs. 4.5 and 4.6).

The three sides of the platform and possibly the northern side as well, as it is presently covered by the steps, are provided with frescoes. Two layers of lime plasters have been applied to the front face and the mouldings of the platform which is made of diaper or sometimes rubble masonry. The lime plaster underneath is in fact added with paints which were covered with a second layer of lime with a smooth surface probably in a later period for unknown reason (Fig. 4.5).

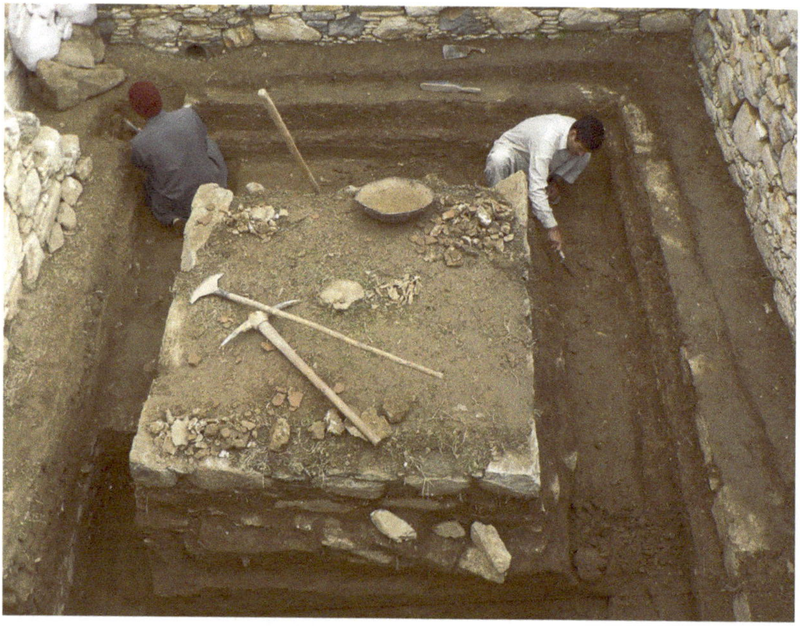

Fig. 4.4 Close view of Fig. 4.3

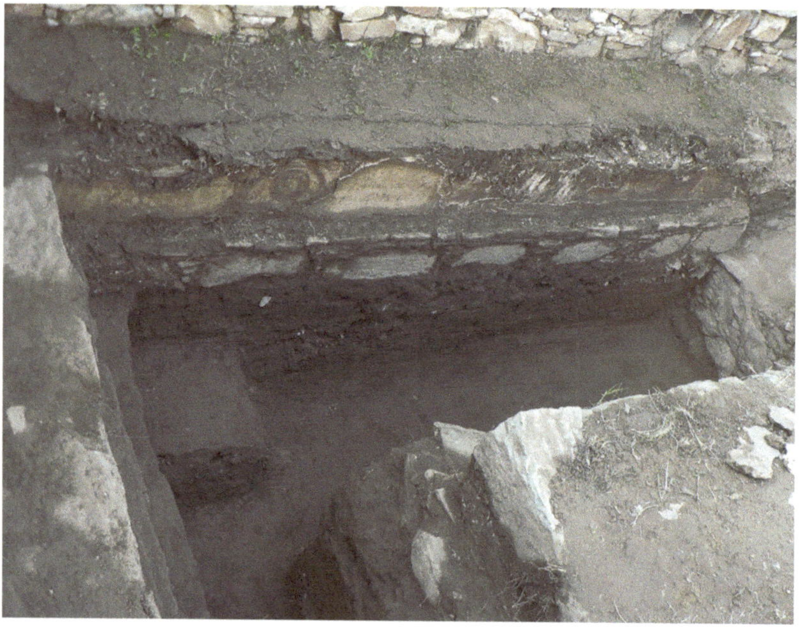

Fig. 4.5 Front of the western podium of Fig. 4.4

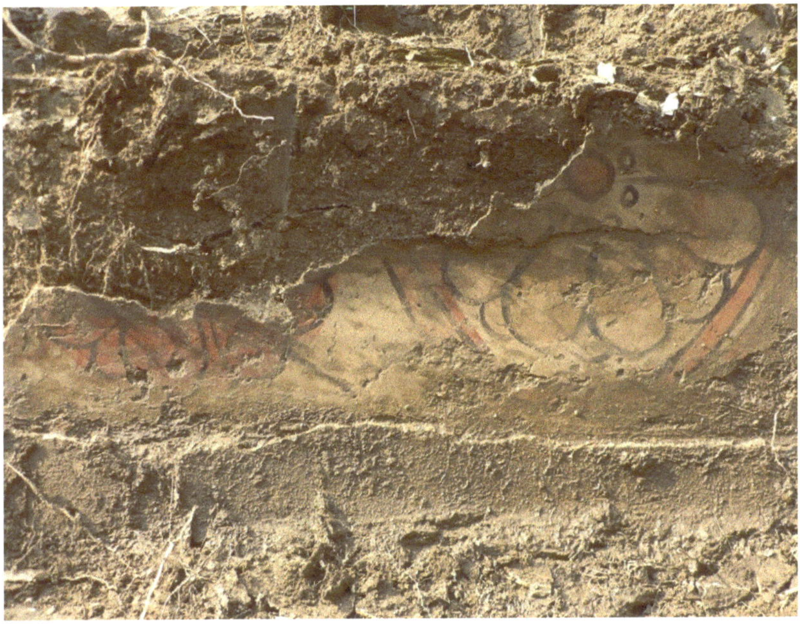

Fig. 4.6 Detail of the paintings shown on Fig. 4.5

Western podium (Fig. 4.5): The paintings seen on the west side of the platform include lotus flowers and a symbol, similar to a sun emblem, located on the south side of the painted surface of the front plinth. Probably, a long band of red colour marked in a zigzag or wavy fashion with black margins is drawn, starting from the right end of the western surface and probably terminates at its southern end. In each arc of the undulating motif, a flower is painted starting with its first curvature on the right side. From this wavy line, another similar band branches off from each arch, which opens downward and probably covers the tops of the white flowers, symbolizing purity for the Buddhists.[5]

The flowers are arranged from right to left and usually have two different shapes depending on their colour application. In the first group, the entire bottom of the flower or surface of the plaster is painted with whitish paint, and then a black line is applied for the outline of the petals giving the impression of a white lotus flower (Fig. 4.6). But the stigma of the flower is marked with a greasy red spot bordered with black. In the centre of the beginning of each petal, near the outer surface of the central circle, another small disc of white colour with a black margin is depicted. The articulation of the two petals at their ends is nuanced with an arc-shaped design painted in black opening on the internal face.

The background of the second group is coloured whitish and for the contour of the petals black paint is applied expressing red colour of the flower. The red flowers

[5] The top of the flowers in the bow fold down is damaged and the shape and purpose of a second strip cannot be confirmed.

are damaged in the centre, and we are not sure about the shape of the stigma and other designs in the centre. But there is much probability that the same pattern is also adopted here as we have for the white flowers. It is possible that the central point remained white in colour with black margins and the other points in the angles are in red with black margins.

The lotus flowers are arranged in a symmetrical and fitting order; each of the white lotus is placed in the down curved of the undulating line while each of the read lotuses in the shadow of the curve bending upwards (Fig. 4.6) following the alternative order of red to white starting from the northern end of the western podium. On that surface, in total, six lotus flowers were observed, three white and three red, but there is a space for four more such flowers, field for two between the last two flowers to the south and a bay for two more between the last flower to the south and the solar-like symbol. To the south of the solar symbol, there is also a room for two more such symbols or flowers.

The solar-like symbol is also damaged and seems quite complex in nature (Fig. 4.7). The background of this symbol is marked with whitish colour whereas the central part of it shows a whitish spot encircled by a large thick band, first painted in red and then black colour is apparently applied to it. The circle covers its top with a thick semi-circular band in red overshadowed with black ochre; this might be part of the undulating band which extends to the left and goes downwards and bifurcates probably into two thick strips; both in red colour with black margins. At the angle of the solar symbol and the bands to the left, there is a spiral-shaped design in red giving the impression of some Pehlavi letters. Above, there is another parallel band which is painted in red but with a lower margin coloured in black; from its outer surface two hook-shaped designs in red and black open and bifurcate to the right. The upper cornice of the plinth is damaged while the lower one is covered with a second coat, nothing can be said about the presence of any sort of drawings in these areas. But it is more probable, as to be concluded from the other podiums, that there must have been some kind of paintings as well.

Southern podium (Fig. 4.8): Unfortunately, the platform is seriously damaged and very little is visible on its remaining part. The only paintings available on this surface are the remains of a lotus flower most likely painted red, the paint which is also applied to the top of the lower plinth cornice below the moulding, found in the southeast corner of the podiums. It can give us an idea of the original look that would have been initially of the lower part of the west podium. The front side of the cornice seems to remain blank. Above and near the corner of the south and east podium is a lotus flower painted red with black ochre outlines. A thick red vertical band is painted in the angle of the podium which descends and terminates at the lower end of the plastered area of the angle.

Eastern podium (Fig. 4.9): As it is the case in the other two platforms, this one is also heavily damaged and very little is preserved from it to study. The top and front sides of the podium were exposed and paint was observed on the top side, front top side and top and some time on the front of the lower moulding. On the upper side, red paint is probably applied without revealing any particular design. The lower moulding also bears a simple painting in red, while the upper facade of the podium

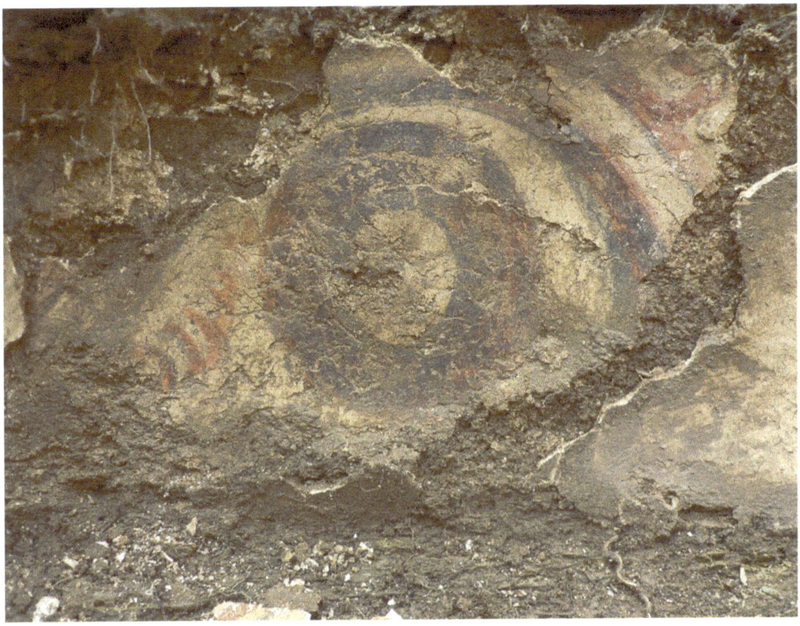

Fig. 4.7 Detail of the symbol painted on the western podium

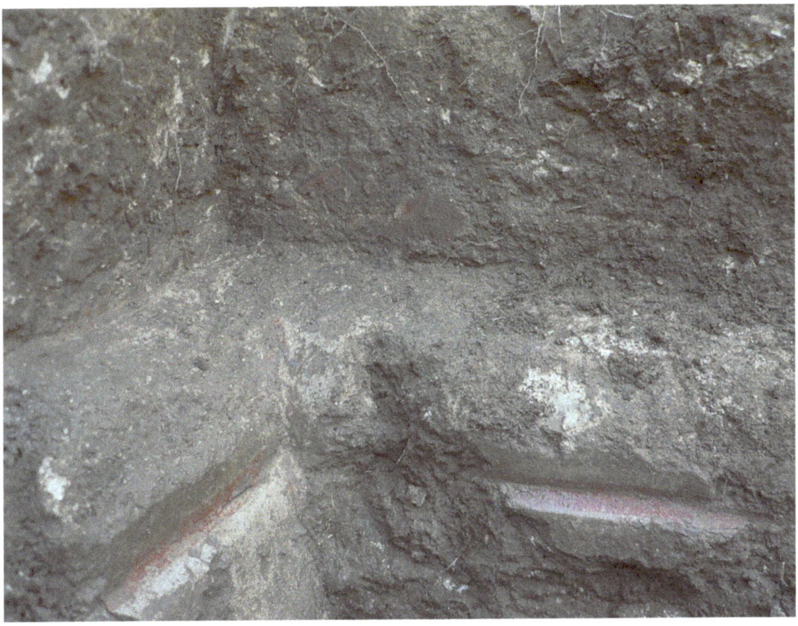

Fig. 4.8 South-west corner of the podiums

is probably painted with the same type of patterns and in the same order as seen on the podium on the west side. On this part of the podium, one could observe, near the southern angle, two parallel semi-circular bands painted in red with black margins. Further north and on the same surface, part of two lotus flowers could be observed. The first to the south is painted red with a black outline for the petals. The northern one, better preserved, is painted white with black outlines for the petals. Details are not available for the central part. Three bands of colour are visible below the floral design. The first, painted in red, is in the form of an arc and goes partially underneath the flower. The other two semicircles below and painted red with black margins may be part of the wavy band. The bifurcation of the wavy band seen on the west podium may represent a second parallel wavy line, judging from current examples, and has also been seen above the sun symbol of the west podium.

The square structure, most probably a stūpa or a platform for an image (?), is 43 cm high from its foundation and is almost square in shape (1.73 × 1.79x1.84 × 1.83 m). The width of the corridor from the foundation of the stūpa to the eastern side moulding is 78 cm, the western corridor measures 80 cm, the northern corridor is 38 cm and the southern corridor is with 80 cm in width. The distance between the floor level coated with lime plaster and the foundation of the stūpa, which is constructed over the floor level, is about 27 cm which gives a total height of 70 cm, measurement taken from the eastern corridor.

The west podium extends approximately 3.4 m in the north-south direction. The south is 3.9 m long and the length of the east podium is calculated to be at least

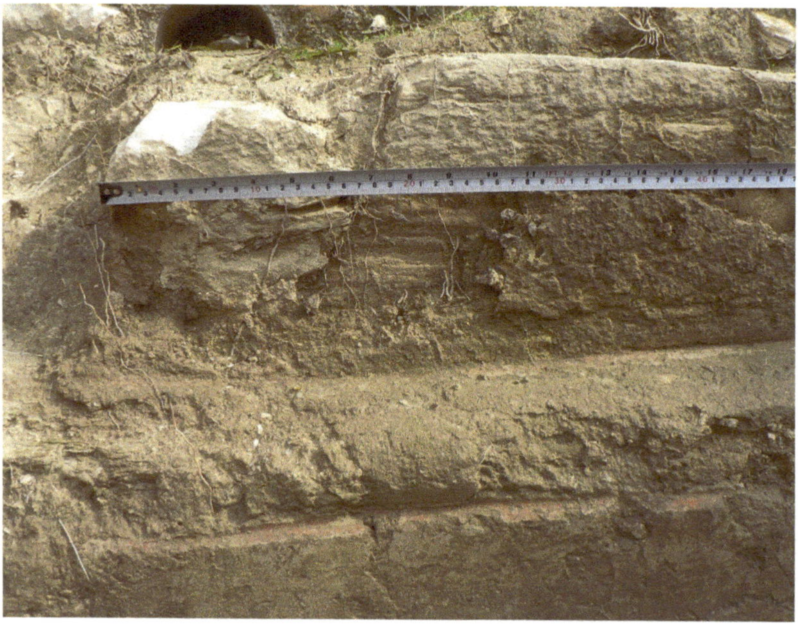

Fig. 4.9 Modern outlet for rainwater

3.4 m. The height varies from one podium to another but the average height remains 30 cm. The heights of the different parts of the East podium are: the first front face of the podium measures 20 cm, the bottom one measures 5 cm high and the height of the last one is 10 cm. The upper face or top side between the first and the second base is 8 cm wide. The distance between the west wall and the edge of the podium is 24 cm.

Regarding the colours, all the paintings of the three podiums are mainly made with three different colours, whitish, red and black. Black is generally applied for the outlines of the designs, except for the sun symbol and related motifs. Red is used for the undulating bands and also applied to the vertical bands probably in the corners and of the lower part of the podium. Red colour is also used in the drawing of the lotus flower to maintain contrast in all painted areas. The whitish is generally used on the entire surface of the lime rendering of the podiums as well as for certain floral designs.

As for the floor of the paint is concerned, the surface of the structure was first coated with a lime plaster which itself is then coated with a whitish-coloured paint or a thin layer of fine lime which has then been painted with different patterns. It seems that the paint has been applied to the wet surface of the lime plaster. Probably, in the following period, these paintings were covered with a new layer of thin lime plaster covering the painted layer; this is largely confirmed by the podium on the west side.

The podium or the platform, originally supporting stucco images of the Buddha and Bodhisattvas,[6] gives a square-shaped design, without the north podium, with sharp corners and the west and east sides with broken ends in opposite directions. It is formed by three walls, the south, the east and the west. In front of the steps, the platform extends in an east-west direction. Of almost the same length and height, another is added to the western end of the southern platform. Opposite the west wall, another of the same length and height is attached to the east end of the south platform, resulting in a "U"-shaped design with acute angles. The east and west walls turn to their northern ends and continue straight under the structures. I could not confirm the length of these extended platforms.

Date and Contextual Study: In addition to all the above information, we still need to sift through previous research work aimed at contextualizing and dating the Aziz Ḍheri murals and placing them properly in their archaeological and historical context.

Excavation of this particular structure was already carried out in 1993 and in a brief note, with a description of the finds, published in the same year, it says, "It is located between Stūpa-I and Stūpa-II. This shrine was rebuilt during the third-fourth century AD as some coins of little Kuṣāṇa are found here. Traces of beautiful red paint are found on the plastered surface inside the shrine. However, the most important feature of the shrine is a broader pedestal provided to its all sides in the interior. This pedestal was made for keeping sculptures. To the western side of the

[6] This is verbally confirmed by Professor Naeem Qazi, one of the member of the excavation team, excavation held in 1993 (see also below). Fragments of those stucco sculptures were found during our excavation as well.

shrine exactly at the centre, floral paintings are found executed on the top flat surface of the pedestal. These paintings are executed on a thick layer of lime pilaster. In the paintings there are shown two lotus flowers where only two colours are used which are red and black. These colours are derived mainly from the natural earth pigments, ochre, minerals, charcoals and black soot" (Naeem Qazi 1993: 77).

Another work published in the same year described the structures of the sanctuary but nothing is mentioned about the murals. The report says, "This shrine is located between stūpa I and stūpa-II. It was built in two phases. The 1st phase indicates the period of great Kuṣāṇa and the 2nd phase belongs to the late Kuṣāṇa on the basis of masonry which can be seen on the northern wall of the shrine. The northern wall is separated by a thick layer of mud. Below the layer, the wall of early phase can be easily identified. Above the layer, the foundation of wall of later period appears to have been added. The entrance to the shrine is provided on the north side. The inner side of the shrine is provided with steps of the same size" (Fazal Sher 1993: 20).

Another report published by one of the excavators of the site in 1993 explains the structures in the following words which are mostly incomprehensible and sometimes based on imagination, "Except the northern side where the stairs are leading downwards, the other three sides make a broad pedestal in the centre of the shrine the structure of which is badly disturbed and damaged. At the centre of the western pedestal, there is a high seat where painting (Plate No. 6a) depicting two lotus flowers is found. It is painted in red and black colours and drawn on plaster surface. Near the painting, a large size toe of Buddha made of stucco is found. It suggests that the high seat was originally decorated with stucco. Figures now mostly decayed and perished. Between the lotus flowers fragments of the Buddha image are also noticed" (Khan 2002: 29). The report further says, "The red colour painted around the rooms on the pedestal suggests that more images had been placed in the shrine. Unfortunately, the illegal diggers looted this important cultural portion of the site. On the outer side of the northern portion, stairs were provided where four steps to each side can still be seen in a fine state of preservation. It is important to mention here that the northern wall (Plate No. 5) of the shrine has a later addition, which has blocked the outer side stairs. Traces of mud layers (Plate No. 6b) are still seen above the stairs and just below the structure added later on" (Khan, S.N. 2002: 29).[7]

In 2007/2008, with specific and precise goals and objectives, we began the excavation in the northern corridor between the square structure in the middle of the hall and the wall to the west. The upper grey soft ground was found quite disturbed and mixed with stone chips, fragments of lime plaster and pieces of stucco with paints, numerous potsherds with few of them inscribed, fragments of bones and other cultural materials were among the inclusions.

After digging for about 30 cm below the surface, we extended our dig area to the west side where we observed a platform with mouldings painted with different colours and patterns. The western side of the platform was cleared and continued exposing it in all directions except the north. The north side of platform was probably covered by the steps ascending to the structure from the north. It is also possible that

[7] These reports came to my knowledge after the campaign of 2007/2008.

there might have not been any extension of the corridor at all. Excavation continued deep in the four corridors around the square structure and at a depth of about 30 cm an undisturbed deposit of grey clay was noticed. Below this level, late Kuṣān coins have been discovered in the western corridors, including a coin of the seated Ardokṣo type of Kaniṣka II (Fig. 4.10a, b) (Nasim Khan 2010, vol. 2: Cat. No. 2.64, vol. 2). A coin belonging to the late Kuṣān period (cat. no. 2.49, vol. 2) was also discovered in the northern corridor above the floor level made of lime pilaster.

A TC oil lamp (Cat. No. 10.ii.2, vol. 2) was found in the southern corridor near the foundation of the square structure. Besides these finds, inscribed sherds in grey ware (e.g. Fig. 4.11) recorded in the western corridor at a depth of about 1 m (Nasim Khan 2010, Cat. Nos. 1.1–1.6, vol. 2). At the same level, many bones and an abundance of potsherds were observed.

At a depth of about 1 m, a floor level was observed in the northern corridor. A very coarse deposit was detected between the foundation of the square structure and the floor level which consists of a thin layer of about 2 cm of lime rendering. The deposit below the floor level was a compact deposit composed of clay and small stone chips. Most likely, the floor was levelled with a mixture of clay and stone chips before laying the floor. The distance between the floor level and the foundation of the square structure, supposedly a stūpa, is about 27 cm. Cultural deposits continued deeper

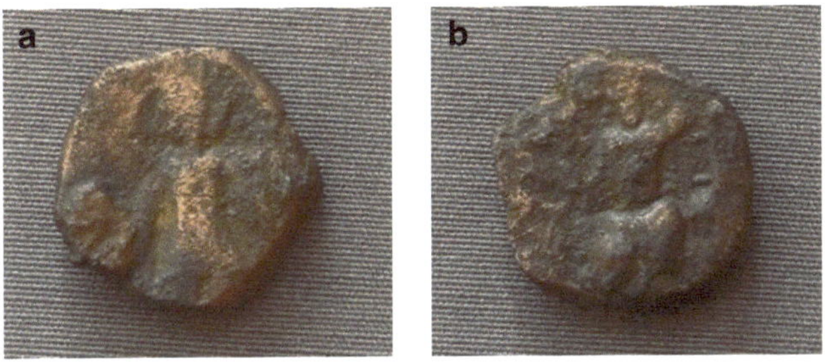

Fig. 4.10 (**a**), (**b**) Copper coin of Kaniṣka II

Fig. 4.11 Grey ware potsherd inscribed with Kharoṣṭhī letters ///*dhaisa* (// /of dhai)

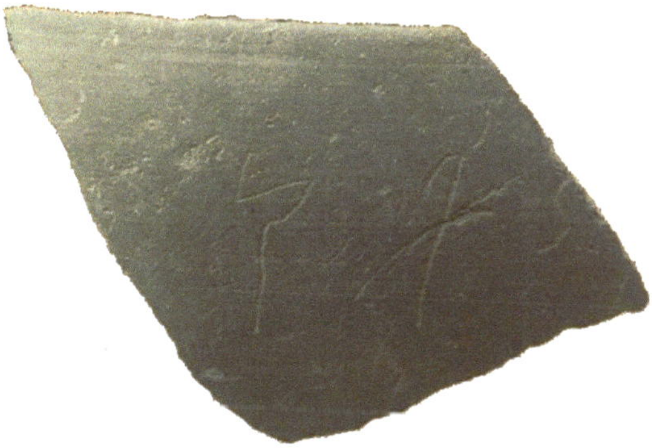

below the floor level but the excavation was stopped at a depth of approximately 1.7 m below the surface.[8]

* * *

To conclude, the floor, the square structure, the podiums and the enclosing walls could have been built in different phases probably during the late Kuṣān or Kuṣāno-Sassanian period; the two usually overlap on each other. The first of these structures seems to be the construction of the floor, in lime plaster, and the second phase could be the installation of the square structure which superimposed the level of the ground. The creation of the podiums around the square structure is either contemporary to the floor or with more possibility to the square structure in the centre. The overlapping of the three walls, east, west and south also indicates that these were made after the main stūpa, but they are contemporary with the rest of the structures in the area in question.

Moreover, the floor inside the room is apparently the continuation of the floor of the main stūpa. If this were the case, one could imagine that the square structure is the base of a stūpa of which the upper part has disappeared. The stūpa was probably built later and was provided with a podium on its three sides on which were placed large stucco figures of Buddhas and Bodhisattvas which were presumably painted with different colours as it was confirmed by the fragments of some the images found during our excavations. The stucco figures and the murals were supposed to be protected from the weather, so the entire structure was seemingly covered using the walls that still surround the square structure and the murals. The discoveries of many sculptures close to the area, fragments of inscribed bowls, coins, bone fragments, etc. are the good reasons to believe that this area of Aziz Ḍheri site was another important premises with a special significance for the Buddhists. The presence of paintings on the podiums and on the sculptures led me to imagine that the stūpa in the centre and inside the walls of the enclosure were probably also having murals which became vanished over time such as the case at the Buddhist site of Jinnan Wali Ḍheri, in Taxila (see below).

For unknown reasons to me, access to the room was provided from the top of the drum of the main stūpa, located to north, through steps that are still preserved. It is possible that this cell was not opened to all visiting the monastery and access to it was only allowed to monks or high-ranking priests. It is possible that after circumambulation around the main stūpa and the dome, the monks had to enter to the cell which sheltered the sacred structure and its murals. There are clear indications for the construction of the north wall at a later period (Fig. 4.12) since this wall also overlaps the floor of the main stūpa to the north. The outer face of the northern wall of the cell can be differentiated from the eastern and western wall of the cell because

[8] Although the discovery of these paintings must be considered unique to Aziz Ḍheri, their proper preservation was posing a serious problem. No immediate action was possible for its proper safeguarding; therefore, the trench was re-filled in and the paintings were covered over to protect them from all natural and human hazards until necessary arrangements to be done for its protection and preservation. The paintings are preserved for future investigation.

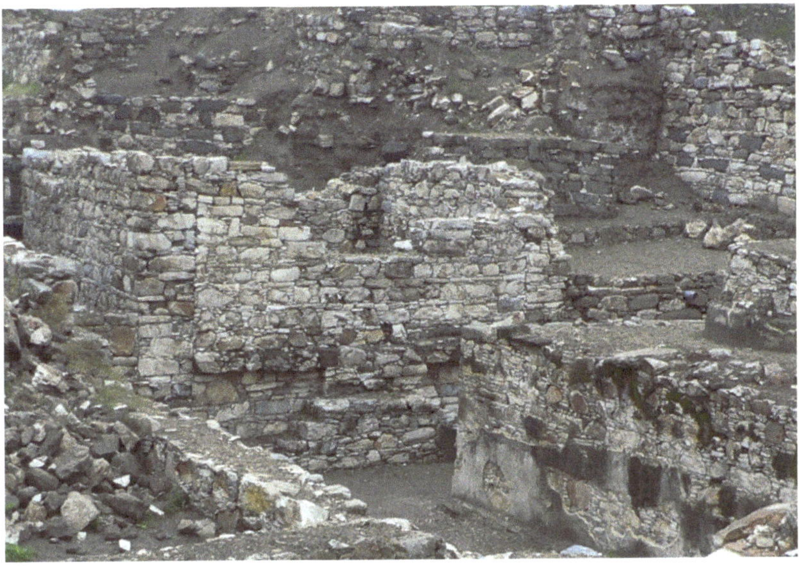

Fig. 4.12 Northern wall shown with joining streaks at both its ends and steps leading to the cell

of the two verticals streaks at its end showing the boundaries of the northern wall. This also suggests that the northern wall is a later addition and the cell was originally covered and surrounded from three sides while the northern side was left open due to the presence of the main stūpa to the north. But as I have already explained elsewhere, the main stūpa itself went through different phases of construction and its last phase may be contemporary with the structures found to the south (Nasim Khan 2010, volume 1: 98).

Further notes:

- The paintings belong to the early Kuṣān period and are contemporary to the original structure of the main stūpa built during the same period.
- The curving festoons are comparable to those found in Butkara I and paintings in Central Asia
- The concept behind the curving festoons and the form of the garlands carried by the *putis* in the Buddhist art of Swat might be the same.
- The same idea is adopted in paintings from Central Asia where the curves opening upwards are filled with human figures; the figures in the lower one support the garlands.
- The curve pattern used in both carvings and paintings might go simultaneously suggesting an early date for the paintings in Aziz Ḍheri.

But Kara 1, Swat

Apart from the ancient rock paintings recorded in the Swat Valley, beautiful frescoes have also been discovered in this region. The Swat Valley has been studied since very early (e.g. Stein 1930; Berger et al. 1941), but more extensive work has been carried out by the Department of Archaeology at the University of Peshawar and the Italian Archaeological Mission to Swat. The main exploration works carried out by the latter organization were the excavations at Bhirkot Ghuandai, Udegram, Panr, Saidu Sharif and the famous Buddhist site of But Kara 1 (Fig. 4.13) of which interesting frescoes have been reported (Faccenna 1980 vol. III.3, Text: 703–718; Faccenna 1981, part 5.1: plates Pl. I, L.). These are the first discoveries of frescoes in the region and which prove the use of this art form in Gandhāra alongside stone and stucco decoration, dated to the second century CE (Faccenna 1980: 718).

The frescoes of But Kara 1 consist of two groups, the human figures—at least two in number, and the decorative motifs in the form of festoons and scrolls. They were found near to the main stūpa of the site. In material and style, Faccenna found the figures on both panels identical and believed them to be of the same composition. He also observes that these figures resemble some from Hadda and thinks that they are embodied in a "Western" tradition of style and composition, but he sees affinities there with the paintings of Miran, in Central Asia. They are painted in red, golden ochre, sky blue and black (see below) and were executed with tempera technique. Faccenna assumes the date between the second and fourth centuries CE (Faccenna 1980: 714–718). However, others have placed these frescoes in the 1st half of the first century AD. Whereas Mahmud, due to his style and physical appearance, placed it in the second half of the first century AD (Mahmud 530), Mahmud develops his theory further and says, "The style of the Butkara painting seems to be quite mature because there is a kind of surety in line and an appreciable craftsmanship. This type

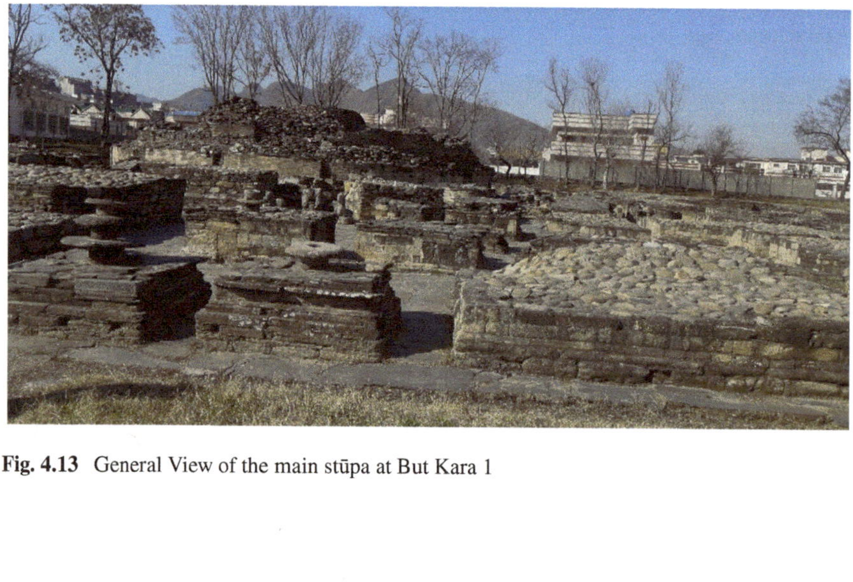

Fig. 4.13 General View of the main stūpa at But Kara 1

of maturity in style, and the developed fresco technique cannot be attained in a short period. Therefore, it appears that much prior to the Huns invasion the art of fresco painting was practised in the Gandhāra region and probably some sort of a school of painting might have existed earlier than the second half of the first century A.D." (Mahmud 530). These two dates seem to me a little earlier for this style of paintings and also because the context in which they were found, may belong to the end of the Kuṣān or post-Kuṣān period. Stratigraphic details are missing otherwise one could assume an approximate date for these frescoes. Selective paints are studied below.

Panel 1 (Fig. 4.14)

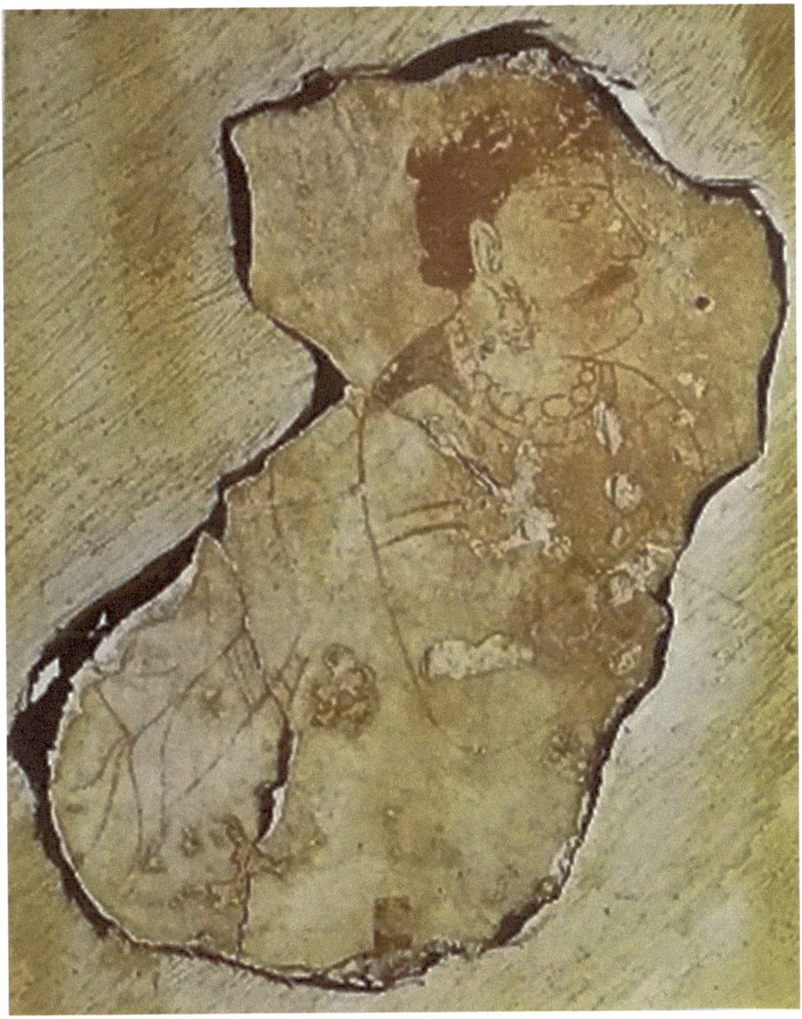

Fig. 4.14 Painting of two images found at But Kara I (Saidu Sharif Museum, Swat)

It was found in the area of Great stūpa 4 and according to Faccena, tempera technique is used in the execution of these paintings. He says, "The panel represents remains of two figures facing right and seen in a three-quarter view. That further to the right is a male figure preserved down to the waist; it is wearing a corselet-type tunic fastened by a band with very short sleeves and semi-circular lower hem. The garment was panted sky-blue and a remnant of this colour is visible on the right shoulder. The figure seems to be wearing a band-shaped armlet (unless this meant to be the edge of the sleeve) and an armilla which is barely outlined at the wrist. Round the neck is a short necklace of round beads which go on increasing in size, the largest in the centre being somewhat elongated. The head is seen in profile and the nose and chin are strong and heavy features. The moustaches are long and straight, while the hair is red and takes the form of a thick compact mass short over the brow and behind the nape where it seems to curl. The ears are free, high and pointed with an elongated lobe to take the large earring which hangs from a small chain and is shaped like a tubular container with thickened ends and a quadrangular end-piece at the bottom. The eye is large and elongated, and the eyebrow is slightly arched and also very elongated. The right arm of this figure is bent forward as though some object is being offered and his expression is attentive and severe. Strength and hardness emanate from this heavy body and massive head" (Faccena 1980: 715–716). The other figure, believed to be a female, is damaged and missing and what could be presumed from the rest is that his right arm is stretched forward and the palm is open. The band of his drapery is clearly marked. Faccena sees an armila on her wrist (Faccena 1980: 716).

The lower body and the hands of the male figure are missing but this does not preclude thinking that this image is with the arms and hands flexed, probably in the gesture of *añjalimudrā*, represented in the same way as the female figure standing aside of which very little is preserved. If we flip this panel horizontally (Fig. 4.15) and compare it to the Yakatoot panel (Fig. 4.16), where the male figure is held at knee level, the position and gesture of these two figures are very similar (see below). It is perhaps the same for the female figure of But Kara 1 where she is most lacking, but one could imagine, in the light of the Yakatoot panel that she is also standing with her hands in *añjalimudrā*. The muscular necks, large elongated eyes, strong and pointed noses, style of moustaches, hairstyles of the male characters show similarities and can display the same way of wearing jewellery (Figs. 4.15 and 4.16). The images are elegantly made like the frescoes of the later Hindu and Sikh period as well as the Mughal miniature paintings Indo-Pakistani subcontinent (see, e.g., Fig. 4.17).

Panel 2 (Fig. 4.18)

This is a very fragmentary image of a person displaying *añjalimudrā*. The most salient aspect of this painting is the dominant golden ochre used to mark the folds of the garment. A fine thin line of reddish or brown colour is used for the outline of the body parts. The preserved portion of the image does not say too much about the exact gesture of the hands, about its gender as well as its standing or sitting posture. From this fragmentary evidence, Faccena concludes, "The other fragment (inv. No. 4312; Fig. 339; pl. 102b; colour Pl. L) comprises the left part of the chest

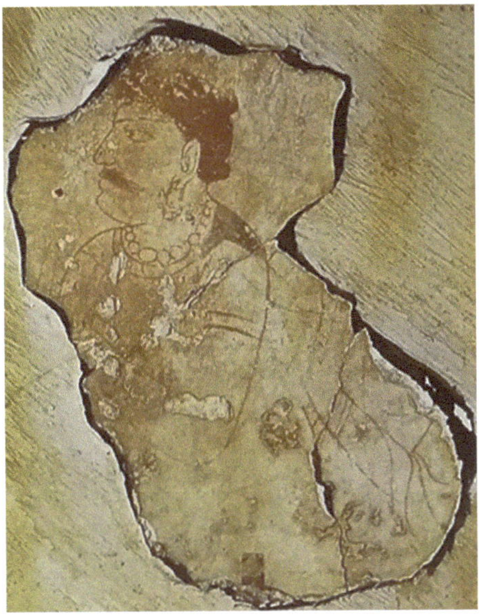

Fig. 4.15 Fig. 4.14 is flipped horizontally

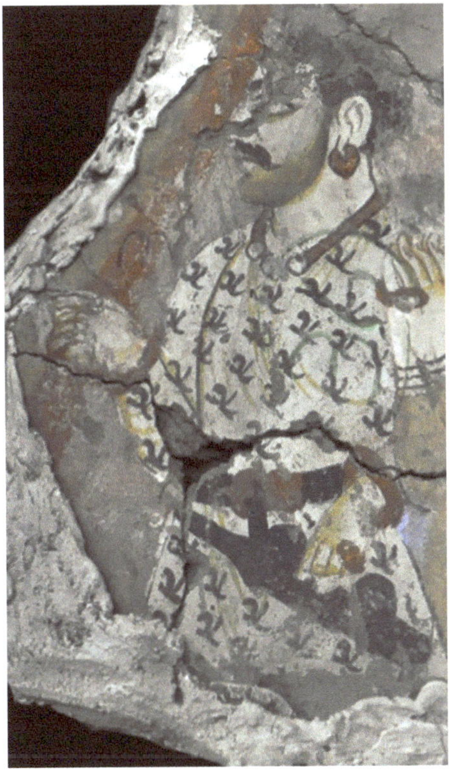

Fig. 4.16 Panel from Yakatoot

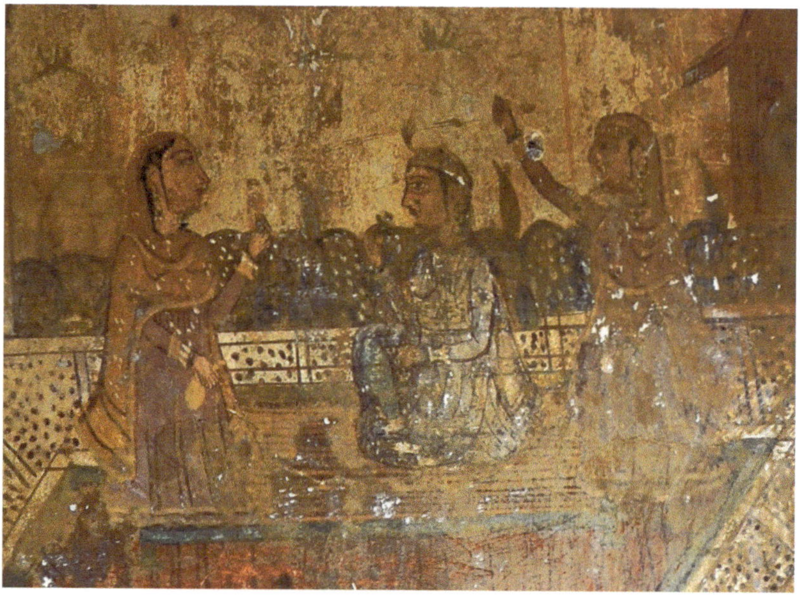

Fig. 4.17 Fresco from a temple at Katas Raja (sixth–tenth centuries AD or later)

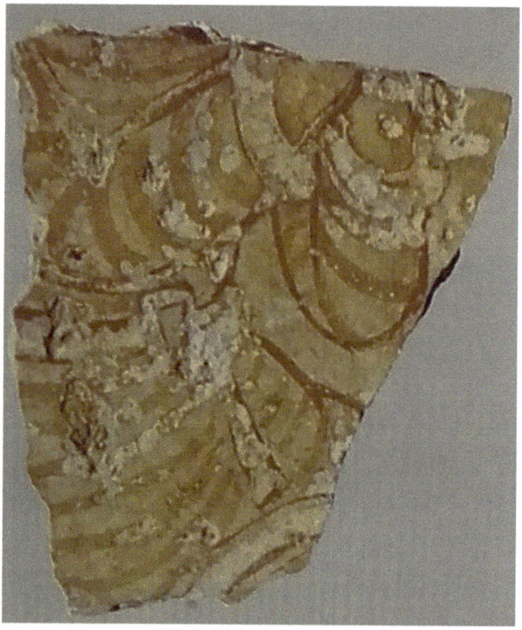

Fig. 4.18 Fragment of painting from But Kara I (Swat Museum) (Photo Zarawar Khan)

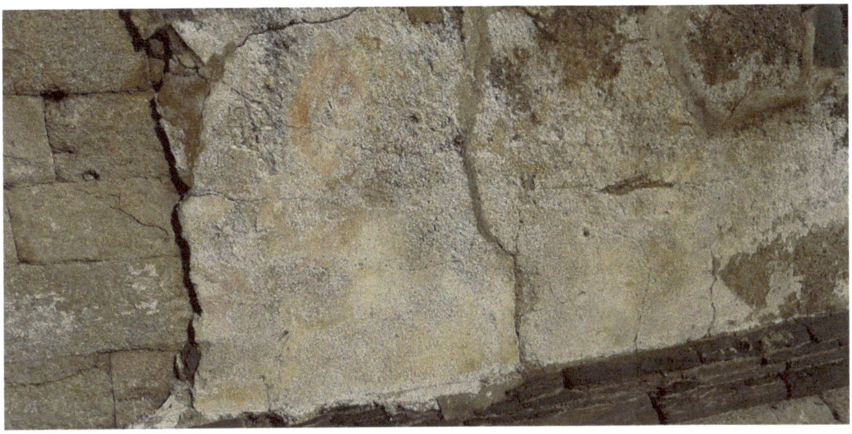

Fig. 4.19 Present condition of some of the murals at But Kara 1

and hips of a mal figure three quarters to right; it is dressed in a tunic with long wide-edged sleeves and perhaps a triangular cut neck (?); as a belt there is a band with a quadrangular fibula from which the end of the band hangs. The line of the left hip and a number of transverse folds in front lead one to imagine that this figure was kneeling, the right knee being on the ground, or sitting in European fashion. The two arms are preserved from the elbow to the wrist, brought to the left-hand side, and bent, with raised hands joined in an act of adoration. Large, recurrent parallel bands of even colour, for example across the arms and body, indicate the folds of the heavy garment" (Faccena 1980: 716).

Penal 3 (Faccenna 1981, Part 5.1, Plates: Pl. F)

These decorations consisted of rectilinear festoons, found extending along the area of the cavetto-torus at Great stūpa 3 (Faccena 1980: 704) and the other developed in a sinuous fashion with lotus flowers placed in the curves alternatively, at top and bottom. Such decorative motifs were added to the lower cylinder of Great stūpa 4 (Faccena 1980: 704) and were also extended on to the stucco floor. They were painted in red, golden ochre, sky blue, green and black.[9]

Panel 4 (see also Faccenna 1981, pl.101.c) (see Faccenna 1980: Part 3, Text, Pl 98b)

The scroll motifs that appeared on Great stūpa 4 are oval and rectangular and belong to group II of stucco floor (Faccena 1980: 708–709). It is formed on acanthus leaves design and is painted in dark red colour. The other group of paintings discovered at Butkara I were the so-called sweeping linear scroll-pattern, with volutes, facing alternatively upwards and downwards (Faccena 1962, volume 1: 107).

"This fact enabled us to observe and to record the existence of painted decoration on level 8 (Fig. 126). It forms a border, o.42 wide up against the base-moulding, and consists of a sweeping lincar scroll-pattern, with volutes facing alternately upwards

[9] For details on designs, form, shapes, colour scheme and techniques, see Faccenna (1980: 706–707).

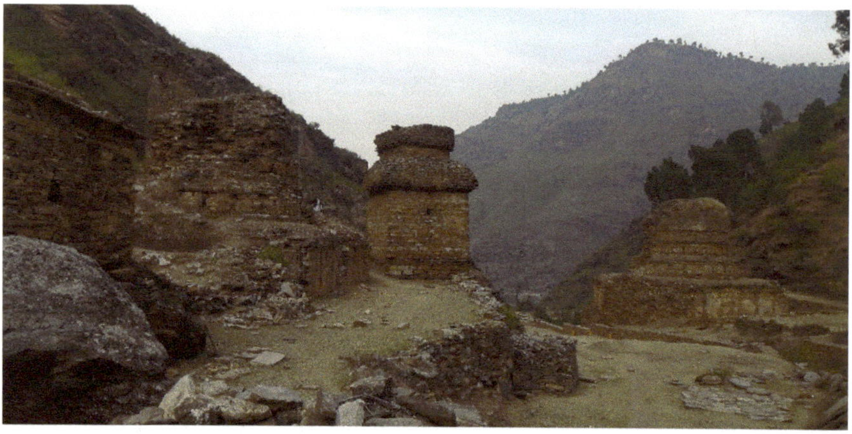

Fig. 4.20 General view of Abba Sahib Cheena Buddhist site in Swat (Photo Dr. Zarawar Khan)

and downwards. It is painted in reddish-ochre, with strokes about 0.015 wide; the treatment is summery, not to say careless. Three alternating volutes were visible within the stretched exposed, about 1 m. in length. A trial-hole near the entrance showed that a corresponding band of ornament ran along the opposite border. Unfortunately, the colour is very faint and difficult to follow, and one cannot altogether exclude the fact that other levels too may have been similarly painted, although no trace now remains" (Faccena 1961: 107).[10]

Abba Sahib Cheena, Swat[11]

During archaeological research in the Swat Valley, ancient paintings have long been observed, but these are usually simple linear representations of human and animal figures or floral and faunal designs directly applied to the surface of rock shelters (e.g. Nazir Khan et al. 1995; Sardar 2016). However, no frescoes have, to date, been recorded inside a rock shelter in the Swat Valley. In contrast, wall paintings have already been reported at the Buddhist site of But Kara I (see above). But these are the few remnants of significant embellishments that may be existed at the site. The very recent discovery of frescoes at the Buddhist complex of Abba Sahib Cheena (Fig. 4.20) is, therefore, another milestone in this field and has to be considered the second most important discovery of mural paintings in the Swat Valley.[12]

[10] On scrolls-patterns on the stucco floor 8 see also Faccena (1980: Part 3, Text, Pl. 98b).

[11] A draft paper about the paintings was published by the present author with https://doi.org/10.13140/RG.2.2.34579.14887.

[12] I am very thankful to Dr. Ghayyur Shahab, leader of the excavation team, for sharing with me relevant information and photographs of some of the images I produced here.

The Abba Sahib Cheena Buddhist site is located inside a valley on the right side of the Barikot-Buner Road and about six kilometres from Barikot town located on the Swat highway. The nearest village to the site is the hamlet of Najigram. The ruins at Abba Sahib Cheena were first mentioned by Aural Stein who visited Swat in 1926 (Stein 1930) while exploring the area in 1938, Barger and Wright were the leading individuals to prepare the first sketch or plan of the structures that were visible at that time. Later on, the site was surveyed by Tucci in 1955 and published a report in 1958 wherein the plan of the monuments was prepared by Prof. V. Caroli, a member of the mission (Tucci 1958: 317–318). Subsequently, the Italian Archaeological Mission to Swat reported the monuments in more detail. The investigation and photographic documentation continued by the Italian Archaeological Mission but the first excavation of the site, besides those made by the illegal diggers, was carried out in 2020–2021 by the Directorate of Archaeology and Museums of the Government of Khyber Pakhtunkhwa. As the site had already been ruthlessly looted and destroyed during illegal excavations, the Directorate of Archaeology and Museums was, apparently, tasked only with clearing the site from debris and to clear the structures for photographic documentation, preservation and preparing drawing of the available structures. Several large and votive stūpas as well as other structures were re-exposed and fragments of sculptures and other antiquities, which were left behind by the illegal diggers, were picked up from the debris.[13] But the most important of the findings are the wall paintings that were exposed at the site and were found in situ (Samad et al. 2021: 16, Fig. 11).[14] These paintings were discovered in two different

---

[13] During his visit to the site, Tucci observed antiquities at the site which he narrates in the following world, "The site of Abba Saheb China is full not only of Kuṣāṇa pottery but also of *debris* of Gandhara sculptures (one was found on the spot) unfortunately it has been unskilfully excavated to satisfy the greet of treasure seekers and dealers from the plain, and also of some Sahibs who for a few rupees induced the local people to undertake clandestine excavations" (Tucci 1958: 318).

[14] The excavation report gives important information and includes some important fragments of sculptures that add to our knowledge about the different themes depicted in the Buddhist art of Gandhara. However, the report some time lacks details which do not help to understand the context of the findings discovered during excavation. The drawing showing the layout of the structures on the site is inexact, e.g., Fig. 11 contradicts Pl.12. In the layout drawing, two of the structures to the left of the steps, which lead to chapel 8, are shown rectangular, although in Pl. 12 they are not either. The map does not reflect the exact location of all the structures vis-à-vis Chapel 8. The identification and interpretation of the structures are unclear. The identification of the antiquities is missing or those provided are generally erroneous. Also, the skeleton (Pls. 13 and 68) needs to be scientifically analysed to know its date because I have a doubt about its age. It may belong to a very late date and has nothing to do with the monastery or Buddhism. The skeleton is mentioned recovered from the top of the stūpa. The exact number of paintings and their finding spots are not clearly mentioned in the chapter on paintings of the excavation report, but if one examines the photographs carefully and reads the report, one can find the precise location of the paintings described. One can also survey other buildings that may be added with the same type of fresco paintings. In the light of the above and many other discrepancies, the excavation report may, therefore, need a drastic overhaul. Above all, the most important in this report is the quick publication of the results of excavation giving the opportunity to the scholars to know and interpret the data in their own context. I hope asking such questions can help the authors overcoming the shortcoming to make their final report more advantageous.

areas of the site; one group of them was found in the shade of the cornice of the steps leading to a sanctuary and the other group inside a cell (Figs. 4.21–4.24).

The report only says, "During the scientific excavations held at the Buddhist monastery of Abba Sahib Cheena, a fair quantity of antiquities have been recovered. The most remarkable discoveries of the site are the fresco paintings of Lord Buddha, the bejewelled figures, and disciples. An ogee arch is provided in the wall, constructed in diaper masonry in front of the chapels and votive stūpas. The ceiling of the arch has been elaborated with fresco paintings. Nine individual illustrations enhance the historical appeal of the Buddhist Monastic Complex of Abba Sahib Cheena" (Samad

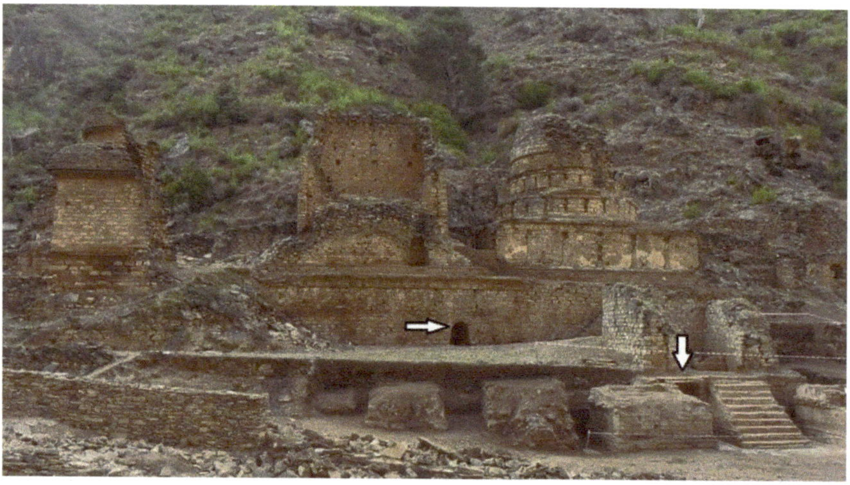

Fig. 4.21 Location of the painting at Abba Sahib Cheena

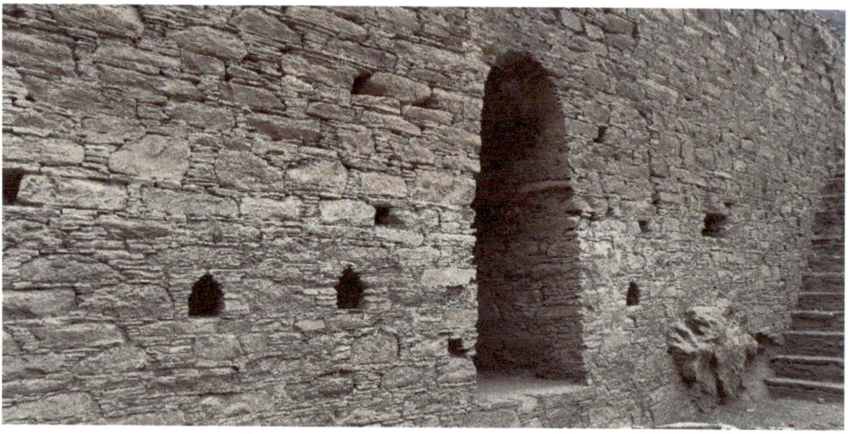

Fig. 4.22 The embankment wall added with niches for oil lamps

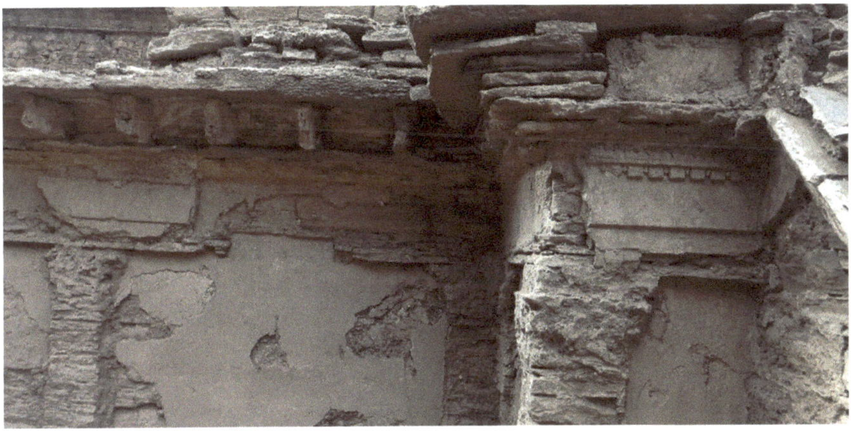

Fig. 4.23 Present condition of the paintings below the cornice of the shrine

et al. 2021: 111).[15] In the context of Chapel-08, it is mentioned, "There are only two fresco paintings separated by brackets to the southern side of the stairs" (Samad et al. 201: 43).[16] Although I observed at least three figures separated from each other by brackets (Fig. 4.25), however, in another place of the report, it is said, "The left part of the head is present, with an oblong ear falling over the right shoulder, bearing an earring. A small part of the neck points towards the position of the shoulder. The facial features are missing (Samad et al. 2021: 113). Here, the report may refer to the third figure. Despite all discrepancies and shortcomings observed in the excavation report, it is worth acknowledging the efforts of the excavation team to bring these important paintings to the scholarly world in order to delve deeper into the history, origin, style and themes of paintings from the Buddhist period in Gandhara.

The above shortcomings led the author to make the following preliminary investigation and share the conclusions which are mainly based on the personal information and observations of the author. After consulting earlier reports and then reviewing

[15] The total number of figures listed in the report is counted nine instead of eight because plates 77 and 81 counted twice although both deal with the same painting. As Fig. 4.60 suggests, the plate may not be included in the report. The nine figures are identified as a Buddha, a winged Buddha, three disciples, a disfigured head, and three jewelled figures.

[16] After analysis of the photographs of the murals and their relevant texts, discrepancies are observed, some of which are noted here. First, the total number of images are mentioned as nine, but only photographs of eight of them are provided; Figs. 4.60 and 4.64 are paintings of the same image which is counted twice. Second, the designs of some images do not exactly match their respective murals (Figs. 4.60 and 4.64) and are also flipped horizontally (see Figs. 4.56, 4.57 and 4.63) which creates confusion. Third, the identification of the images does not seem accurate and the iconographic details are missing. Fourth, the exact location and sequence of the images are also not specified. Fifthly, after the paintings were discovered, they may have been carelessly cleaned with a stiff brush or water, therefore some details are washed out during this process. Sixth, the ensemble is not studied in its archaeological and stratigraphic context, and it is therefore difficult to understand the relationship between the different settlements and their chronology. It would have helped us to roughly date the murals.

published photographs, several different structures may have existed at the site, some of which may have been destroyed in different periods. Most of the structures seem to be decorated with similar paintings, but they kept disappearing for various reasons such as climatic conditions and human hazards. Most of the structures could have been provided with wall paintings, some of them still retain remains of paintings (Samad et al. 2021, e.g., p. 29, pl. 19; p. 43, pl. 39; p. 60, pl. 57). The murals published here were found in two different areas. A group of them was painted under the cornice of Chapel-08 (Samad et al. 2021: p. 43, pl. 39) and the other group inside and on the ceiling of an arch (Samad et al. 2021: p.111, pl. 71). A third group of paintings which is not illustrated in the report was found in the shade of the cornice of Chapels 12–14 (see, e.g., Samad et al. 2021: p. 60, Pl.57). Group I paintings belong to Chapel 08 and would be added to the south side of the staircase. According to the report, this group consists of two figures named Winged Buddha and Disciple 01 while the second group, found inside an arch, consists of seven paintings named, Defaced head, Disciple 02, Disciple 03, Bejewelled figure, Bejewelled figure, Bejewelled figure, and Buddha (Original) (Samad et al. 2021: 111–116). The third apparent group consists of frescoes composed of human or celestial figures or other decorative motifs as seen at Aziz Ḍheri and But Kara I (see above). While no trace of them exists today, similar paintings might have existed in the cells of other Buddhist sites in Gandhara.

The first group of murals were applied to the smooth surface of a lime plaster, specially designed for paintings, which is used below and in the shadow of the cornice of a shrine named as Chapel-08. The two figures that were recorded during the cleaning of the shrine from debris belong to one side of the staircase to the building while the paintings on the rest of the structures are missing. The cornice of the shrine is supported by brackets, and the space between the brackets has originally been frescoed on all sides. The report does not explain how many brackets there were otherwise one would guess the number of images added to each space between two brackets. Our Fig. 4.25 shows that the so-called winged Buddha (Fig. 4.27) precedes the supposed figure of the disciple (Fig. 4.26) which means that the images are counted from right to left. In addition, the photograph shows three images instead of two, two are added on the south side of the staircase and one on the east wall of the square platform to which the staircase is added. Most likely, the third image of this shrine is the one called "Defaced Head" (Samad et al. 2021: 113).

The paintings of the second group were found inside a building called "arch" (Samad et al. 2021: 111, Pl. 71); however, their sequential order and arrangement were initially not very clear because no general image of the group of painted figures is provided. The paintings published here weren't the only frescoes inside the cell, but there were others also that were destroyed before official excavations began or some may have been during the process of cleaning of the site.

The discovery of the paintings was first made public by Mr. Majid F. Masaud on 4 February 2021, through his Twitter account, under the title Fresco Paintings. News of the find then spread and appeared in different digital and print media before being published in the excavation report on Abba Sahib Cheena. Currently, the paintings are in a depilated state; either they are very faded, or in some places they have gone astray due to lack of proper care and conservation. We hope that the Directorate of Archaeology and Museum will do some preservation work otherwise, it's not too far from the fact that they will all disappear in the years to come, due to weather condition and because of human vandalism (Fig. 4.24).

Group I (Figs. 4.25): Apparently, the entire surface between the brackets around the building, below the cornice of the stūpa plinth, was painted with different figures, however, only three of them are traceable. Two of the three figures were somehow preserved at the time of their first discovery while only a few traces for the third were available when the figure was first photographed. Presently, they are all in a very poor state of preservation and are barely visible.

Group I.1 (Fig. 4.26): The first image in the first group also appears to be depicted with wings and be a shaved headed. Only a few traces of the left wing are available. The contour line at the level of his head is used to mark the border of the hair or the scalp in relation to the face. The top line of the outline is shown sunken in its centre, apparently providing space for a design that appears to be missing or may originally does not exist and the that the top of the head is deliberately depicted flat. The outline of the hair is extended towards its earlobes. The space inside the outline is lightly shaded, relative to the face, to mark the hair. This type of representation of the hair is very typical of the headdress of the Buddha's disciples in the Miran murals (see Hansen 2012: plate 5B; China National Museum Catalogue 2019: 246). The pointed

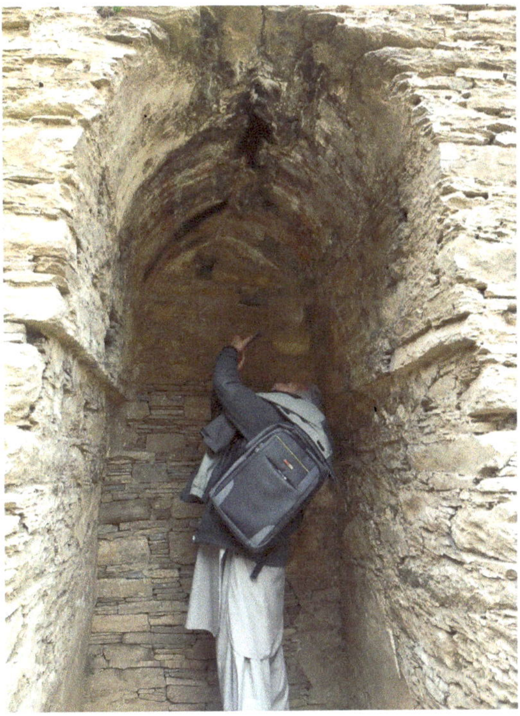

Fig. 4.24 Cell with paintings

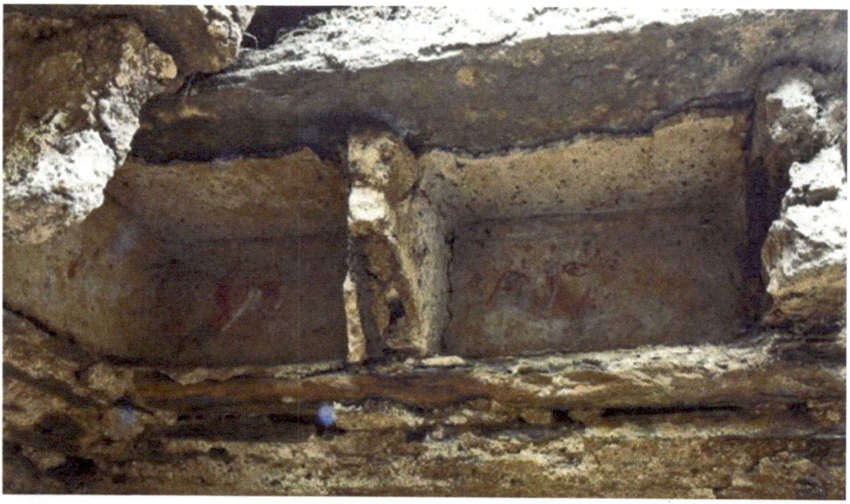

Fig. 4.25 Paintings (Group I) below the cornice of the stair to the shrine (Photo Dr. Ghayyur Shahab)

fleshy nose is somehow intact. The eyes are to some extent also preserved; the iris and pupil are painted black while the sclera is white in colour; his right is intact but the left is damaged. Each eyebrow is represented by a thick brown line. The necklines of the garment, painted dark brown, are visible. The black bands on his right shoulder suggest that the person is probably wearing a black or whitish-coloured monk robe or garment but with black bands (?).

Group I.ii (Fig. 4.27): The second figure of the series, described here from right to left, is painted on the left side wall of the staircase under its cornice. He is identified as a Winged Buddha. The image is shown turned ¾ to its right. The head touches the cornice moulding and appears to have no space for an *uṣṇīṣa* above his skull. However, traces of a lock of hair are available on his forehead. The mesh design is probably extended to and above the figure's right ear, like the figures of angels in the Miran murals (e.g. Hansen 2012: plate 5B). If this were the case, the large solid circle between and above his eyebrows would perhaps not represent the volute of hair representing the *ūrṇā* of the Buddha but probably a net of hair as attested by the murals from Miran (see China National Museum Catalogue 2019: 247) or the garland bears in the Buddhist art of Gandhāra (e.g. Khan, G.R. 2015: n° 114, 116, 120, 124, 120, 125, 128, 129). The eyebrows, eyelashes and iris are delineated by thick and thin lines of brown ochre. His left eye is partially damaged but his right eye is almost intact. As the image is represented at ¾ to his left, his left eye is partially represented but poorly preserved. The right ear is almost intact and is marked with lines in brown paint. He is depicted with wings; the left one is barely visible while the right-wing feathers are in some way preserved and are depicted with brown and black ochre.

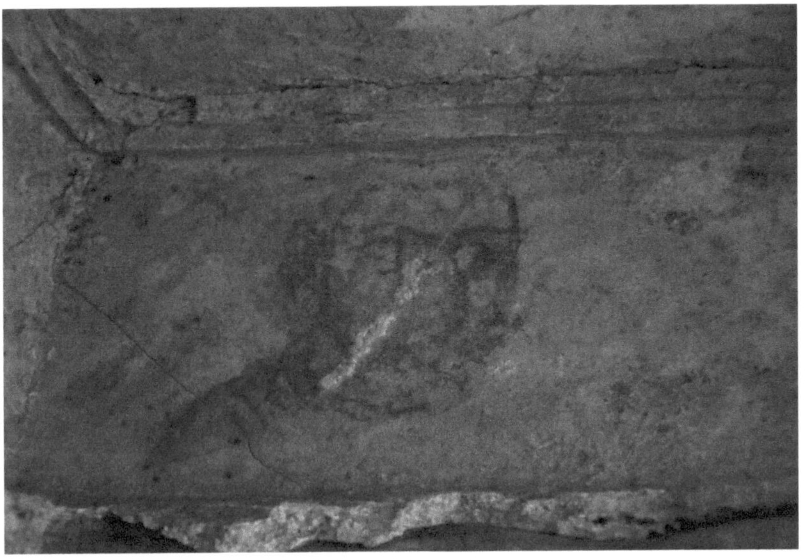

Fig. 4.26 Human figure with shaved head and probably with wings

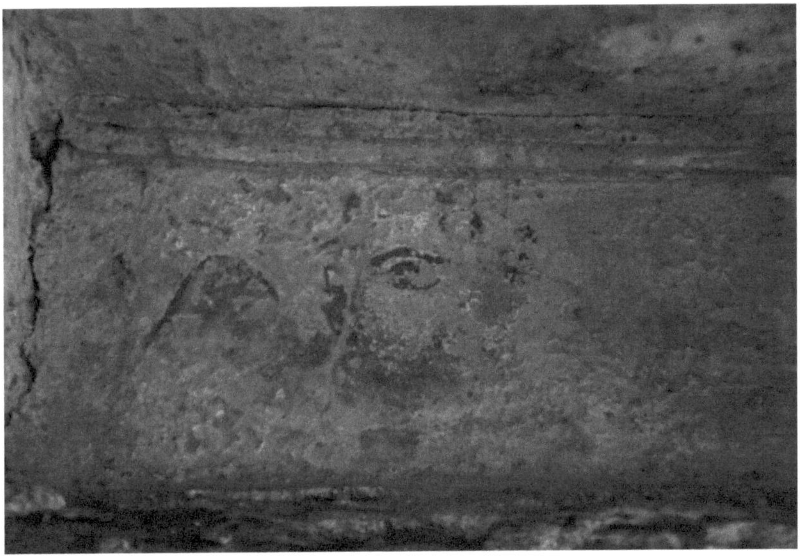

Fig. 4.27 Figure with wings and is probably bald except a mesh of hair on his forehead

Group I.iii (Figs. 4.28 and 4.29): The third and final recorded figure of the first group of paintings is extremely disfigured, and only faint evidence of some of his face is traceable. It is located to the left of the two previous figures and is painted in the same alignment but on the south wall of the building and which is facing to the east. According to the excavation report, "The left part of the head is present, with an oblong ear falling over the right shoulder, bearing an earring. A small part of the neck points towards the position of the shoulder. The facial features are missing" (Samad et al. 2021: 113).

Group II (Figs. 4.30–4.37): The paintings of this group were applied to the intrados or soffit of a vaulted cell which may have originally housed a standing image installed against the facade of the rear wall of the cell. Only traces of the base, made for the image, are available. The paintings inside the cell were part of the overall landscape of the cell. The ceiling and the surface of the side walls were symmetrically divided into several squares or rectangles. A thick straight strip in black or dark red paint was provided which runs horizontally from the rear of the arch keystone to the pointed end of the rear wall (Figs. 4.30 and 4.31). At regular intervals and parallel to the first band, similar black bands were provided on the rest of the lower surface. To divide the area into several square or rectangular blocks, similar bands were painted vertically and equidistant on the intrados and most likely reached to the springer or the springing line or may be drawn down to floor level.

Subsequently, inside each compartment, a character is added facing right, left or nearly facing. Presumably, each area on the side of the central stripe or crown line is divided into at least three fields, by two horizontal stripes, each of which is divided into at least four square or horizontal compartments, every allowing space for at least

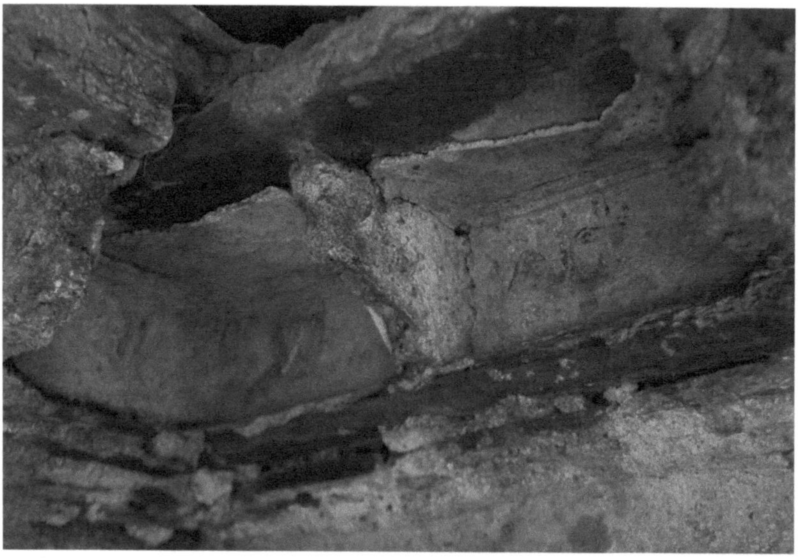

Fig. 4.28 The group of three figures below the cornice of the stūpa

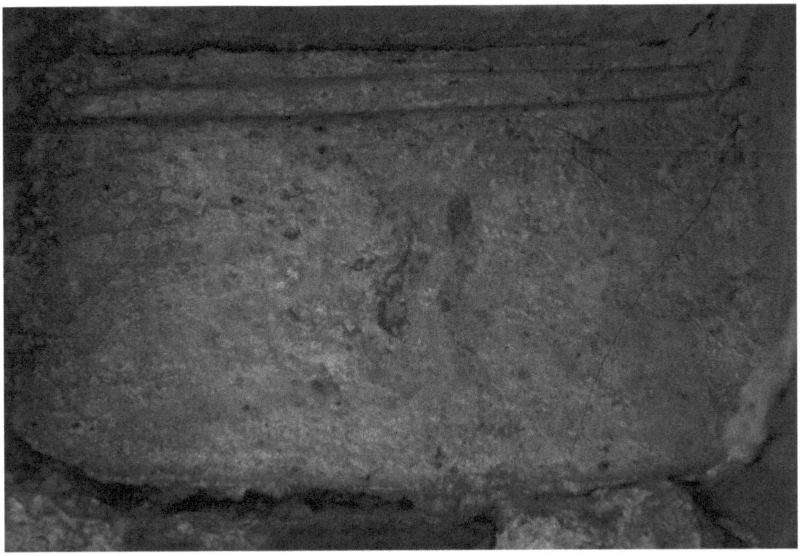

Fig. 4.29 Defaced figure; only part of his left temple is traceable

one image. Apparently, there were not less 24 compartments, at least twelve on each side, originally added to the intrados. However, the two lower fields, one on either side of the crown line, each with four compartments, are mostly degraded and little is preserved. The partially available and preserved units are 12.

In this group, five of the total figures, registered on the site, have been published. The rest of the images are either defaced or missing. Three appeared to be facing ¾ to their right and the other three were facing to their left. These two orientations suggest that three of them were painted to the right of the missing standing or seated figure, or on the left side wall, and the other three figures to the left of the figure, or on the right-side wall of the cell. When first recorded, the images were found damaged and disfigured and some details were missing. But the situation is getting worse because they have not yet been properly preserved. The murals are also faded and crumbled. For the description, the sequence of figures, presented here, is the same as that published in the excavation report (see Samad et al. 2021).

Most of the visible figures are depicted in *añjalimudrā mudra* with their heads facing the side of the back wall of the cell where the supposed image, most likely of a Buddha or Bodhisattva, was originally installed or painted.

Group II.i (Fig. 4.32): Over fifty per cent of the figure is damaged and missing. Part of his joined hands and the left side of his head are traceable. The bust is slightly turned to his right. He has a shaved head but the hair shade is featured by a thick brown line. The outline of his left ear is visible. He probably wears a chunky ear ornament; the ornament can be compared with that worn by Fig. 4.33. The hands are joined and are brought in front of his face displaying *añjalimudrā*. The fingers are clearly marked and are shown in outline with red colour. He is draped in a garment

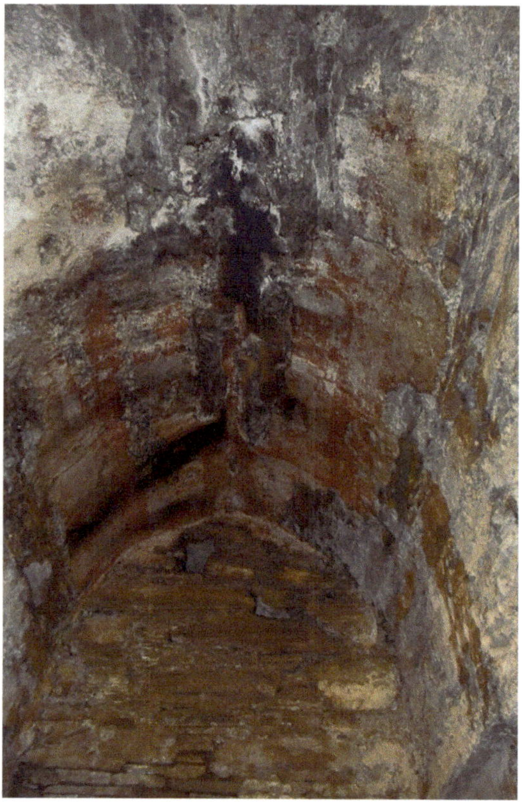

Fig. 4.30 Interior of the cell with paintings

whose folds are marked with red lines. The image has a square whitish background with thick red borders forming the whole like an image inside a frame.

Group II.ii (Fig. 4.33)

Inside the block at the back and on the right side and near the rear wall is the bust of a youthful with his head slightly tilted to his left probably towards the supposed image against the rear wall of the cell? The face and certain parts of the head are highlighted with red colour on a whitish background in lime plaster. The left side of his face is most likely damaged during recent excavation, as indicated by the fresh marks. The head parts are delimited by red paints. He has a small face and his left eye is wide open. He is also depicted with long moustaches. His left ear, which is visible, is adorned with a jewel similar to that worn by Fig. 4.32. The rest of the body is unclear due to dirt or crust on its surface. This youthful-looking face probably has a halo-like design (??) behind its head. This design has a light brown shad and is edged in whitish paint. Its upper part is covered by the border of the frame in the middle of which the figure is placed. The bottom is also painted in light brown colour. The overlap of the top bar of the frame on the halo-shaped design indicates that the image was first painted on the brownish background which was then framed with

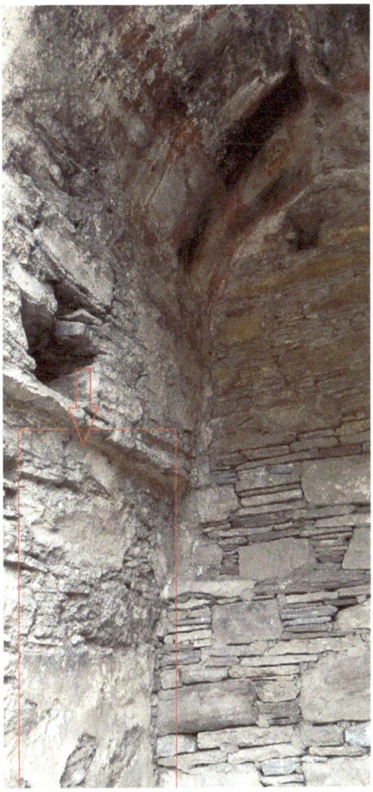

Fig. 4.31 As shown by the lime plaster and traces of colours, the whole interior surface was apparently decorated with paintings

thick square borders of red colour. The photo published in the excavation report does not show the round design. Most likely the head is depicted with a round drawing like a hair mesh or an *uṣṇīṣa*. The necklines of the garment or the neck ornament is visible. The diagonal line that crosses his left shoulder and then his right chest suggests that the figure is wearing a garment like a monk's robe. In the published photograph, the background of the image looks white which is not the case in the photo which was probably taken before clearing the image, most likely done with a hard brush or water. This is why other details are missing inside the frame and in the background.

Group II.iii (Fig. 4.34): Below Fig. 4.29, the image faces ¾ to his left with his hands folded in the *añjali* gesture. Like other figures of group II, this one is also represented inside a frame, with a whitish or light brown background, with thick borders of dark red or brown colour. The image is blurred but we can still distinguish the different parts of his head and his garment. The hair is probably painted black. Its eyebrows and eyes are pale but legible. The iris of each of its eyes is depicted in black while the sclera is painted in white. His hands are brought to his chest level and are apparently folded in the *añjali* pose. The position of the fingers is previously described as follows: "The Index finger of his left hand is intermingled between the

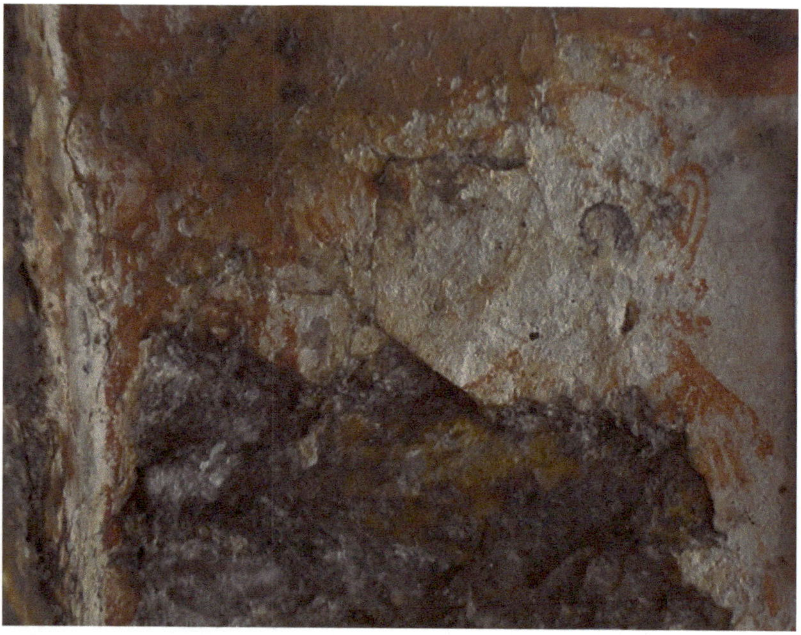

Fig. 4.32 Shave-headed figure in *añjalimudrā*

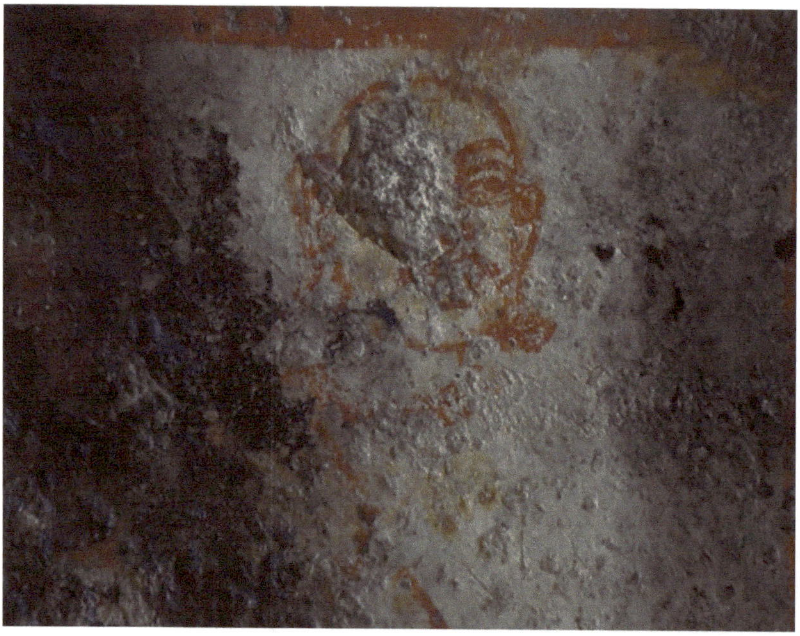

Fig. 4.33 A juvenile face wearing ear ornaments

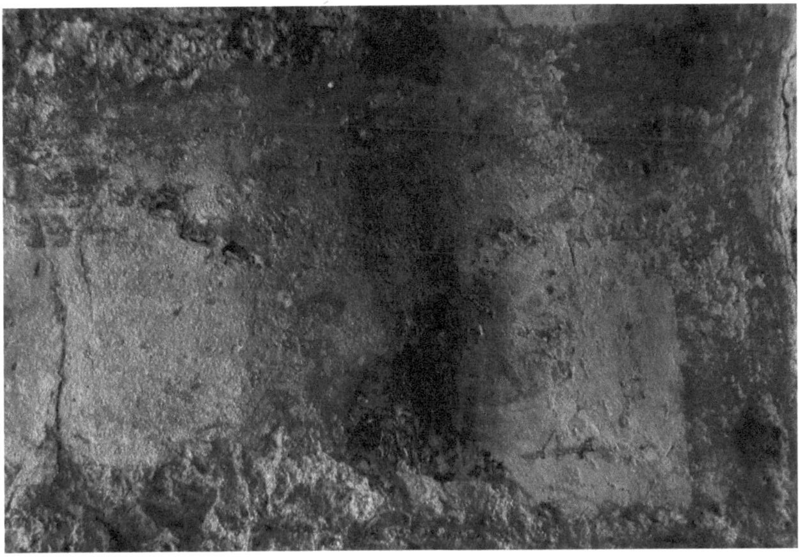

Fig. 4.34 Defaced figure

index and middle fingers of his right hand" (Samad et al. 2021: 115). But I'm not sure that's the case. The tips of most of the fingers are damaged and missing giving the impression that the figure has clasped hands. He wears a garment with fine folds and a thick neckline painted red; the supposed neckline could also represent a neck ornament. The garment he wears covers both his shoulder; the folds are marked with red paint.

Group II.iv (Fig. 4.35): Below and to the left of Fig. 4.34, the bust is painted on a light brown background. The borders of the frame are marked with bands of red colours. The head is damaged and missing. The neck is somehow intact. His body is turned slightly to his left. Like other characters in the murals on the site, the contour lines are painted in red ochre. He is represented with joined hands in *añjalimudrā* and his arms are complemented with four bracelets, two on each arm, and he also wears a neck jewellery.

Group II.v (Fig. 4.36): To the right and opposite to Fig. 4.37, the image is damaged, defaced and partly missing, and it is difficult to deduce and develop any idea about the image from the few available traces. I can only make out his left ear, the two eyes and the top line that delimits the forehead of the skull. Therefore, I only have to rely on the excavation report which says: "The defaced head of a monk with a skull is not marked. His left eye, lips and chin are absent, while his right eye and nose are intact. The left ear is oblong while the right is slightly defaced. The rest of the body is missing" (Samad et al. 2021: 114, Disciple 02).

Group II.v. (Fig. 4.37): In the compartment below of the previous figure are traces of a drawing of an image but it appears to be washed out with water after being exposed and, therefore, the majority of the painted image is lost.

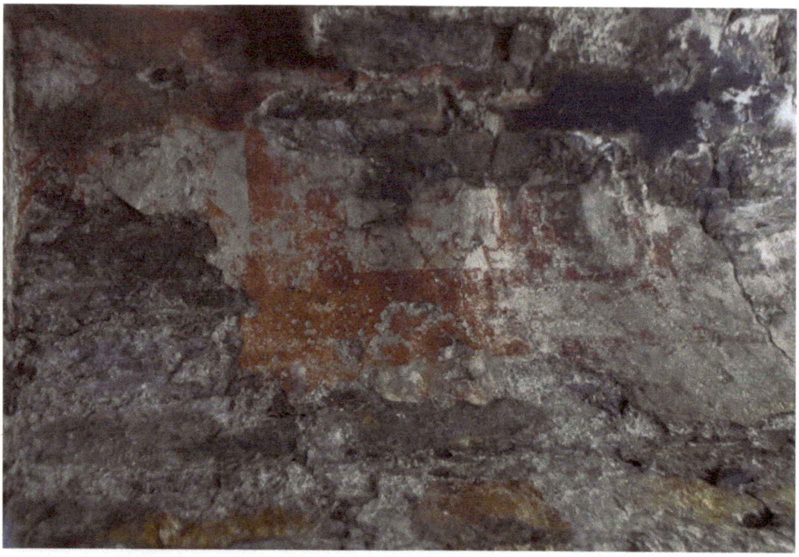

Fig. 4.35 Man displaying *añjalimudrā*

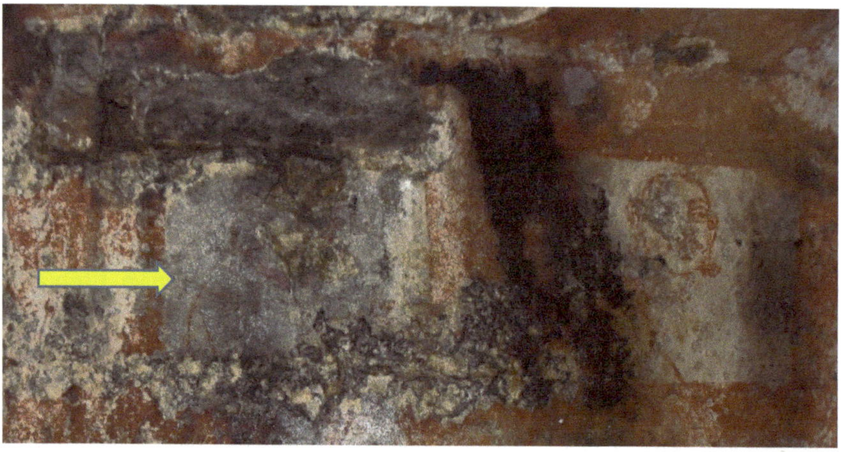

Fig. 4.36 Defaced drawing of a human (?) figure

* * *

The Abba Sahib Cheena's paintings are currently in a deplorable state and urgently need proper preservation. They are either discoloured or damaged or one has been removed from its original location for display in the museum in Swat, but unfortunately the panel, which has been detached, is said broken and is now difficult to reassemble. Therefore, about the technique and colour scheme, I can only refer to the

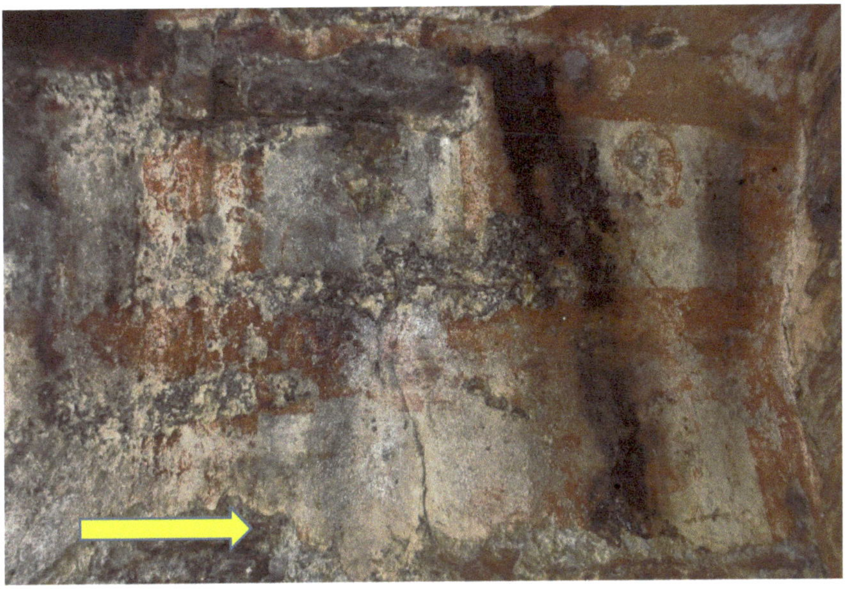

Fig. 4.37 Defaced figure (Fig. 4.36)

few lines added to this subject in the excavation report published in 2021 which says, "All the paintings have been executed in sepia (reddish-brown) and green colour, upon a thick layer of fine stucco plaster. For background manifestations, light brown ochre is applied, and the contours have been marked by a dark sepia colour. A merging shading is done for the prominence of bodily and facial features. The minerals used in the preparation of colour mixtures have been quarried from the nearby hilly areas" (Samad et al. 2021: 116).

Material analysis of the existing wall paintings at Abba Saib Chena would help to add more to the knowledge of Gandhāran School of Painting, provided that they would remain intact. For such an analysis, samples of the paint coat, lime plaster or base coat and coarse plaster or first coat may be required at a minimum. At present, judging from the high-resolution colour photographs taken just immediately after their discovery, the shade combination of paints and their application or method appear to belong to two different groups and may also belong to two different periods, although this may not be with one significant difference. It would be difficult to say which group is older than the other, but from the layout and landscape of the site one can presume that the paintings of the first group are older than those of the second group although the cell seems older than the other sanctuary. The construction of the structures may also not be contemporary with their decoration.

The colours used in the first group of paintings are light and it seems that a thin brush was used in the execution of thc figures. The background prepared for the paints is whitish or light brown in colour and, guessing from the section of the plaster, a thin layer of lime coat is used for the face making a background for the paints. The plaster is apparently made of different materials, including fine husk fibres. The main colour used for the outline of the body parts is red, dark red or brown like ochre and the skin-coloured body is usually shaded while red and green or black is used for the wings. The background is either whitish, light brown or skin-coloured.

The combination of colours and their application is more complex in the second group. Here, each individual figure is placed inside a frame. The colours are red or chocolate or dark brown for the frame (moulding) and white, whitish or light brown for the glass or glazing of the frame on which the surface paints are applied; see also Samad et al: Plate 78. The characters' bodies have at least two colours, usually whitish or light brown and red for their outlines or delineating parts of their bodies. Apparently, a fine brush is used for the outline of the figures whereas from the thickness of the frames or borders of the boxes, I presume that they were made with a thick brush or paint was applied to the canvas with the fingers.

The Abba Sahib Cheena's paintings are of two types. The first group of them is consisted of winged spirits or celestial figures while in the second group they are devotees, each is depicted in a posture of *añjalimudrā*. Each of them is placed inside an individual frame and all are added symmetrically to the intrados on both sides of the crown line of the cell. The draperies that the images carry are not very clear. Apparently, they wear clothes that cover their shoulders; some of them could also be naked. The figures in the first group, painted in the space between the brackets of the Chapelle-08 cornice, are adorned with jewels and seem to belong to a noble class.

Iconographic study of the images of the first group suggests that there seems little parallel with the rest of the paintings from the Gandhara region, as no winged figure in the frescoes in this region has yet been confirmed. However, the depiction of winged figures is not new to Gandhāran Buddhist stone art, where winged figures are represented in various contexts and may also belong to different origins. However, outside the Peshawar, Swat and Taxila Valleys, frescoes depicting winged figures have been discovered in Bāmiyān, Afghanistan (Brentjes 1981: 144, no. 13; Tissot 2003: 286, Fig. 6; Taniguchi and Cotte 2022: 7, Fig. 2, 20–21) and Kucha, Tuopulukedun and Miran in Central Asia. A painting of a small winged cupid, playing a flute-like instrument, was found at a Buddhist site in Kuca, China (Bussagli 1979: 85–86). Likewise, winged Buddha and other figures were found in Tuopulukedun, Hoitan Prefecture, Xinjiang China and Miran, Taklamakan Desert, Xingjian China. The Tuopulukedun paintings were discovered in 2002 (National Cultural Relics Bureau 2003.6: 112–113). While the Buddhist site of Miran was explored by Aurel Stein (Andrews 1948). At Miran, a total of sixteen winged figures have been recounted in Stein's murals, "The wall paintings Stein found were particularly striking; on the lower edge of wall, below waits level, were paintings of sixteen winged figures, with distinctly Western-looking faces…" (Hansen 2012: 54, plate. 5B). A fragment of a winged celestial figure is also kept in the National Museum of Tokyo and is said to have been extracted from the Miran murals in 1911 (Haewon 2013: 169, 167, Fig. 3). To resume, the winged figure of Abba Sahib Cheena is very similar in style to the winged celestials of Miran (e.g. Fig. 4.38) which are dated to the third–fourth centuries AD.

Further beyond the Gandhāra border, among the earliest depictions of winged figures can be seen in the classical period of the Romans and Greeks where such

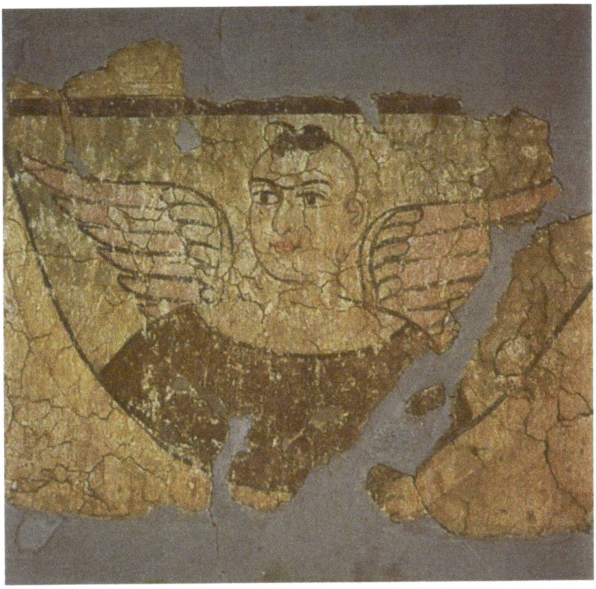

Fig. 4.38 Winged figure from Miran (Ref. Wikimedia commons)

images appeared as part of the decoration of Attic pottery, depicted on coins and carved into stones or moulded in clay, etc. The Greek goddess Nike, the Greek gods Boreas, Eros, Triton, etc., are all added with wings.[17] With the emergence of the East-West connection, this art also reached Afghanistan,[18] proper Gandhāra and Central Asia. In the Buddhist art of Gandhāra, the winged figures are numerous and varied. The most represented are those of Atlas (see Jongeward 2018: 149), Triton (e.g. Fig. 4.39), Aphrodites,[19] and Nike, mainly represented on coins.[20] Besides figures of Hellenistic origin, there are others of unknown origin, such as celestial figures which are depicted in a different context, e.g. accompanying the garland carrying

[17] Some of the earliest evidence may come from pottery of the Attic period, from Hydria-Athens, on which Boreas—the god of the north is depicted, dated to around 440 BC (National Archaeological Museum of Athens (13119)). Another early example of the god Boreas depicted on a clay pot is in the British Museum, London (GR 1931.5-11.1) which was unearthed in southern Italy and dated to 360–350 BC. The figurine terracotta statuette of Nike unearthed in Pella, Greece, is one of the best examples of its representation in clay art of Eros found in Pella from the 2nd/1st century BC in the Museum Pella Archaeological (1983.13) is another good example of a winged figure.

[18] The gold hoard from the Tillya-Tepe excavations depicts several high relief representations of winged figures of Hellenistic association some of which are identified with the Greek goddess Aphrodite, Nike and with Cupid—the Roman god of love, and are dated to the Kuṣān period (see Sarianidi 1985: 48–50–51; nos. 48, 80, 99).

[19] Such as the Aphrodite of Bactria, found at Tomb VI at Tillya Tepe; now in the National Museum of Afghanistan.

[20] There are also examples of winged figures that are part of the Bodhisattva Jewellery decoration (see Tanabe 2007: 92–93, No. II-6 and 94–95, No. II-7).

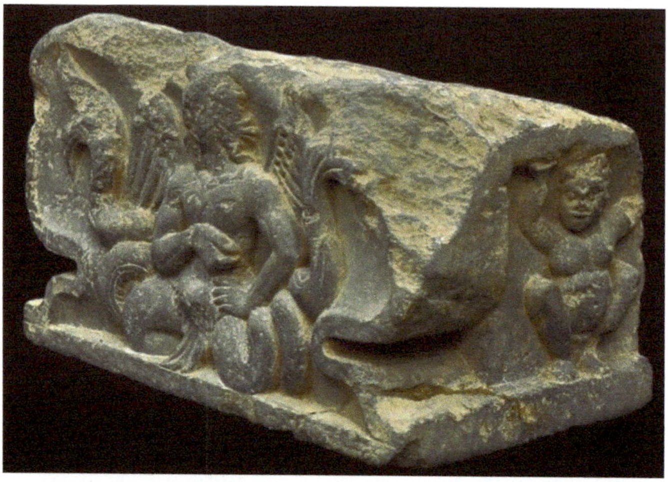

Fig. 4.39 Triton Dir Museum Chakdara

ceremony (Figs. 4.40 and 4.41).[21] Other examples of winged spirits, both male and females,[22] are those who carry an offering in their hands (e.g. Fig. 4.42). One of the winged spirits is depicted in a kneeling position, probably Heracles, with hands in *añjalimudrā* (Fig. 4.41) like those in Abba Sahib Cheena's Group II paintings. Besides the above two groups of figures, there are native figures or symbols which are depicted with wings; these are e.g. a *triratna* symbol (Fig. 4.43) representing the Buddha's first sermon[23] and the figure of a bodhisattva (Fig. 4.44). The seated figure of a Bodhisattva from Aziz Ḍheri shows wings which were previously identified as flames emitting from the Bodhisattva's shoulder (Nasim Khan 2010, vol. III: 306, cat. no. 3887). But the design behind is triangular in shape with straight lines in the middle and looks like wings rather than wavy flames. The shape of the bodhisattva's wings is comparable to those that appear on the wall paintings of Tuopulukedun, Xinjiang China (see National Cultural Relics Bureau 2003: 112–113).

The combined study of the evidence discussed above suggests that the Abba Sahib Cheena wall paintings may belong to the late Kuṣān period. Iconographic features,

[21] Banerjea, who already identified such figures in Bharut, Sanci and Gandhara, says, "To refer to one or two typical cases from Bārhut, Sānci and Udayagiri: The flying garland bearers on the oftreproduced Bodhi-tree shrine from Bārhut and similar other figures on the lintel of the eastern gateway of Sānci are hybrid in appearance, the lower halves of their bodies are bird-like while the upper halves are human with wings attached to their shoulders or waists. But the elaborately dressed flying figures on either sides of the Toraṇas in the animated scenes on the friezes of the rock-cut temples at Udayagiri are entirely human ….But they seem to have gradually discontinued the practice of making use of both these motifs; they retained the human flying figures. By the Hellenistic craftsmen of Gandhara also the garland bearing cherubim and female flying figures were frequently employed (Banerjea 1936: 53–54)".

[22] For the female winged-spirits see Tanabe (2007: 78, No. I-70).

[23] In an example, preserved in Hirayama collection, Buddha stands and touches the shaft of the *triratna* symbol while two winged-spirits are seen above (Tanabe 2007: 34–35, No. I-25).

Fig. 4.40 But Kara III

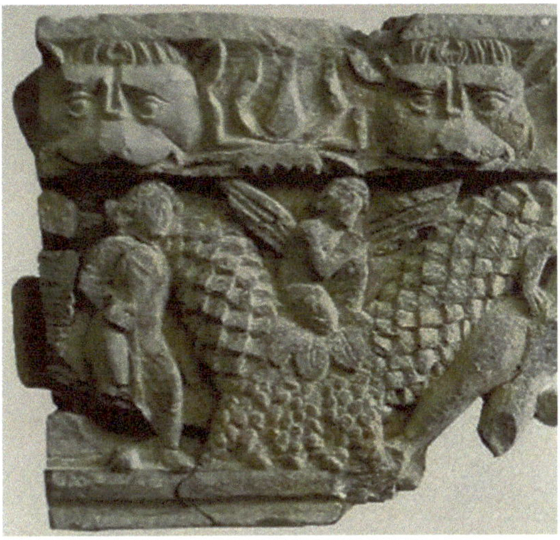

Fig. 4.41 But Kara III

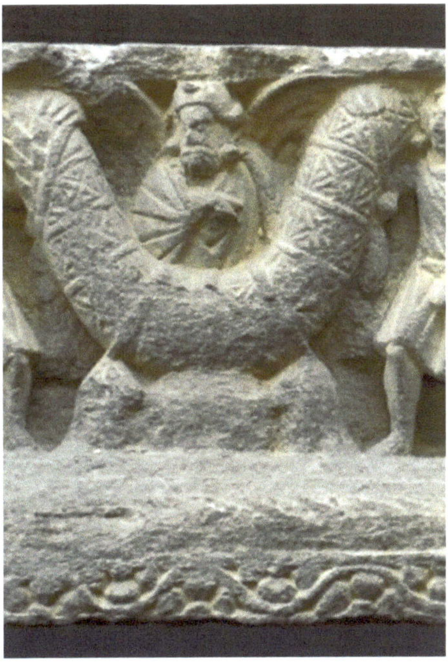

such as winged figures with a tail hairstyle on top or on the side of the skull while the rest of the head is shaved, are already known in Gandhara Buddhist art, see Tanabe 2007: 54, n °.I-36 and 201, our V-43 and V-44. In the last two cases, both are considered children. A similar representation of the hairstyle is attested in the various panels discovered in the Buddhist site of But Kara III (e.g. Khan, G.R. 2015: 175,

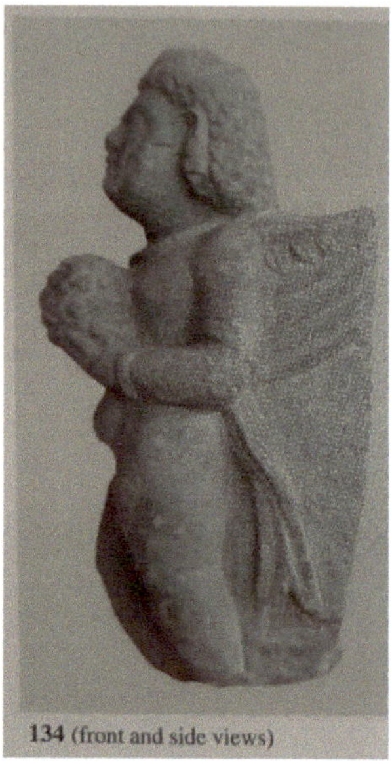

Fig. 4.42 Cupid from But Kara III

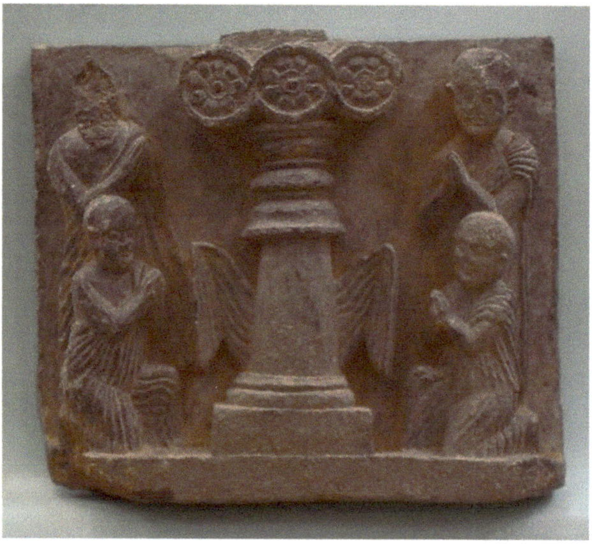

Fig. 4.43 Triratna from But Kara III

Plate 125, 181, Pl. 128). Each of these panels represents human figures, naked or draped in fabric, which carry a large garland. In the corners of some of the garlands, winged figures are also represented (Figs. 4.45 and 4.46). Such a hairstyle is also attested in the clay art of Greater Gandhāra (e.g. Fig. 4.47). These elements suggest that winged figures and figures with a tail hairstyle are typical of Gandhāra, especially

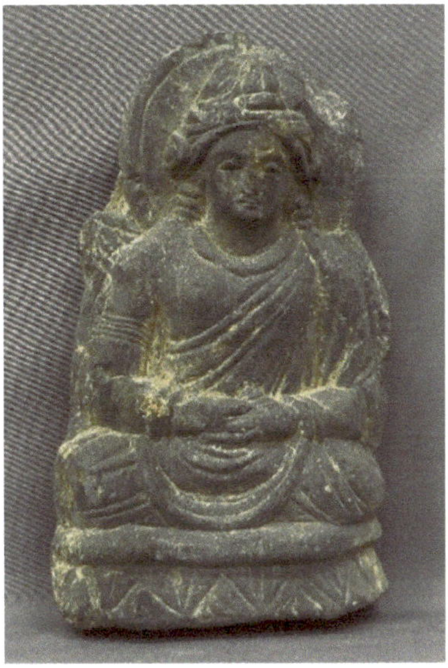

Fig. 4.44 Sculpture from Aziz Ḍheri

in the Swat Valley which played an important role in cultural exchanges between China and Gandhāra (see Nasim Khan 2011, Fig. 11).

The colour used in Cheena's murals are red, dark red or dark brown, white and whitish, black, and possibly green. These pigments are also used in other Gandhāra

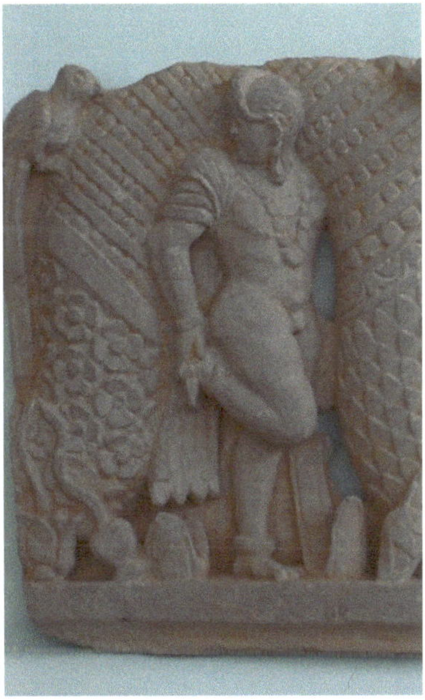

Fig. 4.45 But Kara III-garland bearers

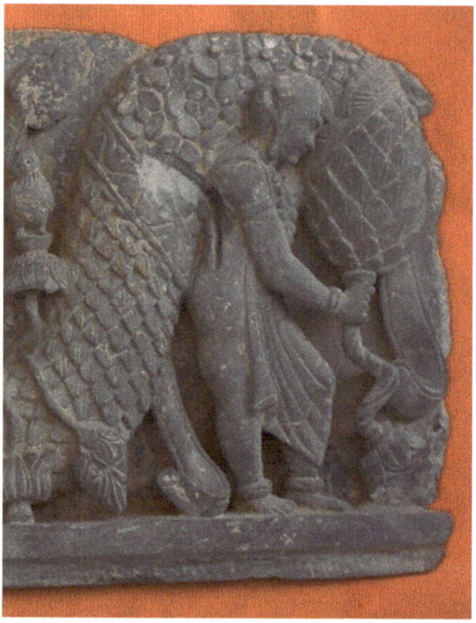

Fig. 4.46 But Kara III-garland bearers

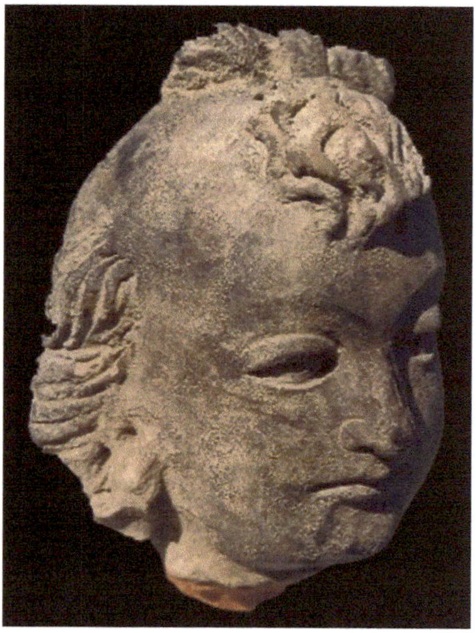

Fig. 4.47 Terracotta head from Gandhāra

murals. In all of these paintings, red, dark red or brown and skin colours are dominant shades except in the Yakatoot paintings where white, black, skin colour and blue are the dominant shades. In Jinnan Wali Ḍheri's paintings, brown, dark sepia, various shades of red, white, black, yellow and blue were used.

Buddhist paintings inside caves or cells are also attested outside the frontier of Gandhāra (e.g. Fig. 4.48) and I presume that, if not all of them, some of the rest of the cells at Abba Sahib Cheena or found in the rest of the Buddhist sites in Gandhāra (e.g. Figs. 4.49 and 4.50), should have also been provided with some sort of frescos decoration that could not survive either due to weather condition or may be because of some other reasons such as due to improper scientific investigations of such sites.

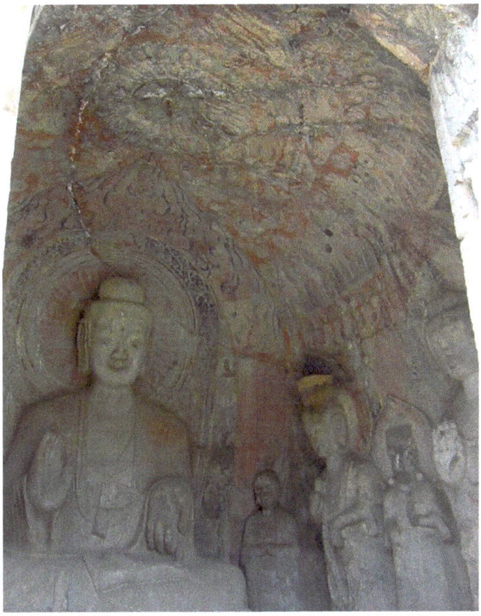

Fig. 4.48 Entrance to Central Binyang Cave, 508–523 C.E. Longmen Caves, Luoyang, China (image Wikimedia commons)

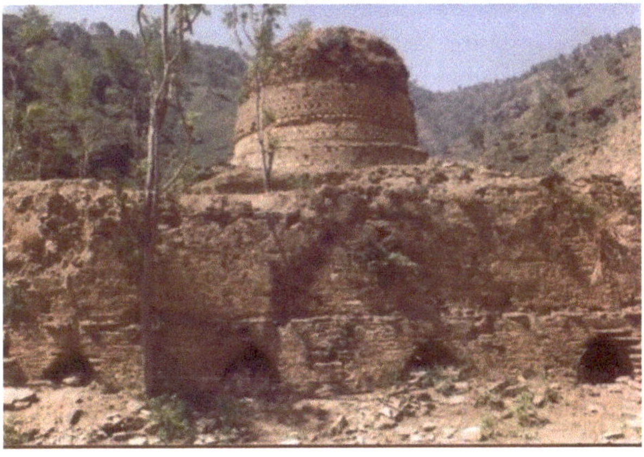

Fig. 4.49 Naji Gram stūpa provided with cell

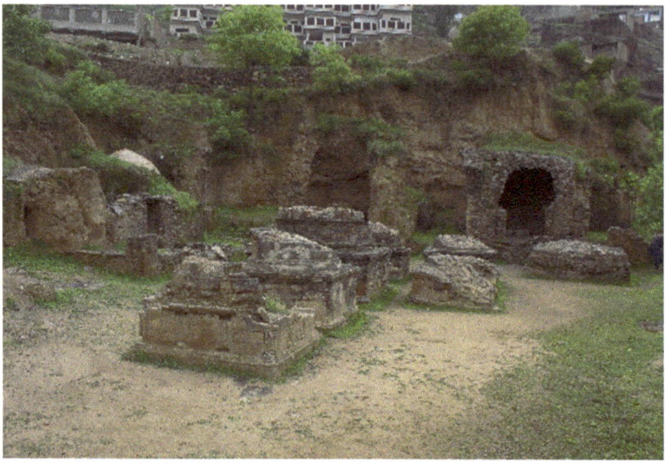

Fig. 4.50 Cells at But Kara III

Date: So far, there is no concrete evidence to precisely date the paintings of Abba Sahib Cheena. At the moment, the only benchmarks are the contextual, circumstantial and iconographic analysis of our chronology of the murals. The coins collected on the site belong to the Indo-Scythian,[24] Kuṣān and Islamic period (Samad et al. 2021: 101, 103; 451–453). They were collected from the surface and were found in trench C, the area of the paintings, except for the single piece of Azes which was found at ground level of stūpa E, trench E&F. Other datable elements are the few inscribed sherds (Samad et al. 2021: 426–427). They are written in Kharoṣṭhī script of the late Kuṣān period. They were also recovered from trench C of the excavated area. The coins and the inscription mostly come from the same trench C and were generally found at the surface level and are, therefore, of little use in dating the wall paintings. However, the layout of the structures suggests that the buildings at the site do not belong to the same period but may have been built in different times. The niche, provided with paintings, is built in the eastern wall of the platform on which the Stūpa C and Vihāra D are built. The votive stūpas located in front of the niche and the Chapel-08 built against the platform and to the left of the niche are probably among the later additions.

The other element that can be used to approximate the dating of the paintings is the circumstantial evidence. The frescoes discovered, so far, come from very few Buddhist sites in the Gandhāra region. These include paintings from But Kara I site, dated to the second–fourth centuries AD, paintings of Paṭvano Gaṭai—dated to the fourth–sixth centuries AD (Nasim Khan 2000), paintings from Aziz Ḍheri, dated to the third–fourth centuries AD (Nasim Khan 2010), paintings from Jinnan Wali Ḍheri—dated to before third century AD (Khan and Mahmood-ul-Hassan 2008: 306)

[24] The presence of Indo-Scythian coin does not mean that the site belongs to that particular period. This is not the only exception, the finding of early-period coins in a late-period Buddhist establishment is already known from other Buddhist sites in this area (e.g., see Nasim Khan 2010).

and the Yakatoot paintings—dated to fourth–fifth centuries AD (Nasim Khan 2016a, 2016b). To give a general date to these previously known Buddhist wall paintings from Gandhāra, they might be placed somewhere between the second and sixth century AD. However, there are other Buddhist paintings, though not frescos, which have been executed around the first and second century AD, or earlier, such as the Kala Tassa paintings in Hazara and the Parlai Ḍab paintings in Swabi (see above). This would suggest that the tradition of executing Buddhist paintings in this region was not really a new phenomenon for the Buddhist to add such an art to their places of worship but this faith was already in existence long before the art of frescoes became known to the scholars in this field. Therefore, the circumstantial evidence would suggest placing the Abba Sahib Cheena murals in the general context of the Gandhāran School of Buddhist painting which probably lasted from the 1st, or even earlier, to the sixth century AD. The Abba Sahib Cheena paintings might belong to the third–fifth century AD.

Jinnan Wali Ḍheri, Taxila

During the long period of archaeological excavations in the Taxila Valley, no significant Buddhist wall painting have so far been revealed except for the very rare evidence of paintings which were found at the Buddhist site of Jinnan Wali Ḍheri in Taxila. The discovery was made between the years 2002–2008[25] at this one of the most important Buddhist sites in the Taxila Valley (Figs. 4.51 and 4.52). The first official excavations at the site were conducted by the Federal Department of Archaeology and Museums, Government of Pakistan, which continued from 2002 to 2008 (Kakar and Khan 2008: 6). Later, in March 2014, a small-scale excavation was carried out at the site under my supervision as Director of the Directorate of Archaeology and Museums of the Government of Khyber Pakhtunkhwa (Muhammad et al. 2018: 96). But the 2014 excavations has revealed no significant finds due to the focus on a very limited area of the site. The recent archaeological survey was conducted, in 2017 and 2018, by a team of archaeologists from the Taxila Institute of Asian Civilizations, Quaid I Azam University Islamabad (Suleman Khan 2018). During first excavation, the courtyard of the stūpa and the area of the monastery were discovered from where several antiquities were unearthed, including inscriptions, coins, a treasure of jewels, wall paintings and other cultural objects. After their finding, some of them, especially the inscriptions, were shown to the present author for identification by Mr. Bahadur Khan, the director of the project. Its reading and translation were subsequently published in 2008 (Kakar and Khan 2008: 6).

[25] There are two different views about the starting date of the excavation at the site. According to Ashraf Khan, it was started in January 2003 (Khan and Mamood-ul-Hassan: 2008: 303) while Kakar and Khan believe that the starting date of the excavation was 2nd November 2002 (Kakar and Khan 2008: 13). In any case, for us, the excavation and the discoveries are more important than the exact starting date of the excavations.

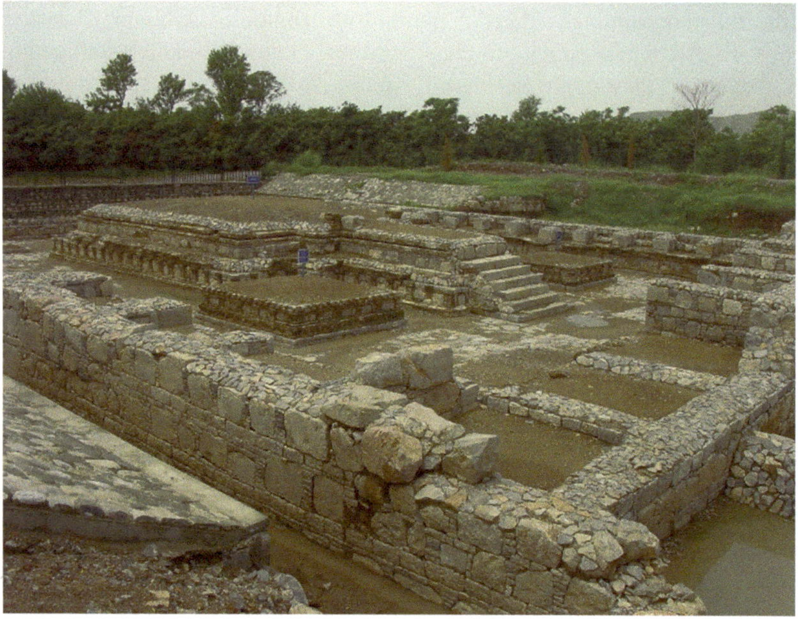

Fig. 4.51 The main stūpa complex at Jinnan Wali Ḍheri

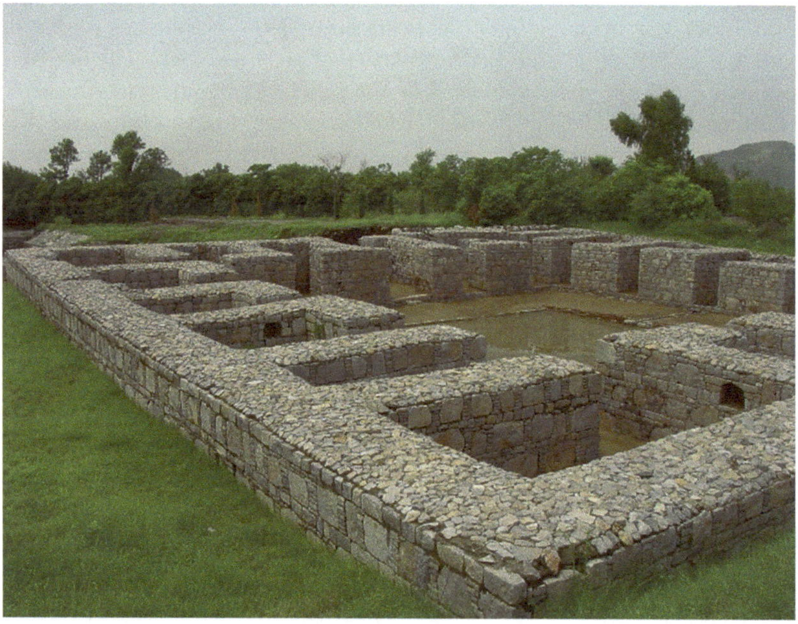

Fig. 4.52 Monastery area of the Jinnan Wali Ḍheri site

Among other discoveries made at Jinnan Wali Ḍheri were the wall paintings which are presently preserved in the Taxila Museum. The paintings were first published in 2004 (Khan and Mamood-ul-Hassan 2004) and then in 2006 (Tanweer 2006). Subsequently, they were republished in 2008 (Kakar and Khan 2008) and in 2011 by Khan and Mamood-ul-Hassan generally with the same interpretation already submitted. They are dated to the fourth/fifth century AD (Kakar and Khan 2008: 23) or second–fifth centuries AD (Khan and Mamood-ul-Hassan 2008: 305).

The paintings were found in the area of the monastery located in front of the main stūpa area. According to the excavators, "The most remarkable discovery from Jinnan Wali Ḍheri, is the fragments of mural paintings, painted on the walls of the western corridor of the monastery, which leads to the upper court and subsequently to main stūpa court. The fragments of the paintings were collapsed when the monastery was destroyed by the Whit Huns in the fifth century AD. During excavation a large number of fragments found lying on the floor of the corridor (Pl.8.a). Most of the fragments of the paintings have been defaced due to heavy fire and weathering, but luckily a few fragments of paintings were recovered in much better condition, described as below:..." (Kakar and Khan 2008: 21). A total of 36 pieces with paintings were noticed and then consolidated. Five of the fragments/pieces have already been published (see above) and explained in detail except for Fig. 4.5. All these published fragments are revisited and reinterpreted here with the following notes (Figs. 4.53 and 4.54).

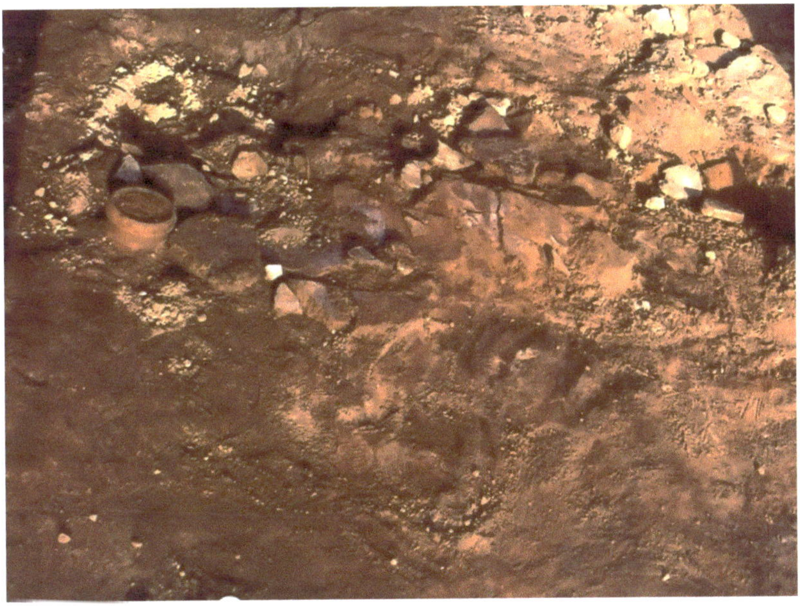

Fig. 4.53 Photo showing paintings before their detection and identification (photo courtesy A. Lone)

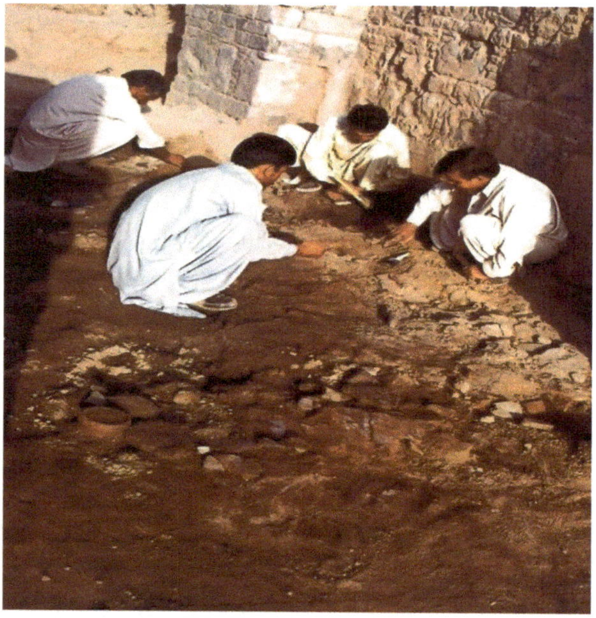

Fig. 4.54 Cleaning of the paintings is in progress (Photo courtesy A. Lone)

Fragment 1 (Fig. 4.55) (20.5 × 53 × 2.2 cm/coating 4 mm) (No.317-JWD/04-E-10-6) (Khan and Mamood-ul-Hassan 2004: Plate 4; Kakar and Khan 2008: Plate a)

The photographs provided by the previous authors show that, like other pieces of the murals, this fragment is also cracked at several places. The image also shows that it was probably photographed in situ and before necessary conservation work. The fragment depicts the remains of at least two busts (?). The one at the left end of the panel is identified as bust of a monk (?) (Khan and Hasssan 2004: 19) whose left side of the head and shoulder are missing. He is shown from the front but his head is little tilted to his left. He has half-closed eyes and a large pointed nose with alar rim retraction or stretched nostrils. The lips seem joined. His left ear is visible. Skin colour is used for the body; however, the eyes, ears, nose and lips are shaded white. The hair is shown black in colour and the eyebrows are in light brown or painted in light black. The figure and the colours used in this painting are said, "Fleshy face with full chin, heavy lips treated with white colour, broad nostril, wide open eyes, eyeballs, nose and ears are painted in white colour, eye brows and wrinkles on the forehead are shown in black colour, long curly hair touching shoulder. Background is brown. Rest of the fragment is decorated with floral motifs in red colour, dark brown, white and blue colour for sky is also used. Colours are faded and pieces are missing therefore, exact description cannot be given" (Khan and Hassan 2004: 19). He wears a robe that covers his preserved shoulder. The garment is shown brown while the background of the image is depicted as yellowish or light brown. The figure

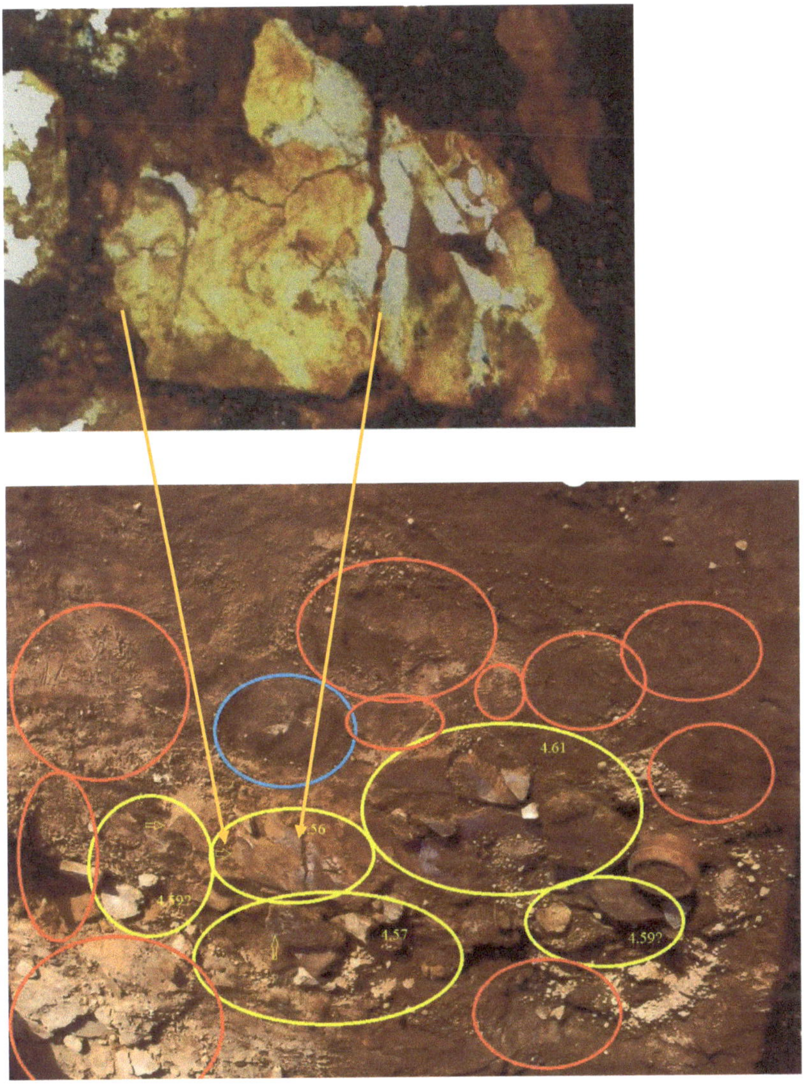

Fig. 4.55 Panel showing Buddha and some other unidentified figures to his left. (**a**) Exact finding spot of Fig. 4.55. Figure 4.53 is shown here in upside down position

to his left is just a human head which is titled to his left[26] and is added with a halo with double band rim in white colour. The head has brown or black hair while the face features a light brown colour. The photo shows that the figure's head is aligned

[26] Almost all figures in Jinnan Wali Ḍheri paintings are shown frontally but the head is titled to one's left or right. Same is the case in the Dandan Oilik Site in Xinjiang (for comparison, see the report published in 2009 (Beijing) by the Cultural Relics Press).

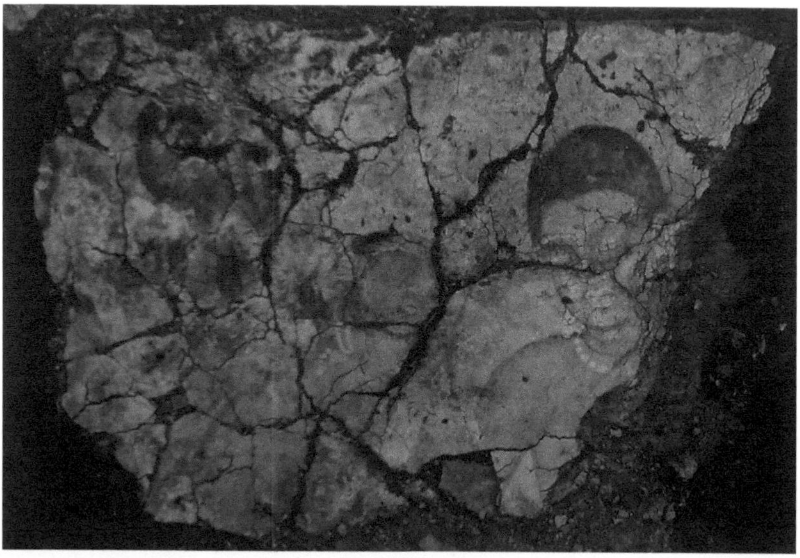

Fig. 4.56 Temptation of the Bodhisattva by Mara's daughters (?)

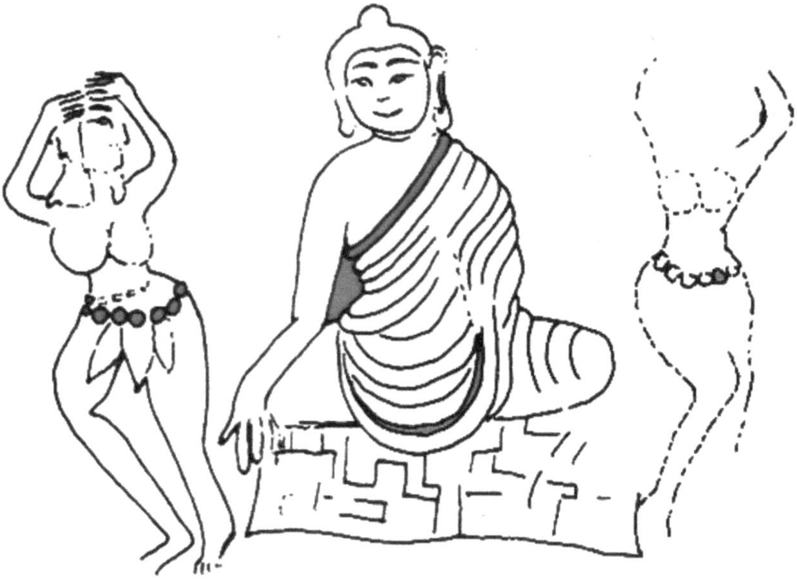

Fig. 4.57 Temptation of Mara's daughters on the Buddha (after Jettmar and Thewalt 1991)

with the level of the first figure's neck, suggesting that the central figure in the scene could be the first image of this fragment or the one, which is supposedly missing, towards the left to which the head is tilted.

Fragment 2 (Fig. 4.56) (33.4 × 53 × 2.2 cm/coating 3 mm) (No.314-JWD/04-E-10-6, Bodhisattva in *dhyānamudrā*) (Khan 2004 and Mamood-ul-Hassan: Plate 1; Tanveer 2006: Fig. 3; Kakar and Khan 2008: Plate 8b; Khan and Mamood-ul-Hassan 2008: 306, Fig.9)

Three figures are identified on the surface of this fragment, a supposed Bodhisattva in a meditation posture and two others, one seated and the other standing and are facing to the Bodhisattva. The main pigments used in the paints are the skin colour identified for the body and white is applied for the lips, nose, eyelids and eyebrows.[27] The neck is marked with red colour and the hair is originally painted black. The background and the halo are white. The folds of the garment of the figure, who is seated close to the Bodhisattva, are in white colour.

The bodhisattva figure is said to be seated in *dhyānamudrā*, however, this may not be the case since the position of his right hand suggests that he is seated, probably cross-legged, with his right arm positioned away from his body as the space suggests. Most likely, his right hand, which is missing, originally crossed over his right knee while making a certain gesture. Apparently, the Bodhisattva wears a tight beaded necklace around his neck, and a similar ornament is also added to his upper right arm. He is also adorned with ear ornaments as can be guessed from the remaining part of the ornament added to his left ear. His right shoulder is bare, suggesting he is wearing a robe that only covers his left shoulder.

The male figure seated (?) near and to the right of the Bodhisattva is faded and all there is to say would be only a guess. His head is completely defaced and only his lips and the tip of his nose are probably visible and which are painted white. The figure seems wear a beaded neck jewel like the other figure explained above. His head seems drawn at the same level as the Bodhisattva's right shoulder. The presence of its right shoulder can be guessed from the folds of its drapery; the folds are painted white. The third figure, probably a female, is in a standing position and is shown in the foreground. This person is also damaged due to visible cracks all over the body but it is somehow traceable. It is a female who stand facing forward, the head turned towards the Bodhisattva. Both arms are bent towards the head in a dancing posture. The right shoulder is defaced, but only the outlines of the arms are traceable. The fingers of her right hand are also clearly visible. The figure is standing in a *tribhanga* pose or dancing gesture and wearing a short lower garment where the beaded girdle is traceable. The garment is painted in brown and the folds are shown in dark brown colour. The upper garment is unclear; it seems that this character is naked. If so, it would remind me of the temptation of the Buddha by Mara's daughter as depicted in the carvings of the Upper Indus Valley (Fig. 4.57).[28] In this case, a similar figure

[27] In paintings from Mogao Cave 254 in Dunhuang (Northern Wei Dynasty) (Fan 2017: 49) Mogao Cave 428 (Northern Zhou Dynasty) (Fan 2017: 68; Agnew and Reed 2016: 7, Fig. 6) shows that white colour is used for the eyes, nose, lips and probably for moustaches.

[28] The presence of the Bodhisattva here may create doubt about the identification of the scene.

on the left of the Bodhisattva should have been existed. But in our case, it is not the figure of the Buddha but a Bodhisattva is represented. Anyhow, at the time of Mara's attack or of the temptation of the Buddha by Mara's daughters, Śākyamuni had not yet attained enlightenment and was not a declared Buddha.

At the extreme left of the panel and next to the first female figure, there is another standing female figure (?), probably of the same nature as the previous one. It is partly preserved; the rest has disappeared with the missing part of the panel. Only his head and upper left body are somehow visible. She stands facing forward with her left hand on her left hip. The face is painted in skin colour and the eyes and hair are depicted in black.

Fragment 3 (Fig. 4.58) (40.5 × 21.8 × 2 cm/coating 2 mm or 4 mm?) (No. 315-JWD/04-E-10–6, Buddha in *dharmacakramudrā*) (Tanveer 2006: Fig. 1; Kakar and Khan 2008: Plate 8c; Khan and Mahmood-ul-Hassan 2008: 306, Fig. 8)

This panel shows a damaged Buddha figure, which is also partially missing. Buddha sits cross-legged with his feet uncovered and the soles turned upwards, but his left shoulder is covered with the robe. The forearms and hands are also uncovered, and like his feet, they are painted white or light brown or the same skin colour as the rest of his body colour. The drapery is depicted with a brown colour while the pleats are painted with dark brown ochre. The hair is painted black. The gesture of his hands, approaching his chest, is interesting. The tips of the index and thumbs of his right-hand touch in a gesture of arguing (*vitarkamudrā*) and are covered by the hooked fingers of his left hand. The little finger of his right hand is stretched backwards while the finger between the little finger and the middle one is tilted towards his

Fig. 4.58 Buddha seated in preaching pose

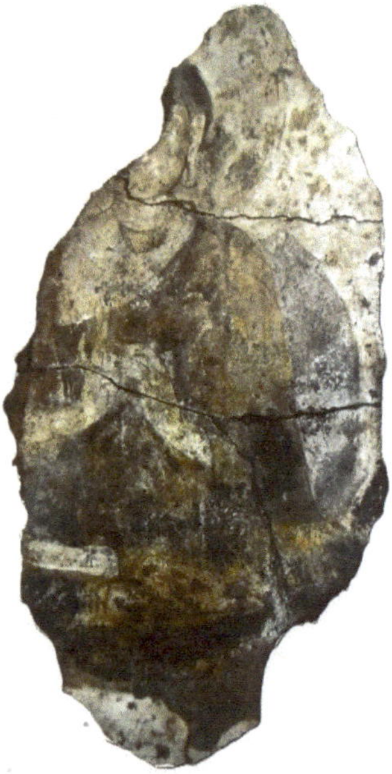

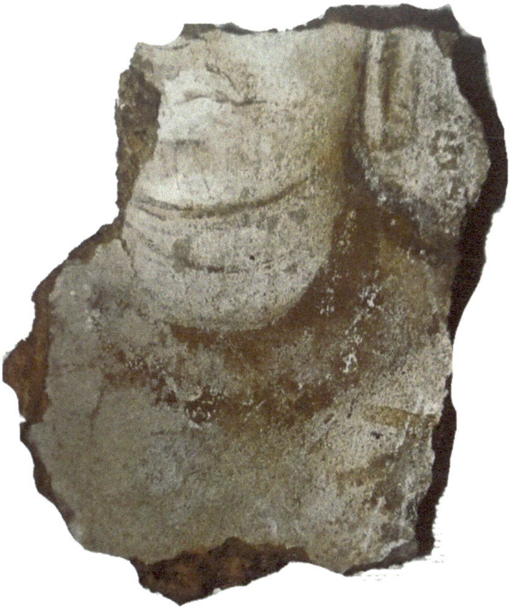

Fig. 4.59 Probably bust of the Buddha with long ear lob

left hand. The middle finger is left straight. Buddha is added both with the halo, behind his head, and the aureole behind his body. The margin of the halo is marked with double parallel lines shown in white. While the margin of the round aureole is marked with a wide band of white colour. According to Khan and Mahmood-ul-Hassan 2004, "Hallow is of white colour and shown with brush lines" (Khan and Mahmood-ul-Hassan 2004: 18).

Fragment 4 (Fig. 4.59) (12.5 × 9.5 × 2 cm/coating 4 mm) (No.316-JWD/04-E-10-6, Bodhisattva) (Khan and Mahmood-ul-Hassan 2004: 18, Plate 3 (?); Tanveer 2006: Fig. 3; Kakar and 2008: Plate 8d; Khan and Mahmood-ul-Hassan 2008: 307, Fig. 10)

This mutilated and mostly missing figure in the panel is identified as the bust of a bodhisattva due to the supposed presence of a necklace made of round white beads (Khan and Mahmood-ul-Hassan 2004). My guess is that the character is not wearing jewellery and it may be the figure of a Buddha, shown frontally, who is depicted with a long earlobe without any ornament. The bust is largely missing and only the left side of the face, the left ear, the fleshy neck and part of his chest are preserved. The body is painted in skin colour or light brown while the lips are apparently depicted in white. The thin dark lines show the throat wrinkles while the dark shade under the neck delimits the neck area from that of the chest and reflects an aesthetic concern of the artist. Khan and Mahmood-ul-Hassan (2004) sees a halo behind the head and says, "Hallow is in white colour and a black line separates hallow from the body".

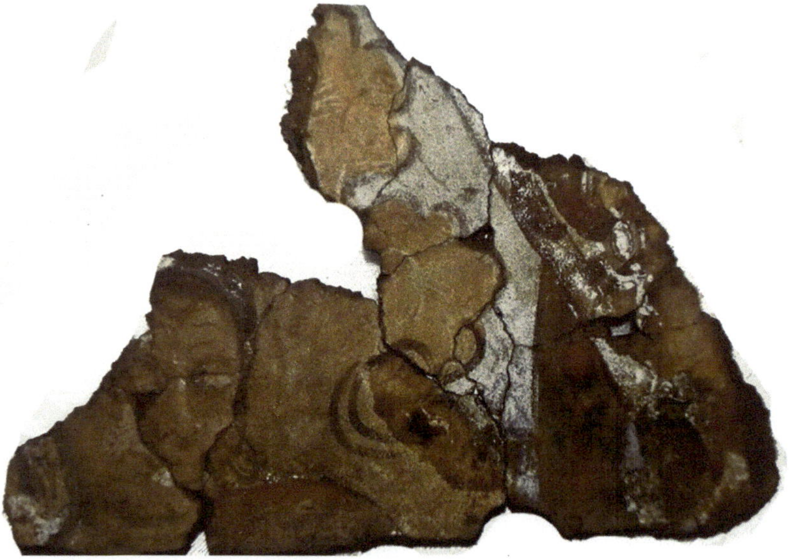

Fig. 4.60 Buddha and some unclear drawings

Fragment 5 (Fig. 4.60) (20.5 × 53 × 2.2 cm/coating 4 mm) (No. 317-JWD/04-E-10-6, Monk?) (Tanveer 2006: Fig. 4; Kakar and Khan 2008: Plate 8e; Khan and Mahmood-ul-Hassan 2008: 307, Fig.11)

The panel probably shows different images. All are mutilated and partly disappeared, however few of them are recognizable by certain of their features. For example, the figure on the extreme left of the panel, which is previously identified as an image of a monk (?), is probably a Buddha represented from the front with the head tilted slightly towards his left shoulder. The cracks in his face area caused damages to his right eye and mouth. The area above and to the right of his head is missing. The preserved left eye is half open; the sclera painted white, and the iris and pupil black. The figure shows a fleshy face with a big nose, a long lobe of his right ear. The distinction between the body and its clothing is made with the shades of paint, light brown is used for the body and brown for the drapery which covers its preserved left shoulder. The hair is painted black, and the eyebrows are depicted with a brown shade. Apparently, a halo is depicted behind its head, and its margin is marked with two parallel white lines. To the left of the Buddha image, the floating motifs form concentric circles. Above, there is another blurred drawing of a human figure. At the other end of the panel, there are other unidentified designs painted in dark brown colours.

To reassemble all the fragments together and also to reconstruct the missing and defaced images with underlying presumptions, the context of the whole group seems much more complex than one might have to guess. However, one thing which seems certain that the set of the images most likely represents any obvious theme from the life of the Buddha. But still, unfortunately, good parts of the panels are missing and it is therefore difficult to access the exact facts. The colour used in the paintings, according to their excavators are explained as, "For the background light brown ochre was used. Colour of the body is varied, light wheat colour in the case of Pl.8b and dark chocolate for two other figures, hair is painted in black or dark brown colour with red shades, contours of the body are depicted with dark sepia colour. Eyes, nose, lips, ears and ornaments are depicted in white colour, black lines are used for separating figures from the background. For borders decoration red, white, dark brown and blue colour is frequently used. Black, white and yellow colours are found in their natural form in the Khri Murit hills" (Kakar and Khan 2008: 22).

Location of the Paintings

The paintings were said to have been found near the side walls, either upside down or in prone position, and to have fallen from the still level wall below the of the walls where they were originally applied. However, the photograph (Fig. 4.55) shows that they were found face up in the centre of the hall, the monastery entrance, which may contradict the proposed theory. Second, they were probably mounted on the ceiling rather than to the side walls, since they were in the midpoint of the entrance hall. Third, the site may have been illegally excavated and antiquities seekers may have attempted to remove it from the top of the side walls, but could not have removed it intact due to the fragile condition of the paint. The paintings therefore remained there after being removed from the surface of the walls by illegal diggers until they were discovered in 2002/2003. Another possibility, given the location of the paintings, is that the entire walls on either side of the entrance were provided with paintings and for some reason they slipped off the walls and lost their position.

Date

These paintings were found in a certain context and an approximate date wouldn't be a big deal provided that the other antiquities from the site are considered contemporary to the paintings.[29] The two types of dated materials found during excavations are the inscriptions and coins. The three short inscriptions are written in local scripts, one in Kharoṣṭhī (Fig. 4.61) and two in Brāhmī characters (Figs. 4.62 and 4.63). The first is carved at the base of a stucco image, now missing, which, according to the excavators, was installed at the northeast corner of the main stūpa and near the entrance of the monastery from where the wall paintings were recovered. The inscription reads as follows:

> [proṭha]hianaṃ e danamukho
> "This religious gift (image) has been fixed"

The other important discoveries are coins, eleven in number, which belong to different periods (Kakar and Khan 2008: 26 and Khan and Mahmood-ul-Hassan 2011: 5452–54). They are essentially associated with the Kushan era except for

[29] These antiquities could also belong to different periods because the Buddhist sites in Gandhāra had generally been used for a very long period of time and the antiquities found at the same site are dated to different periods.

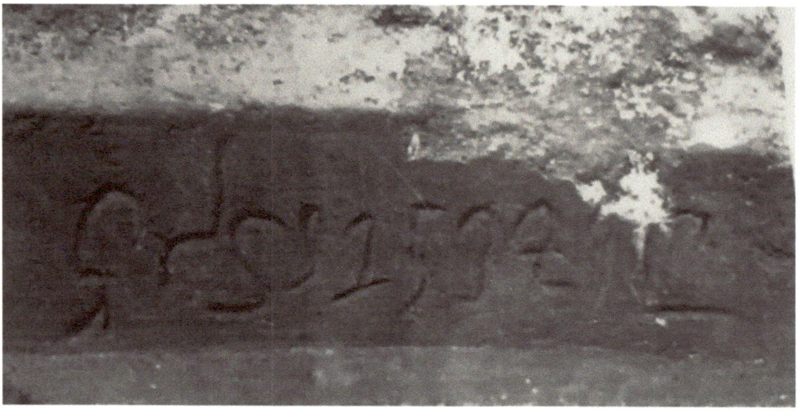

Fig. 4.61 Kharoṣṭhī inscription carved into the pedestal of an image

Fig. 4.62 Bangle inscription in Brāhmī

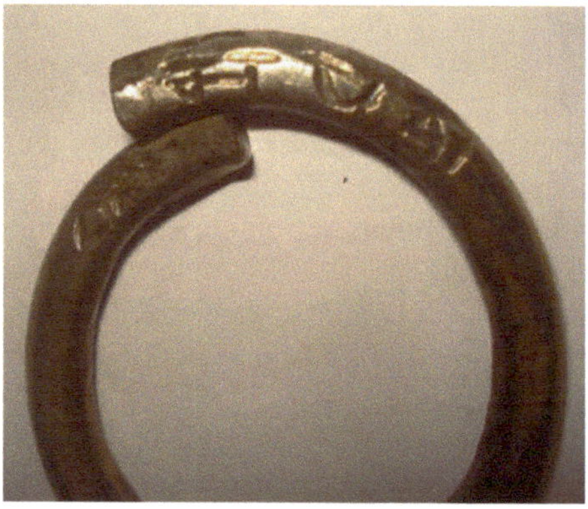

Fig. 4.63 Finger ring inscription Brāhmī

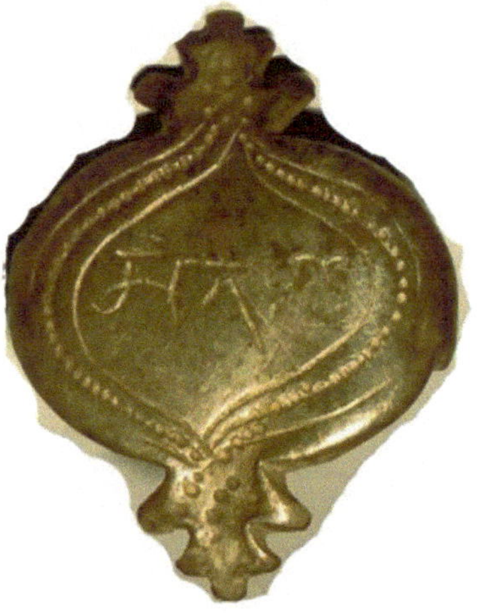

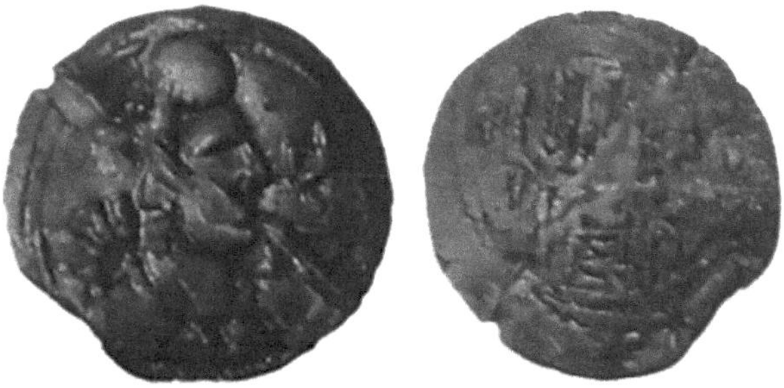

Fig. 4.64 Alkhon coin

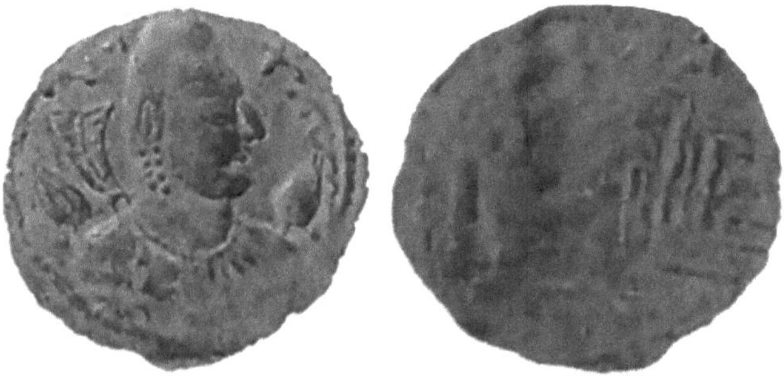

Fig. 4.65 Alkhon coin

three which belong to a late date. The latter are rarely attested in the Buddhist sites of Gandhāra. One of them is a square-shaped coin weighing 4.3 g. It is associated with the Gupta period (Khan and Mahmood-ul-Hassan 2011: 54). The other two are silver coins (Figs. 4.64 and 4.65) (Kakar and Khan 2008: 26, and Khan and Mahmood-ul-Hassan 2011: 52) and are said belong to the "White Huns". In fact, all the three coins belong to the Huns period.

In the presence of the above antiquities, also discovered at of Jinnan Wali Ḍheri, one can surmise an approximate chronology of the site. The epigraphic evidence may be more reliable, especially the Kharoṣṭhī inscription as it is still in situ and in its original context. This inscription seems contemporaneous with the construction of the stūpa, which may belong to the third–fifth centuries AD. The two Brāhmī inscriptions, also discovered at the site, belong to the fourth/fifth century AD. As far as the numismatic data is concerned, these are coins fitting to the end of the Kuṣān and post-Kuṣān period and which can, in general, be placed between the third and fifth centuries of our era. Therefore, based on the above epigraphic and numismatic evidence, the Jinnan Wali Ḍheri site was most likely established during the late Kuṣān period and which remained functional even during the Huns rule over Gandhara.[30]

[30] If so, the theory of Huns hostility to Buddhist establishments in Gandhāra might be considered redundant. The Huns period is generally seen a time of aggression and desertion towards the Buddhist

The Jinnan Wali Ḍheri site appears to be contemporary with the Buddhist site of Bhamala and can be dated to the third–fifth centuries AD. If so, the wall paintings at the site belong to the third–fifth centuries CE.

Yakatoot, Peshawar

The acquisition history of Gandhāran antiquities has a very long history and the museums' collections in Pakistani are mainly based on three sources: purchase and donations—largely acquired before partition of the Indo-Pakistan subcontinent, archaeological excavations, and the museums are enriching through seized materials. The Peshawar, Mardan and Hund museums' collections are mainly based on the latter source and as a result the exact provenance for most of their objects is unknown, especially those transferred to the Peshawar Museum after devolution of the Federal Department of Archaeology and Museums in 2011. After the establishment of the Directorate of Archaeology and Museums, Government of Khyber Pakhtunkhwa, in 1993, the number of antiquities has been increasing enormously both through archaeological excavations and during antiquities traffic control process. Thanks to the vigilant attitude of the law enforcing agencies, the custom authorities and other organizations in Pakistan, the number of these seized materials has been increasing consistently. And in this process, during a police raid on a house in the Yakatoot area of Peshawar city (Fig. 4.66), a group of more than one hundred antiquities consisted of sculptures both in stone and stucco, coins, metal objects, etc. were seized by the law enforcing agency which were later on handed over to the Directorate of Archaeology and Museums Government of Khyber Pakhtunkhwa.[31] Among these antiquities some beautiful panels representing fresco paintings were also moved to the Directorate of Archaeology where they were lying in the reserve collection of the Directorate before this publication. These antiquities do not come from legal excavations; therefore, their exact provenance, context and date pose problems.

The area of Yakatoot, which is part of the old Peshawar city, is famous for such kind of accidental discoveries and deliberate activities as well because it is built over ancient remains the date of which goes back to the Achaemenid period (Durrani et al. 1997). Rich in antiquities, whether these are the graveyards in the city of Peshawar or the old house or other premises in the area, these areas are also the main target

establishments in Gandhāra, which seems not to be the case here and, like some other Buddhist sites in the region, the establishment of Jinnan Wali Ḍheri may also show the opposite. The other good example of the sensitivity of the Huns to the Buddhist faith is the construction of the Bhamala stūpa, also at Taxila. From the centre of this stūpa, a hoard of coins belong to the Huns period has been recovered, suggesting that it was deposited during the construction of the stūpa, most probably by the Huns and if not or if it was constructed in a later period this would pose another question about the history of Buddhism in Gandhāra and about the chronology of the Gandhāran Buddhist art.

[31] A detailed report on sculptures in stones and stucco is published in my article published in Gandhāran Studies, volume 9 (Nasim Khan 2016a).

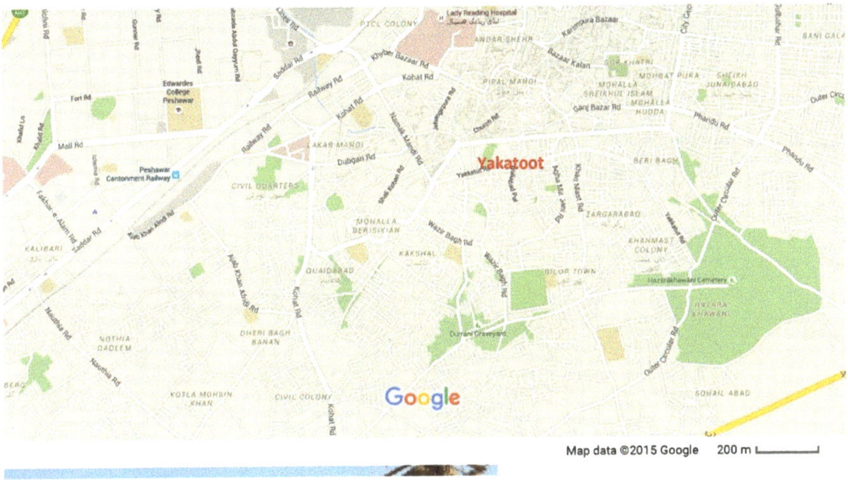

Fig. 4.66 Location map of Yakatoot area in the Peshawar city

of the antique seekers living in the area.[32] The Yakatoot paintings were recovered from one of the houses in that area. These paintings consist of four panels which represent male and other designs which are executed both in aesthetic and in artistic manners and are good addition to the rest of the paintings found in Gandhāra. One of the panels is added with a Brāhmī inscription (Fig. 4.68) that can also help us to approximately date the paintings.

The panels are somehow in good state of preservation. It seems that after removing from their original place, the illegal diggers have tried to preserve them from all sides by using lime plaster but, they still need further better treatment for long term preservation.

Panel I (Fig. 4.67), DoAM-75 (1)[33] Measurement: 52 × 38 cm

A weathered ancient Brāhmī inscription painted in black on a cracked white background. The mural shows signs of age with visible cracks and erosion, surrounded by a rough, textured surface. The inscription is partially obscured by the mural's deterioration.The panel is broken and making irregular shape. Part of the painting is

[32] Rumours say that old houses in the city are either dismantled in search of antiquities with a pretext of a reconstruction work or sold them out to antique dealers with very high prices. It is also believed that some of the inhabitants in the old part of Peshawar are digging themselves inside their houses in search of objects of worth. Rumours also circulate that some of the houses are rented to dealers and are became veritable store rooms for antiquities. The multiple antiquities recovered from a house in the Yakatoot area may also be making part of such accounts. As per report, in pursuit of the criminals, the local police received information that some fugitives were hiding inside a house in the Yakatoot area of Peshawar and after a raid on the targeted house, the police recovered from there these superb paintings along with other antiquities while illegal diggings inside the house was in progress. The illegal excavation was told happening inside the rooms and in the courtyard area of the house at the time of police raid.

[33] The number in bracket represents the police station registered number.

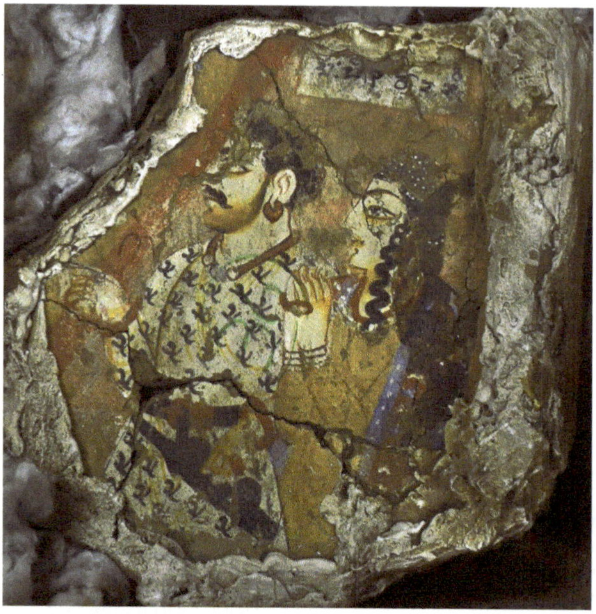

Fig. 4.67 Panel 1 showing a couple facing left

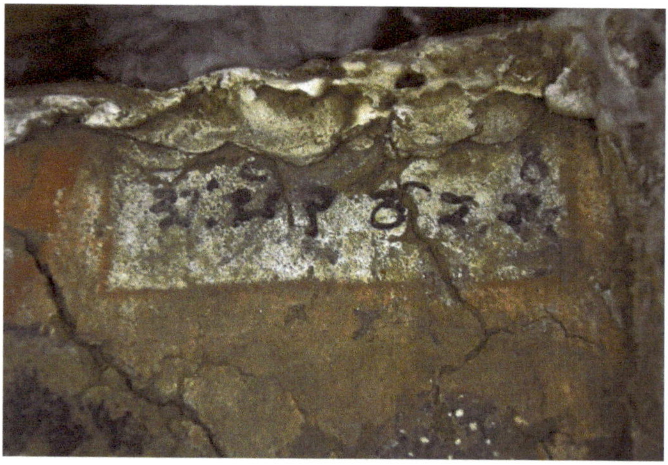

Fig. 4.68 Close-up of the inscription of panel 1

missing from all sides such as the three white dots in the right field indicate that with the missing portion of the panel some drawings are lost. The preserved portion shows a couple and a Brāhmī inscription; the latter one is painted in the upper part of the panel. Both figures are painted with white pigment on a yellowish or golden colour background and are shown in profile facing left. The male figure is bareheaded and is with short hair which is probably combed downwards. The hair of his head and the moustaches are painted with black colour. The shaved face is painted with dark brown colour while the shad of his fingers and his eyes are in brown pigment. He is shown with open almond-shaped eyes and a fleshy pointed nose and is having a large muscular throat like an Alchon or a Gupta period king. His right hand is extended frontward with fingers turned towards his palm and the gestures of his index and thumb show that he is probably carrying a flower (??). His left hand probably grabs his weapon attached to his thigh.

The man wears a long tunic like white silky dress with cross-shaped floral designs painted in black colour. The belt with a clip or buckle is round his thigh and the sword or any other such kind of weapon, attached to the hooks of it, is also painted in black. The weapon and the way it is carried can be compared with the Panjikent painting (Azarpay 1981: 74, Fig. 36).

The jewellery the figure is carrying on his body are: a pair of leaf-shaped earrings, a torque-like plain neck jewellery with open ends and a pair of hoop-shaped plain bracelets, one added to each of his wrist; all these are painted in golden or with dark-brown colour. He is also wearing two finger rings with the same colour, one to each little finger. In his front a thick strip in red pigment is added in slanting manner.

His female counterpart is standing or sitting behind with both hands joined in front in *añjali* pose. She has an elongated face with a large pointed nose and almond-shaped eyes. Her lips and the shades of her eyebrows, eyelashes, chin, throat and fingers are marked with brown colour. The long curly hair drops on her back, shoulders and temples. She is wearing a plain golden colour silky dress or frock and an overcoat in brown colour. The brim or border of the overcoat is shown in blue colour strip with white spots depicted with regular intervals; they may either indicate jewellery such as pearls or buttons of the overcoat. The silky scarp covering her head is also added with white pearls. She is bedecked with different kinds of jewellery such as a torque or round collar in hoop shape, a row of round and plain bracelets, finger rings added to her two little fingers. Each of them is inlaid with a precious stone marked in white colour.

In the upper part a whitish rectangular band is prepared for depicting a Brāhmī inscription written with black paint. The inscription is written in Gupta Brāhmī characters and probably reads "maḥhirevādasya" or "maḥhirevāḍasya". The stroke attached to the letter "ra" could also be for the medial vowel "i". The cracks above the head-mark of the letter "ma" in the beginning give the impression of the medial vowel "o" or "i". Above the head-mark of the ligature "-sya", there is a letter "va". With less probability, it is also possible that the author forgot to write the said letter and therefore, after realizing his mistake he added the sign later. If it was the case, then the reading of the inscription would be "maḥhirevādavasya", a proper name in genitive case. The upper part of the panel is covered with a lime pilaster, and it is more possible that the inscription was written on at least two lines and the proposed letter "va" is in fact the last letter of the preceding line whereas the rest is covered with the lime pilaster used by the dealer for conservation purpose. In this case the reading would be (Fig. 4.68):

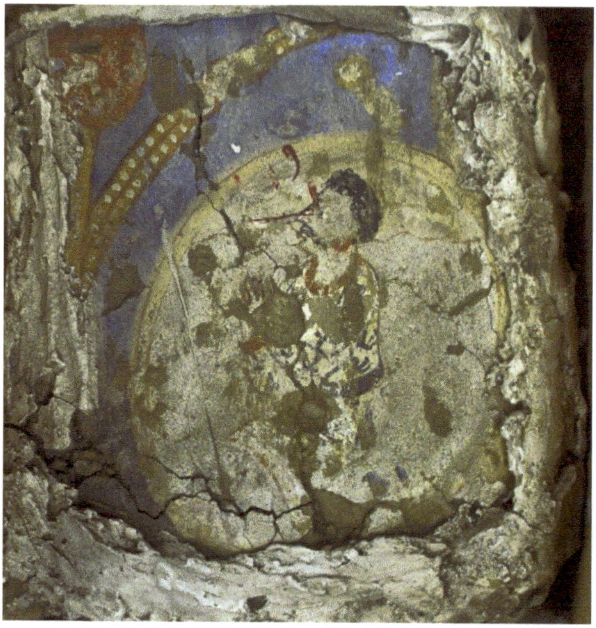

Fig. 4.69 Panel depicted with a male figure portraying *añjalimudrā*

/// ...va
maḥ hirivādasya.
///...vama, of Hirevāda or Hirivāda

The name is Indian and is composed of two elements: hiri-vāda-. The first component is also attested in combination with other Sanskrit words such as hiri-śipra which means "golden checked" or having a golden visor applied to Agni and Indra or in composition with hiri–śmaṣru- which means golden bearded. If the name is read as Maḥhirivāda-, it may be a mistake for mihira-vāda-. Mithra-vāda.[34] If the letter after visarga is read as "mi" then the reading would be "Miravadasya". Mīravāda could be an hybrid Indian name whereas the first component would stand for "Mithra" attested in Kharoṣṭhī and Brāhmī inscriptions such as the names Yola-mira and Vakha-mira (see Humbach 1976: 36ff). The name Mira-boyana is attested in a Kharoṣṭhī inscription from Gandhāra (Konow 1929: 62). In Sanskrit, Mitra is used as a first component in proper names like Mitra-gupta, Mitra-vinda, etc. while the word "mīra" in Sanskrit means "the sea, ocean, etc.". The name could be half Iranian (Mira) and half Indian (Vada). Names with similar formation such as "Mira-Varma" are attested in the Upper Indus Valley inscriptions (Nasim Khan 1994: 207, no. 37).

Panel II (Fig. 4.69), DoAM-76 (2) Measurement: 25 × 26 cm

[34] For Mihira and Mithra see Fussman and König (1997: 135, 17.4) and König (1999: 239, 32.4).

The panel shows a male figure painted inside a round medallion shape design in whitish colour but having double contours margin marked by thin lines in brown colour. The area between the lines is in golden colour. The preserved portion suggests that most probably another circle or ornament in brown colour with pearls or beaded design is added around the medallion. The background is painted in blue colour. Above the head and outside of the circle, there is an unclear design extended from the outer surface of the medallion and is painted in white and brown pigment; it could be a constellation or be a part of another design whereas remains in form of a curve painted in light brown can be seen on the right side of the unclear object or design.

The short hair is painted and is combed downwards. The moustache is marked by a thick black dark curved line. The elongated shape eyes are left open. He has a long pointed nose and a small chin. He is also wearing a similar kind of silky dress with cross-shaped designs, painted in black, as wearing by one of the figures in Panel 1 and he may also carry the same type of weapon. In the present case, the brim of the upper dress is visible which is marked with double lines in brown colour. He is wearing a pair of hoop-shaped earrings and a round-shaped neck ornament like a torque. Both ornaments are marked in brown colour.

In front and attached to the outer circle, there is a drawing probably of a tree with a trunk in golden colour and the pigment used for the branches is dark red. The man inside the medallion is seated on his knees with hands in *añjali* pose and looking towards the tree. The whole may represent the scene of veneration or adoration of the Bodhi-tree. In Gandhāra art, compare to other symbols, adoration of the Bodhi-tree is not very well attested but in Sanchi, India, the worship of a stūpa, wheel of the law and the bodhi-tree is well depicted (see e.g. Marshall 1960: Plate 3).

Panel III (Fig. 4.70)

The right-side part of the panel is damaged and cracked due to which details of the figures are missing, particularly the female figure sitting behind his male counterpart. The background of both the figures is painted with whitish colour while that of the medallion is in blue colour. The preserved portion shows a round beaded design or ornament in brown with rows of pearls painted in white colour. A barrel-shaped bead with two large-sized pearls, one on each side of the bead, are added in the top left portion of the ornament. Inside the medallion the couple is kneeling on their knees with hands in *añajli* pose. The female figure, sitting behind, is not very clear and only the outline of the dress and blue colour spots, may be traces from the brim of the overcoat as worn by the female figure in Panel I, are visible. The male figure is bareheaded and is shown with long pointed nose and elongated eyes. The whole body is painted in whitish colour except his short curly hair which is in black and the contour lines that mark the different parts of the body are in represented in brown colour. He is probably bedecked with a torque like neck jewellery, bracelets and probably wears the same type of garment as worn by the male figure in Panel I. Unlike the other male figures in the paintings, the neck ornament is shown in white colour with brown outlines. The belt round his thigh is also marked in white with brown colour margins. An unclear round design painted in white with brown margin is visible in the left lower side and in front of the knees of the male figure.

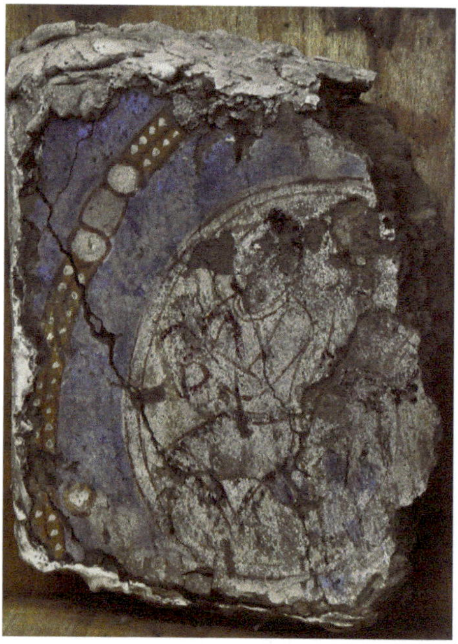

Fig. 4.70 Panel III showing a couple of human figures

Panel IV (Figs. 4.71 and 4.72): DoAM-77 (3) Measurement: 30 × 25 cm

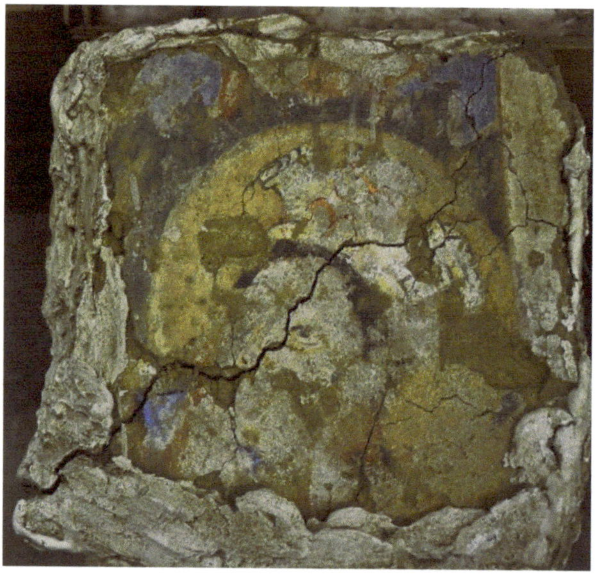

Fig. 4.71 Panel III. Female bust with animal's skin headdress

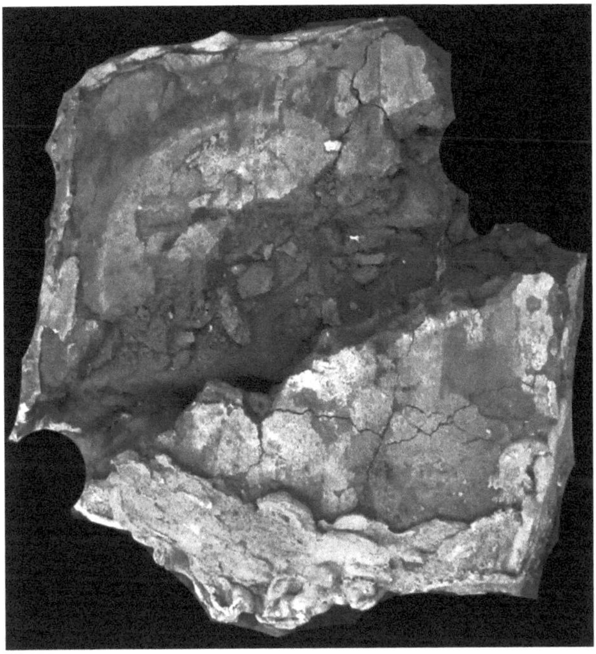

Fig. 4.72 Present condition of the panel

This panel shows a male or probably a female bust which is partially defaced and damaged due to several cracks in the panel. The head of the bust is having a crown or a kind of bulky headdress with folds in the rim and is made or surmounted with an animal skin marked with black curved strips arranged on regular intervals on the whitish colour skin. The rest of the headdress seems in whitish colour with geometrical designs made of black bands and orange colour designs at the front portion. This reminds me the figure of Heracles with lion skin, found together with the painted panels (Nasim Khan 2016a: Fig. 18).[35]

The bust is facing left. The eyes are opened and the eyebrows are marked with black pigment while the eyelids are painted with golden colour. The halo behind the head is also marked with golden colour but with white margin whereas the rest is coloured with whitish paint. The figure probably wears a scarf, painted in bleu, over his head. Traces of brown colour used in the background suggest that it is overlapped by a blue which itself is superimposed by a blackish shade.

It is not very clear whether the golden round background behind her head is part of the image or it is the background of the image, which I believe so. The other subject is the form of the headdress which is not very clear. It may be formed from tiger skin, because of the strips, or snake-like creature but in this case, it would seem to me somehow bizarre. In any case, the headdress is most probably formed on an animal

[35] See also, e.g., Zwalf (1996, vol. II: pl. 293) and Tanabe (2007: 180).

design. Similar fashion is also noticed in an example from the Central Asian paintings (see Fig. 4.73). The painting of the female donor with a ram's horn headdress was found on the south-western wall of the central court. According to Lo Muzio, "The fragment actually preserves the representation of a female worshipper wearing an eccentric headgear crowned by ram horns. So far unknown in Kuṣān iconography, this type of headdress is witnessed in Sasanian dynastic and aristocratic imagery, to begin with a silver drachm of Shapur II (309–379) (Gyselen 2004: 58–59; 114, no. 212, type IV / 2a, and fig. A) and, later on, on other Sasanian, Kushano-Sasanian and Kidarite numismatic productions and art works including a sardonyx seal on which this particular headgear crowns the head of a woman, who is a concubine of the Sasanian king Shapur III (383–388) (Gyselen 2006: 207, no. 156) (Plate 3.14)" (Lo Muzio 2014: 130).

Exact Provenance of Yakatoot Paintings

The Yakatoot paintings is one of the most important acquisitions of seizing objects of the Directorate of Archaeology recently made in the Gandhāra region, however, the exact provenance of the panels with paintings and the other antiquities is not yet clear. We still do not know whether these paintings were actually excavated at the area from where they were seized by the police or they were brought from somewhere else and had stored there. The uncertainty about the exact finding spot of the Yakatoot paintings is not the only exception but such question also exists for some other antiquities which neither came from proper archaeological context nor being acquired through reliable sources but they are preserved in different museums in Pakistan. It is always challenging to believe what the owner narrates about the provenance of their antiquities. Usually, the original owner does not unveil the truth simply because they are either just ignorant or are not willing to share that sort of

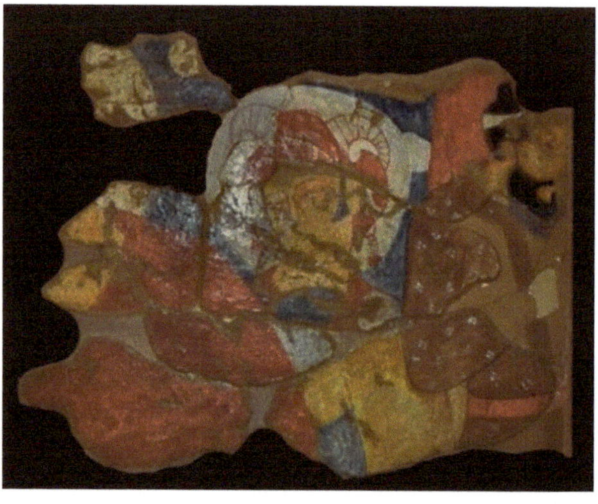

Fig. 4.73 Mural Fayaz Tepe (Southern Uzbekistan) (Reference: Wikimedia commons)

information because of the fear that the other will also dig at the site. Moreover, if the original source is exposed to the government official, this will also create problem for the owner. We are, therefore, confronted here with the same problem of how to associate these paintings to a certain area because they are seized materials and the option that rests is to rely on the statement of the police or those government officials to whom the panels were handed over or the information gathered from the rumours associated to these objects by the locals. In fact, neither the police report could help much to be sure that these paintings originally were excavated at the site of Yakatoot nor the officials of the Directorate of Archaeology and Museums could help us in this regard. The only thing that can be said for sure that illegal diggings were happening inside the house at the time of the police raid. But that would not help even to say for sure that these paintings were found during these illegal diggings because the multitude of antiquities seized by the police consists of different objects that belong to different cultures and dates and should not had been found composed until and unless they were together as a hoard at that particular place.[36] Although it is not yet sure whether these panels were dug out at the place where they were seized or they were brought from somewhere else and stored had there, their discovery is still very important for the history of Buddhist period murals in Mahāgandhāra.[37]

The facial features of the figures are generally Indian such as the almond-shaped eyes, long pointed nose, elongated face and the way the moustache are presented. The costumes, particularly the long tunic, are generally Central Asian in style though such type of dress is also attested in the late period Indian art. The jewellery shown in the Yakatoot paintings is of four kinds: pearls in the headdress, earrings, neck jewellery, bracelets and finger rings. The earrings are very much similar to those worn by Rustam in Panjikent paintings (Azarpay 1981: Plate 8–9). In Bamiyan paintings, a Bodhisattva is adorned with a plain torque opening on his chest (Azarpay 1981: 85, Fig. 38) while in the Balalyk-tepe paintings both men and women are bedecked with twisted torques (Azarpay 1981: 88, Fig. 40). They can also be compared with the earrings excavated at Sirkap (Marshal 1951, Vol. III: Plate 190.g = 9, 10) and Kashmir Smast (Nasim Khan 2006: 202–203, figs. 190–194), and also with those depicted in the Hindu art of Gandhāra (e.g. Nasim Khan 2006a: figs. 3, 6; Ghose 2003: 369, plate 319), even if they are not exactly of the same type. A stele from the Buddhist site of Mohammed Naṛi, Mardan, shows a very similar type of torque worn by a female figure (Haesner 1999: 450, Fig. 12b). A bronze pot of the Alchon period, found at Kashmir Smast, depicts certain images where two of the busts are wearing similar type of earrings as well as hoop shape neck ornament (Nasim Khan 2006: 80–81, figs. 76, 77). Similar torque, with open ends, is well attested in the sculptures

[36] Questions may also be raised about the authenticity of some of the sculptures in stone.

[37] Fresco paintings have already been found during clandestine activities in the vicinity of Yakatoot. An eyewitness said that recently some more such paintings were observed in the Hazarkhawani cemetery, an extension of the Yakatoot area, the graveyard superimposes a Buddhist site covering an area of more than one square kilometre. It is said that most of the paintings were either destroyed or damaged during illegals diggings while few of them were saved and are most probably lying in private collections.

and paintings of ancient Greek and Persian (e.g. Becatti 1968: 226, Fig. 207; Porada 1962: 172, pl. 51).

Dozens of sealings found in Gandhāra and in the surrounding regions that belong to the Huns period also demonstrate such type of earrings and neck ornaments (e.g., Callieri 1997: Pls. 22–26; Lerner and Sims-Williams 2011: p. 33, Fig. 3; p. 108, AB 3.4; p. 123, AB 7.1; p. 124, AB.125). The numismatic data also provides enough evidence of the use of almost similar type of rings and a neck ornament worn by the Huns kings (Pfisterer 2013: 77, Kat. 64–1). Those worn by the female figure in our Panel I are of the same type as that of the male figure except the addition of a pendant hanging from the ring and is very similar to those in Hirayama collection (Tanabe 2007: 247, VI-80, 81) or those recovered from Sirkap, Taxila, that are dated to the first/second century AD (Khan, F.A. 1969: 141, n of P. 23, fig, 6). Interestingly, such type of earring is worn by a female figure in stucco belonging to the same collection (see Nasim Khan 2015).

Apart from their physical features and costumes, the other important subject in these paintings is the colour scheme. In contrast to those paintings previously discovered in Gandhāra, the Yakatoot paintings demonstrate brilliant blue colour which is almost missing in the other paintings where the dominant colours are generally the red, brown, golden, white, black and chocolate.[38] However, blue pigment is very well attested in the Buddhist period paintings in Central Asia (Blänsdorf et al. 2009; Tissot 2003, p. 286, Fig. 6) and the same colour is not only used in the wall paintings found in Afghanistan but it was also used in painted glass such as the famous goblet from Begram (Afghanistan) that belong to the second century AD (Dupree 1974, p. 29, illst. 6). In paintings from Sogdiana,[39] blue is used both for the background and to define exposed flesh (Azarpay 1981: 165–167). In other Central Asian regions wall paintings such as Miran, Kizil, Khotan, green is also used alongside blue pigment (Bussagli, Mario. 1978; Zin 2013a,b). Like in the paintings from Central Asia, blue colour is very prominent in the Yaktoot paintings, except in Fig. 4.70 where brown is used in the background while the colour blue is only used in the costume of the female figure. Although the perishable indigo blue, of vegetable origin, is considered to be of Indian origin (Azarpay 1981: 163), the colour used in the Yakatoot paintings is a brilliant blue derived may be from lapis lazuli. While in Ajanta paintings beside yellow, red, brown, green, white, black etc., soft and clear blue are also used (see, e.g., Singh 1965: 171, 176, 186).

One of the panel is added with a Brāhmī inscription, the script which was rarely used in Gandhāra before the fourth century AD but later on the use of this script in the region is attested by the discovery of a large number of Brāhmī inscriptions found at Kashmir Smast and Aziz Ḍheri as well as some scattered Brāhmī manuscripts discovered in Gandhāra such as those excavated in Taxila at the Buddhist sites of

[38] I could not judge from the colour photographs where blue colour is used in the Jinnan Wali Ḍheri and in the Butkara I paintings or not. For these paintings see Kakar and Khan (2010: 22) and Filigenzi (2010: 392).

[39] The earliest among the Sogdian paintings are from Panjikent dated to fifth century AD and the latest are those come from Samarkand (Afrasiab) belong to sixth–seventh centuries AD (Azarpay 1981: 185–203).

Dharmarajika and Jaulian (Marshall 1951, vol, I: 287, 387) or some fragments which are preserved in the Peshawar Museum as well (Accession No. PM_03195). Nevertheless, at the same epoch, besides Kharoṣṭhī, Brāhmī was also in use in Central Asia such as proved by the Buddhist remains at Termez (see e.g. Fussman 2011).

Despite the several characteristics and distinctive elements that belong to different cultural milieu, the Yakatoot paintings were most probably excavated at the area where they were seized by the police and may belong to the Gandhāra School of Paintings. The fusion of elements coming from different zone of cultures such as the facial features, costumes and the colour schemes may be justified by the geographical and strategic position of the Gandhāra region, as already seen in other mediums of the Buddhist art of Gandhāra. Being situated at the cross route of civilizations, Gandhāra has always played and has still been playing an important role in this cross-cultural communication.

Setting and Subject matter: Since the Yakatoot paintings do not come from a proper archaeological context, therefore it would be difficult to say for sure in which context these paintings were found. They may belong either to a residential area such as a house, palace, or they were found in a Buddhist complex which is the case for other such paintings in Gandhāra. But judging from the gestures of hands of the figures which are mostly in *añjali* pose and the way they are sitting with their heads slightly raised in adoration and reverence, it is possible that they were found in a scared area, most probably in a Buddhist context as to be ascertained from the scene of adoration of the Bodhi-tree in Panel II.

Date: As far as the date of the paintings is concerned, it would have been difficult to precisely date the paintings by using other agents such as iconography of the figures, technical and stylistic features, colour schemes, without the presence of the Brāhmī inscription added to one of the panels above. Although fragmentary, the inscription still helps to place these paintings between the third and fifth centuries AD. A Kuṣāno-Sassanian period coins hoard, consisting of about 50 coins that makes part of the same collection, also suggests a third/fourth century date of the paintings provided that the coins hoard and the paintings were found in the same context.

Chapter 5
Painted Vessels from Bajaur

Paintings on household or ritual pots has probably a long history in Gandhara and its surrounding regions. The earliest evidence of this art may come from the proto-historic site of Rahman Dheri site in DI Khan from where pottery decorated with multiple and diverse drawings of animals and plants have been reported (see Durrani 1988). But we have very examples of Buddhist sites from where such an art has been reported. Among the very few of the Buddhist sites are the site of Aziz Ḍheri and Damkot Buddhist site in the Lower Dir district. The Damkot site pottery is of particular interest since it shows a variety of designs and drawings which have recently been reported from other sites in the area. Judging from their decorations, fabric and texture, they apparently belong to the same group of culture. The latter are mostly discovered in the Mohmand and Bajaur areas of ancient Gandhāra (Nasim Khan 2023). Very little work has been devoted to their study although the number of which is not only increasing in the region of Gandhāra in Pakistan, such pottery were also recovered from the Buddhist site of Mes Aynak in Afghanistan (Noori et al. 2019). The Bajaur painted pottery is of special interest which carries a variety of different floral, faunal and human figures that may belong to the Buddhist culture or at least to the Buddhist period. There are examples of pots which are decorated with images and at the same time contains ancient Buddhist manuscripts (see Solomon 1996: 80).

Bajaur district (1,290 km^2) consists of several tehsils or administrative subdivisions and is bordered to the west by Afghanistan, to the north by Lower Dir and to the south and east by Mohmand and Malakand regions. The area is rich in archaeological remains starting from the prehistoric times to the Mughal period. Many of these finds have already been published and are considered one of the main sources for reconstructing the history and culture of the region. About two decades earlier, I had the opportunity to photograph cultural objects which, according to their owner, were recovered from a Buddhist site in the Bajaur region, except a mask (see Nasim Khan 2006: 68, Fig. 61) which was also found in the same area, but it does not come

M. Nasim Khan, *Gandhāran School of Buddhist Paintings*,
https://doi.org/10.1007/978-981-96-9310-8_5

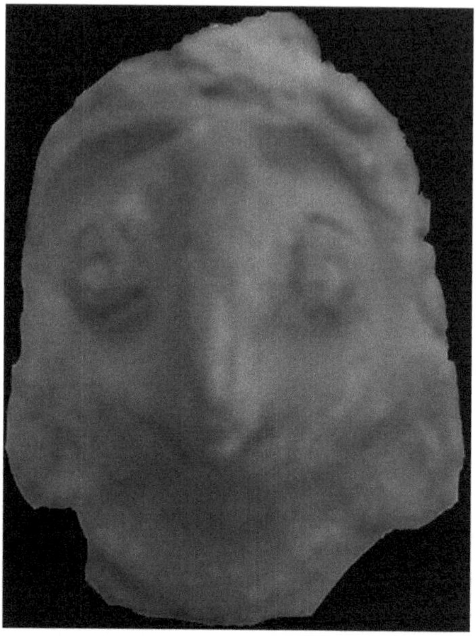

Fig. 5.1 Terracotta head

from the same site. These objects included TC figurines (Figs. 5.1, 5.2, 5.3, and 5.4), a wine condenser and the present painted vessels (Figs. 5.5–5.24).[1]

The three objects selected for this study belong to vessels of large to medium size, while only the edges as well as the neck and their shoulders are partially preserved; the rest are missing.[2] One of them appears to be a large jug (Fig. 5.20) while the other two are medium-sized vessels, each with two side handles. I was initially unsure of the authenticity of the jars or their exact location as the owner constantly changed his statement about their location. For these reasons, and since then, these objects have remained unpublished. But, in the meantime, articles on similar pottery are published by Brancaccio (2010) and Ali and Rahman (2005) which gave me the idea to write a preliminary note on the current pots. The pottery published by Pia Brancaccio is housed in the Metropolitan Museum while that listed by Ali and Lutfur-Rahman is

[1] For lack of time, I was not able to study these objects in detail on site. Additionally, the photographs were taken so hastily and also with a low-resolution pocket camera, that the quality of the images, produced here, may not be good enough to capture all relevant details to comment on the ceramic technique. For this reason, it is also difficult to discuss enough iconographic details and character traits and place the elements of flora and fauna in a sure context. The photographs were also not taken to scale, so their size can only be guessed. Some of them are taken in groups and can be measured against each other.

[2] The Bajaur region has already yielded some important discoveries, especially with regard to the Buddhist religion and history. The present group of pottery found in this area is part of various collections of the same type of ceramics which are kept in various private collections and some museums in Pakistan and abroad. Some of these potteries represent hitherto unknown images and an attempt is made to study them here, both in their historical context and at the same time in their iconographic framework.

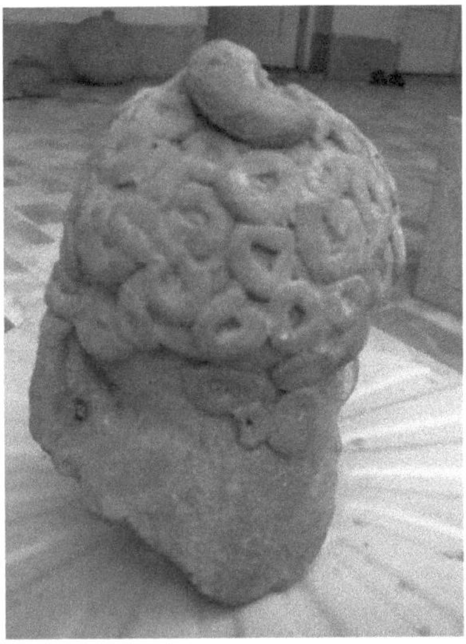

Fig. 5.2 Back and top view of Fig. 5.1

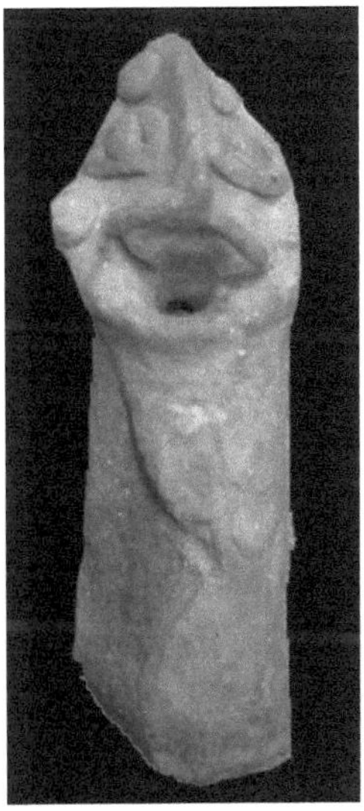

Fig. 5.3 Terracotta bust

supposedly in the Directorate of Archaeology and Museum, Government of Khyber Pakhtunkhwa, and the Department of Archaeology, University of Peshawar.

According to Ali and Rahman, most of the pottery which are randomly collected from the surface of the sites, are fast-wheel thrown which, according to them, are characterised by red, dark red, brownish and pal red slip. They also claim that the group of pottery is predominantly of thin fabric (Ali and Rahman 2005: 75) and propose a provisional date of the 2nd secondary BC believing that the tradition of

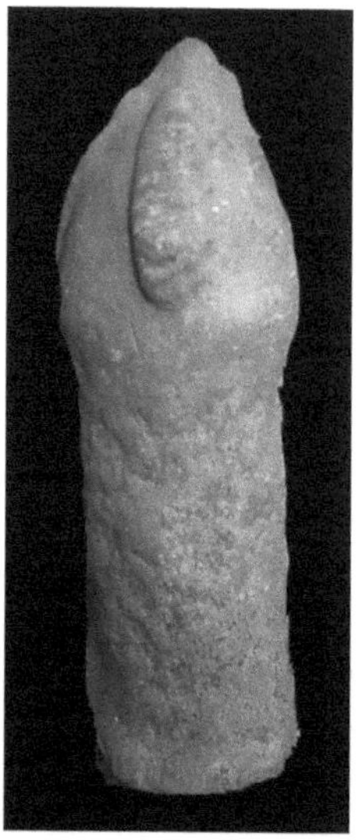

Fig. 5.4 Back side of Fig. 5.3

this style of pottery continues till the rise of the Hindu Shahi era (Ali and Rahman 2005: 76).

About the function of the vase published by Brancaccio, she thinks that it is not an ordinary container and believes that, as its shape indicates, it was mainly used for drinking purposes (Brancaccio 2010: 333, 336). The figures identified on the pot are said female figures and the painted twigs and fruits are depiction of Ephedra plant and its berries. Brancaccio says that such plant produces an intoxicating juice and is identified with the Haoma/Soma drink of the Indo-Iranian people (Brancaccio 2010: 333). The date proposed by Brancaccio is fifth and sixth century CE.

Comparing the style and paintwork of the pots shown here with the so-called Thin sectioned ware or "Bajaur wares" previously published, gives the impression that they were all fashioned in the same workshop(s) whose exact location is difficult to determine or which may come from different sites of the same cultural background. But it is unclear which particular area of Bajaur or Mohmand Agency the workshop(s) should be associated with. Or to be more generous in asking further questions, one also needs to be certain that the pottery original home is only Bajaur-Mohmand region or if they also have sources beyond Bajaur-Mohmand regions (see below). A systematic excavation of more than one site can help us answer these questions. In regard to the date or dates, to reconfirm the proposed dating which was obtained by thermoluminescence examination, an iconographic study of the figures and a stratigraphic excavation of a well-preserved site may also be necessary.

The more material we would have, the more we would be able to know the nature, the role and the iconography of the characters, the meaning of the scenes, the use and function of the pots, etc. Thus, the three pots presented here could help us to delve deeper into the above questions and seek, if possible, logical answers.

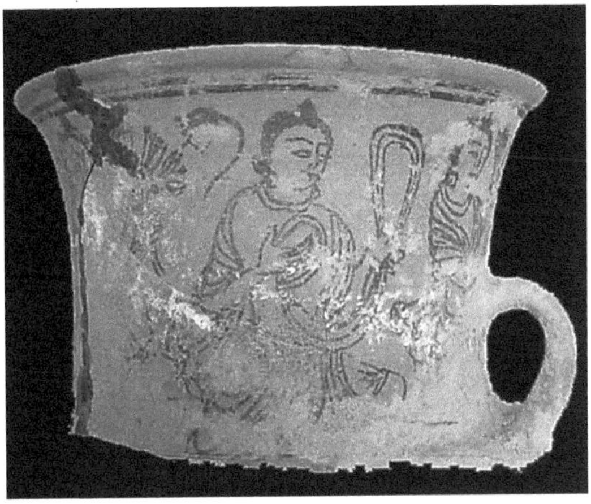

Fig. 5.5 Rim of Pot_I

Pot_I (Fig. 5.5)

Only the flanged neck and one of the handles are preserved. Traces of the second handle, fixed opposite to the first, are available. Between the fields of the handles and around the neck and probably the shoulder of the pot is decorated with seven different human figures arranged in a row or procession, three on one side and four on the other. They are shown frontally but their heads are positioned slightly to their right. All are shown standing. Due to cracks in the neck of the pot, the figures are damaged and the lower bodies are, sometimes, partly lost with the missing part of the vase. Besides the human figures, the other decorations consist of flora, birds like goose, fish or some kind of mythical animals and some unidentified drawings.

Pot_I_1 (Fig. 5.6): The first of the seven human figures of Pot-1, starting from the right side of the intact handle and towards the left, read from left to right, stands ¾ to its left. He has a round face with a small chin and a small nose, a small closed mouth, wide-opened eyes, each with a visible iris, and nearly straight long eyebrows. His hair is short with a tuft of hair at the top of his skull or it may be a skull bump (*uṣṇīṣa*). He brought his right hand close to his chest with a speaking- or teaching-like gesture. In his left hand he probably holds three lotuses or blue iris or even water lily.[3] One of the flowers is tilted towards his face and it seems that he smells and enjoys the fragrance of the blossom. One of the other two is stretched towards the male figure standing in front and on his left side, while the third, which seems faded, hangs down. In the last two cases, the flowers seem detached from their stem or stalks. One of them is above the shoulder of the person on the right and the other detached flower is seen between the legs of the two figures. It is possible that these two flowers are not of the same nature as the third; the stem of both flowers may also be disfigured.

[3] Lotus leaves float above the water while water lilies float directly on the surface of the water. The lotus and the water lily are not part of the same family. Lotuses belong to the genus Nelumbo and the family Nelumbonaceae. Water lilies belong to the Nymphaeaceae family and generally include the Nymphaea and Nuphar genera. On the difference between the lotus and the water lily see Vassal (2022: 342–343).

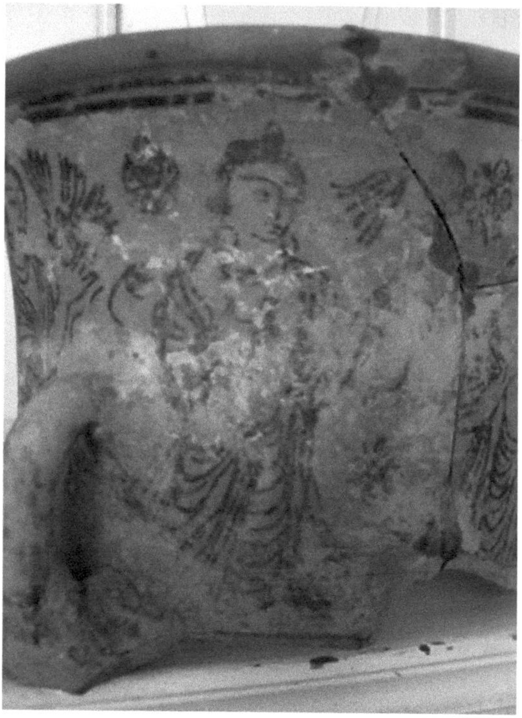

Fig. 5.6 Detail of Pot_I_1

It is possible that these two detached flowers have nothing to do with the bouquet the person is holding. An unclear design is also visible behind and above his right shoulder. Is this a drawing of a fledgling bird? Because whose head with beak and eye are traceable (see below).

He wears both the lower and upper garments. The lower one, with wide pleats, falls loosely on over his feet. The upper garment covers both of his shoulders but his chest is left bare. The set looks like made of a single piece of unstitched fabric. He is adorned with jewellery on the ears and neck. The ear ornaments look like rings in a round shape while the neck jewel is probably a collar or a torque which gradually reduces its width towards its end; it is represented in outline.

Pot_I_2 (Fig. 5.7): The second figure is depicted on the right side and stands in the same style and gesture and wears the same type of dress as the previous person except that the right shoulder here is more exposed. The gesture of his right hand is also the same except that in the previous case he makes a bowl shape while here the hands are stretched outwards. The facial features of the two characters are comparable. He carries four flowers in his left hand; two of them are similar to that retained by the previous figure while the other two are analogous to those found between the two figures. The lotus or blue iris flowers are shown leaning towards its face and it looks that the figure enjoys the fragrance of the blossom. One of the other two flowers is placed near to the head of the next character. The fourth is dangling. Behind his head,

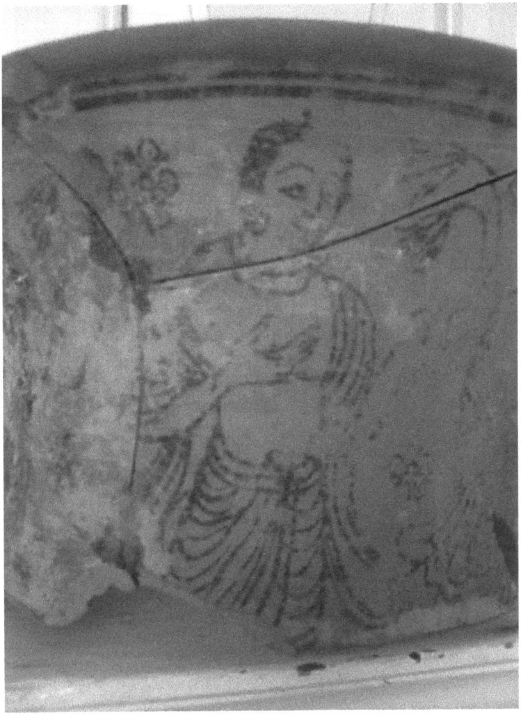

Fig. 5.7 Close-up of Pot_I_2

the same type of flower or a drawing of a fledgling bird as observed in the previous case is seen. The other similar drawing is located between the lower bodies of the previous figure and the current figure.

Pot_I_3 (Fig. 5.8): This image is faded. Due to a vertical crack in the pot, it is also damaged but most details are still visible. It is also depicted in a standing position with its body turned slightly to the left. The image is draped in the same type of dress and has similar characteristics to the two previous figures except that here the torso is probably covered. The heavy folds of the clothes that cover its legs are clearly visible. The character tries to catch the stem of the four flowers that are sticking out of the ground. Two of the flowers bow over its shoulder, one stands almost straight, and the last hangs down as seen in the two previous cases. Below and in the shadow of the broken handle is another similar flower which is emerging from the ground. The upper garment suggests that this image must be of a female figure. The lower legs are not clear. It seems that she is not added with ear ornaments. There are two flowers or designs of two fledgling birds, one is depicted near to the back of her head and the other one is close to her right elbow.

Pot_I_4 (Fig. 5.9): It is the first character in the next field and is painted on the right side of the broken handle. The character, probably a female, is standing, the body more turned towards the left. She wears the same type of dress as in the previous case, except that the upper garment or perhaps a sash covers both of her shoulders.

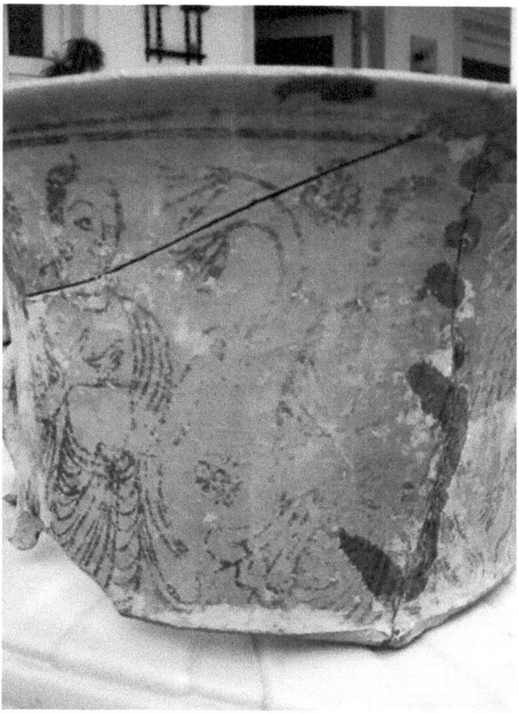

Fig. 5.8 Close-up of Pot_I_3

Her chest is almost covered while her stomach and navel are bare like the one who wears a *sari*. She is adorned with a large-sized earring and a necklace. In addition, his eyes are shown half-open. Instead of carrying flowers, she catches with both her hands a goose-like bird. The bird, with its high and tortured neck, is turned towards the flowers emerging from the ground. It seems that there are still two or three more flowers of different heights also sticking out of the ground. They are twisted towards the figure with the bird.

Pot_I_5 (Fig. 5.10): It is damaged due to a vertical crack in the preserved portion of the pot. In addition, a large part of the vessel is degraded or covered with crusts. Despite these issues, the style and gesture of the figure are traceable. He is represented almost full face and wears the same type of clothing and is in the same style as the first two figures of this pot. He holds a lionfish or a puffer fish or even the head of a mythical creature (see below). Above, there is a flower with a stalk that bends towards the animal that the man is holding. Below and to its left are some unclear drawings.

Pot_I_6 (Fig. 5.11): He stands ¾ to his left and has a round face with a small closed mouth, a small nose, wide-opened eyes, and nearly straight eyebrows. The iris, turned towards their left, of each of his eyes is visible. He appears to be with curly hair and is depicted with a tuft of hair on the cranium. He wears both the neck and ear jewellery and is dressed in the upper and lower garments. The lower one

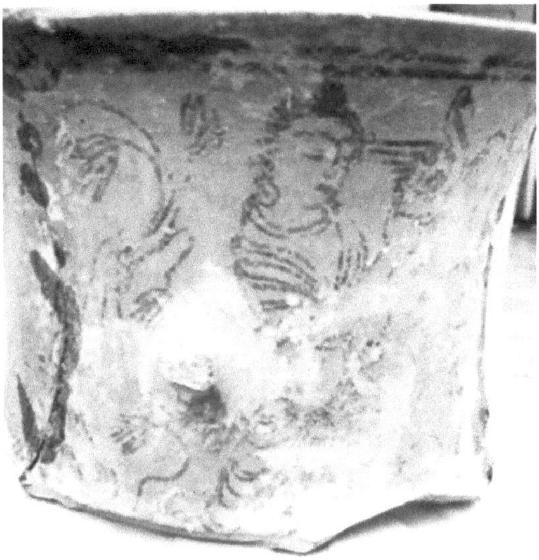

Fig. 5.9 Close of Pot_I_5

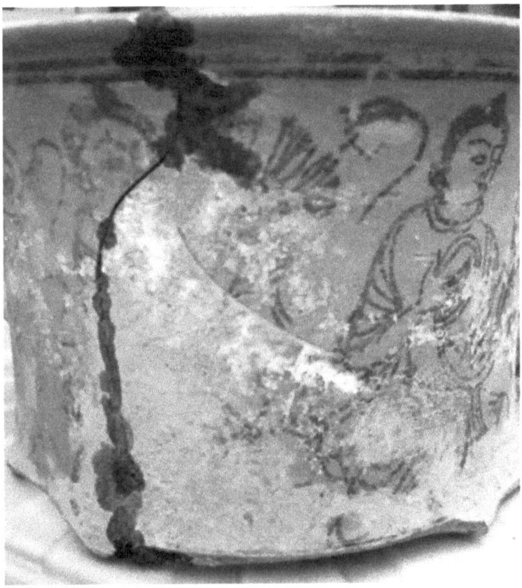

Fig. 5.10 Close-up of Pot_I_5

looks like a *paridhāna* while the top one is like a monk's robe that covers both of his shoulders. However, the front of the torso is left bare. The upper garment passes over his left shoulder and over his right shoulder and upper arm and falls over his right thigh as in the first two figures depicted on the same pot. With his left hand, he probably holds the fold of his drapery or an unclear object that is held with both hands. The object in question has two ends, each ending in a loop. The one, which

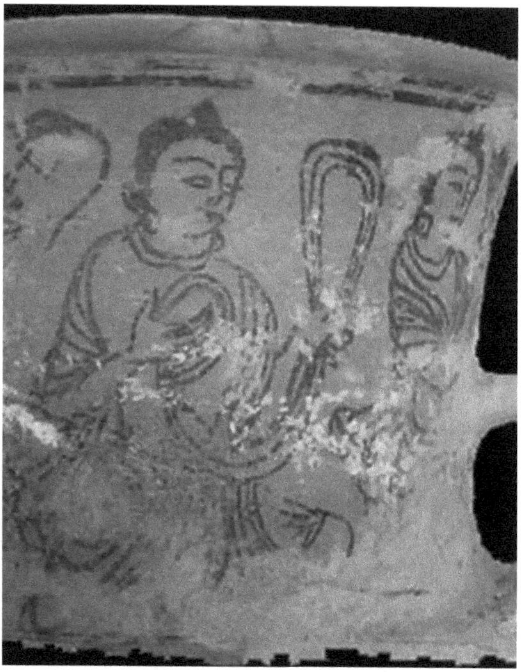

Fig. 5.11 Pot_I_6

is held in his left hand and stays away from his body, forms a large oval and floats to his left. The other forms a circle and is shown against his chest and is probably held in his right hand. Could this object in question be an animal catcher like lasso? His right hand can also be in the gesture of teaching and comes closer to his chest and opens towards his body. Near his left thigh, there is a flora that emerges from the ground and is tilted towards his left thigh. A second flower can be seen near and above his right shoulder (see Pot_I_5).

Pot_I_7 (Fig. 5.12): The last human figure in this series is probably of a female figure which is painted near the intact handle. She wears a dress very similar to Fig. 5.9 painted on this pot. Here both her shoulders are covered with the upper garment, apparently a scarf or part of her *sari* like garment, but the belly and navel are left uncovered. She has a hair tuft or a knot on her skull and wears earrings and a flat necklace. Most likely, she is holding a similar (?) animal or fish with both hands, as in Fig. 5.10. The feathery head, or Native American-like headdress, shows a round face with large open eyes having a prominent dotted iris, a scalloped nose or an indented nose with widely opened nostrils or nostrils apart, and probably an open mouth. Due to the crust on the pot, the lower body of the female is not very clear.

Since most of the pot is missing, the context in which these images are presented cannot be explained precisely. Neither can it be restored until the missing parts of the pot are available. The exact function of the pot is also unclear. However, the presence of two laterally positioned handles attached to the area between the neck and the shoulder of the jar, the wide funnel-shaped mouth and the remaining part of

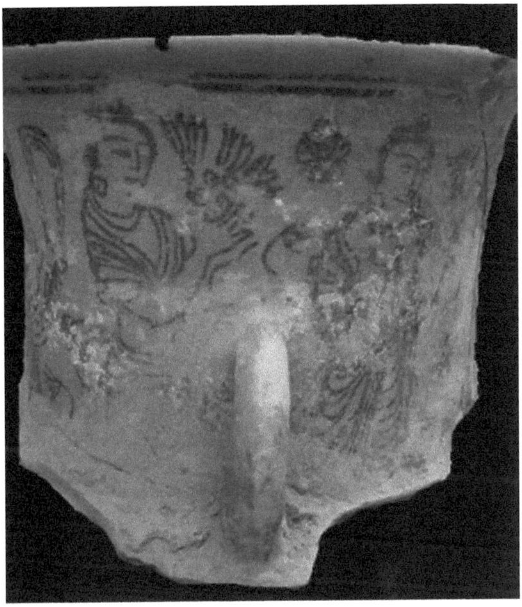

Fig. 5.12 Pot_I_7

the shoulder indicate that the jar was originally a low, squat, probably flat amphora. Its original size is also unclear. The pot, which has a fine and thin texture, has a red slip and is painted with black patterns. The area between the rim and the collar is decorated with two parallel lines that go around under the rim. The neck and the body of the pot are delimited by parallel lines probably similar to those between the rim and the neck.

Of the seven human figures, five are male figures and two are female. The difference is made by the way the upper garment is worn (see above). The three figures (Figs. 5.5, 5.6, and 5.7) in the first field are shown bare-chested and carry flowers in their left hand while the right is brought closer to the right chest. Three of the characters in the second field (Figs. 5.8, 5.9 and 5.11) carry birds, fish or mythical animals in both hands and are represented with their chests covered. Two of the three characters in the second category are images of women. The only figure that does not share all characteristics with the other figures depicted on the pot is Fig. 5.5. He doesn't carry flowers or a bird or a mythical animal, but he wears a rope like object with loops, one at each end. What is the meaning and significance of the rope and the loop is unclear.

The characteristics of the seven figures reside mainly in the style of their dress, in their hairstyle and in their facial features. These are the elements which suggest that the figures are of Indian origin and are probably of a Buddhist period or may be nature. None of them are added with a halo behind the head, otherwise they could be easily confirmed as figures of Buddhas, Bodhisattvas or other affiliated images since the rest of the features fit very well in that context. They could also represent a group of royal figures consisting of both male and female characters.

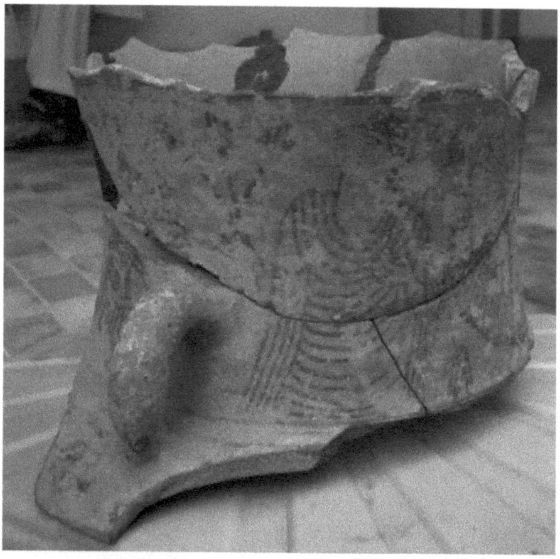

Fig. 5.13 General view of Pot_II

Pot_2 (Fig. 5.13)

The rim and the body of the pot as well as fragments from the neck are missing. The two handles are intact and are added in a lateral position as is the case with the Pot-I. The fields between the handles are decorated with three human figures and three floral or geometric motifs in a continuous and alternating series. Below the rim and above the neck the area shows a band of two parallel lines with a zigzag designs added between the two lines. The gender of the human figures is unclear; they can be male characters. Three parallel lines run around the shoulder of the pot which originally separate the designs of the missing body from those of the neck. Only a few traces of paint on the shoulder are preserved.

Pot_II_1 (Fig. 5.14): From right to left, a human figure is painted to the left of one of the handles. The body above its thigh is depicted while the lower body, just below the stomach, seems to hide behind the lines which are painted on the shoulder of the pot and which pass under the curve of the handle. The figure appears to be standing in a pond. He is standing almost frontally but with his head turned to the right and his eyes raised to the sky. He has a chubby face with a large, fleshy, pointed nose and wide-opened eyes. He has a fatty large-sized neck. The eyebrows are long and almost straight. His hair is short in front but long behind and seems to fall over his shoulders. At the level of his skull is a tuft of hair that ends in a tail-like pattern and is similar as the Hindu *śikhā*, a tuft of hair specifically kept by Vaiṣṇavas and Brahmans at the back of their head.[4] His body is fully covered in a single sleeveless pleated dress. He probably also wears a scarf that goes behind his body and around his arms at the elbows. The two ends of the scarf fall, one on his right thigh and the other on his left.

[4] The coiffure is also comparable, to some extent, to the Manchu hairstyle of the Qing dynasty in China. In this case, the hair is shown long but the front of the head is shaved.

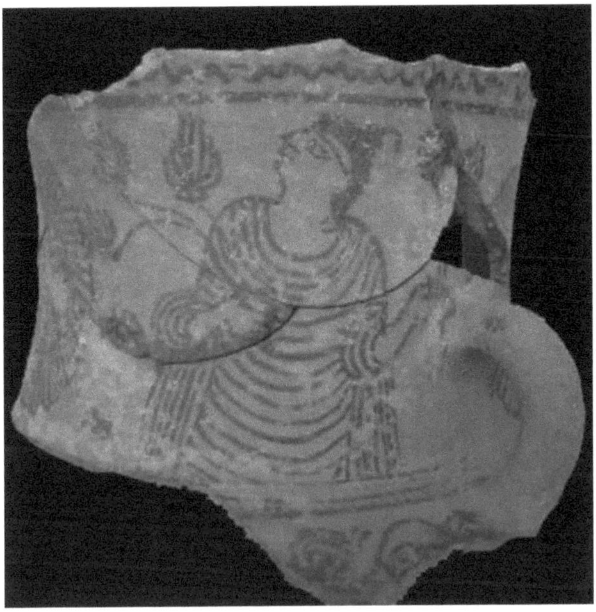

Fig. 5.14 Close-up of Pot_II_1

In his right hand, which is close to his right chest, he holds a bouquet of three stem flowers, each with a long-curved stem. In his left hand he also appears to carry the same number of flowers and is equally depicted in the same style. To his right, there are two floral motifs arranged one above the other but with a certain distance. Between the previous figure and this drawing, there are two floral motifs, each one of seven petals.

Pot_II_2 (Fig. 5.15): The drawing next to the previous one is a large wheel-shaped drawing. It is mainly composed of three parts like a wheel, a pad or the central bore, the spokes and the rim. The runner is made up of two consecutive or concentric circles which are connected by small bars. The core is connected to the rim or inner frame, which is made up of two parallel lines in a circle, through nine spokes. The design in the centre also looks like a spider-shaped design. The outer surface of the outer rim has elongated wedge and point patterns which may represent flames if the pattern represents something other than the wheel. In the case of a wheel, the concept is not very clear. It is possible that the wheel is depicted in motion resulting in flares like the flames of the wheel. This design could also be of a sun-like flower.

Pot_II_3 (Fig. 5.16): The next and last drawing in this field is of a man who is depicted in almost the same form and with a gesture similar to Pot_II_1. Their facial features and clothing are of the same type. It also bears the same number of flowers and in the same manner as in the other example. The only visible difference between the two figures is that the man here has his mouth open as a gesture of expectation,

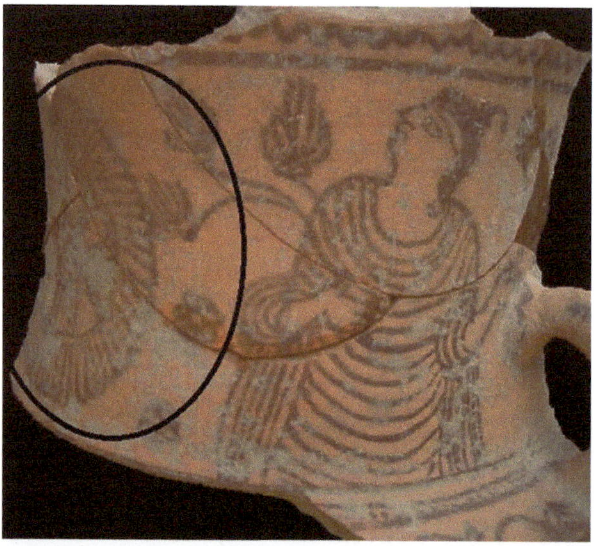

Fig. 5.15 Pot_II_2

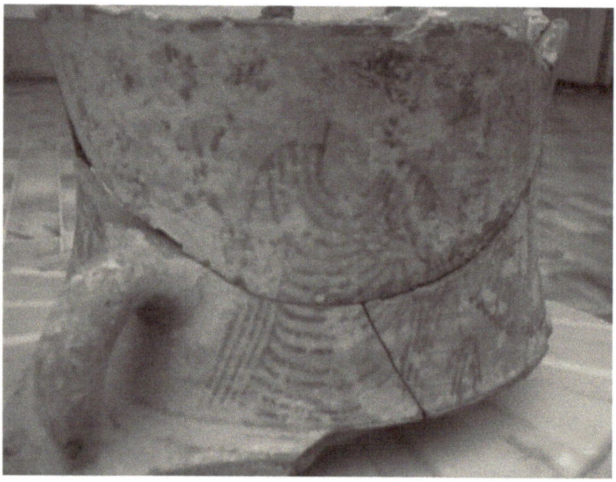

Fig. 5.16 Pot_II_3

shock or astonishment. In the lower field and on its right side is an unclear object, possibly a floral design.

Pot_II_4 (Fig. 5.17): The second field, the area between the two handles, is badly damaged and part of it is missing. The first drawing on this side is the painting of a wheel, probably of the same shape and nature as the previous one (view Pot_II_2).

Pot_II_5 (Fig. 5.18): The following human figure is also damaged and partly missing. However, from the remaining part of the drawing, it seems that the figure

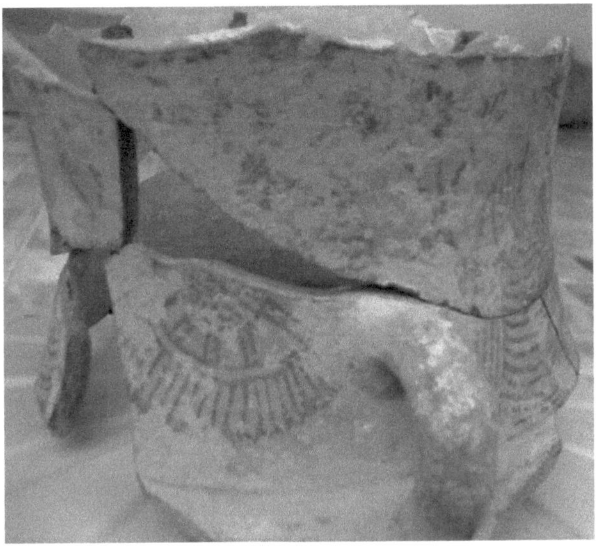

Fig. 5.17 Pot_II_4

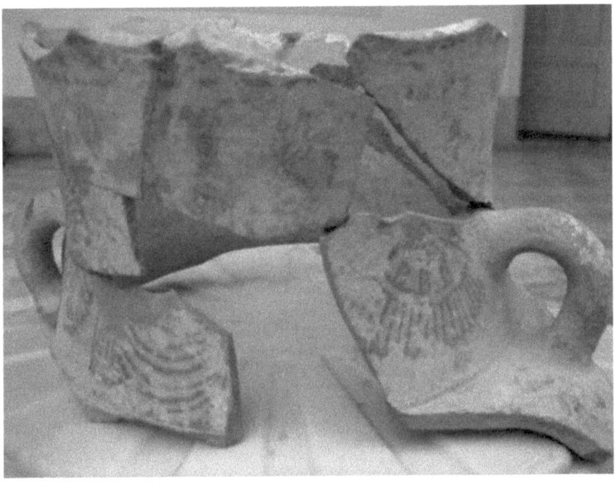

Fig. 5.18 Pot_II_5

is very similar in gesture, in style, etc. to the two previous human figures (see Pot_II_1 and Pot_II_3).

Pot_II_6 (Fig. 5.19): This wheel-like design is similar to the other two depicted on the same pot (see above).

Pot_III (Fig. 5.20)

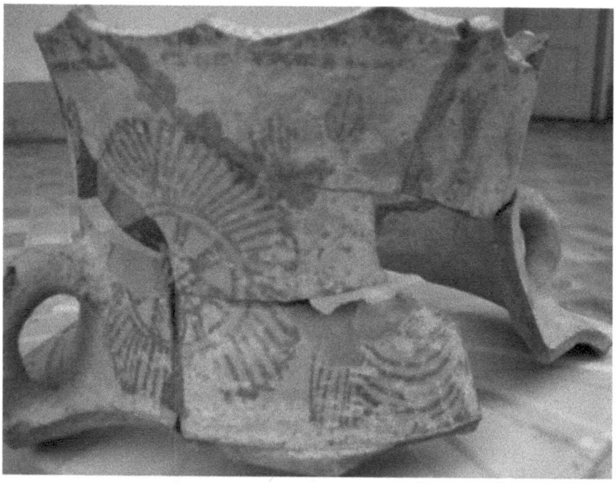

Fig. 5.19 Pot_II_6

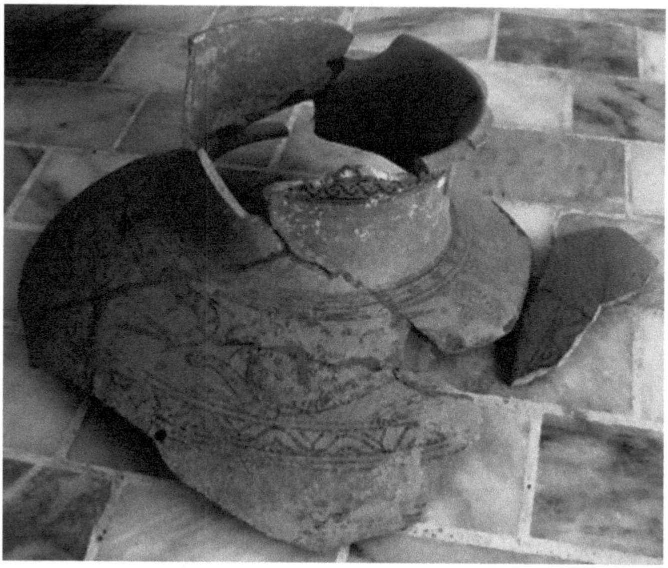

Fig. 5.20 General view of Pot_III

Only part of the rim, collar and shoulder are intact. The rest of the vessel is missing. The available part of the pot is also damaged due to many cracks found on all its sides. It resembles a large pitcher and is decorated on its shoulder with a geometric band around and below the rim. The remaining part of the band suggests that the shoulder and belly of the pot were originally divided horizontally by three wide decorated bands. The band that separates the neck from the shoulder is formed

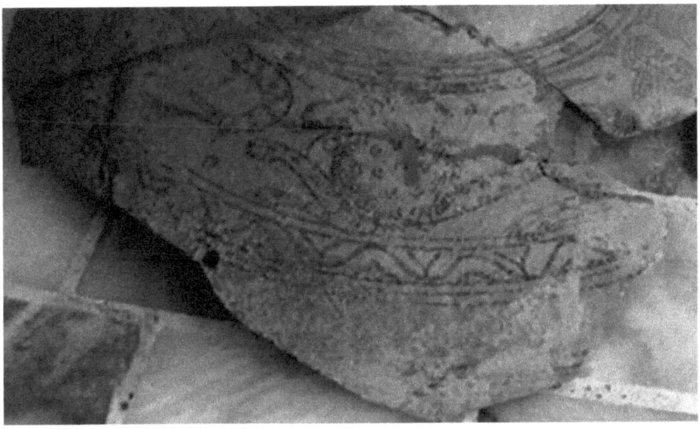

Fig. 5.21 Pt-III_1, 2

by at least four parallel lines and the empty space between the lines is filled with small circles arranged at regular intervals. The second band is wider compared to the rest of the two and separates the shoulder from the belly of the pot. The strip is made up of five parallel lines, two above and three below. The central field of the band is decorated with a wavy pattern consisting of two parallel wavy lines. In each angel of the curve that opens to the sky is added with a "V" shaped design. Only traces of the lower band are visible. The area between the upper band and the middle band is decorated with flora and fauna. The animals, four in number, are three lions/cats and a fish.

Pot_III_1 (Fig. 5.21): The pantherinae is shown in full stride running position; the body is marked with small circles. The tail is raised and folded towards its back with a tassel or tufted end. His mouth is wide open with prominent teeth and tongue out. His left leg is raised and making the gesture of attacking the catfish in front of him.

Pot_III_2 (Fig. 5.21): The fish is shown bent in the middle, its tail and head appearing to advance in an effort to escape. The pelvic fin, dorsal fin, anal fin and fin ray as well as the tail are clearly marked. Near his fin ray is a small circle.

Pot_III_3 (Fig. 5.22): The following drawing is that of a lion which is represented in the same gesture as the previous one. He appears in the gesture of pouncing on the lion standing in front of him (see below).

Pot_III_4 (Fig. 5.23): The last lion of the three depicted on this Pot_III is mostly damaged, but I suspect it may have originally been shown in a different style and gesture than the other two. Here the body is short and unstretched, and the lion appears to be in a standing position.

Pot_III_5 (Fig. 5.24): On the other side of the vase, only part of the floral motifs are preserved. The flora appears to be a combination of stem tendrils or leaf tendril patterns with flower stalks. Are they aquatic shrubs like money plants? Somc of the money plants' family have white and cream flowers with a strong fragrance. The

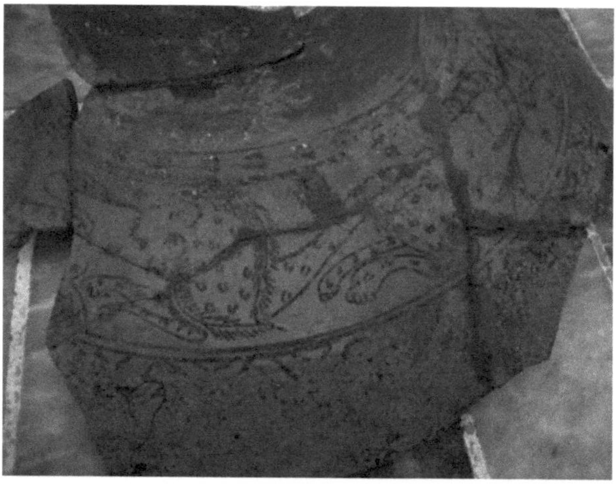

Fig. 5.22 Pot_III_3

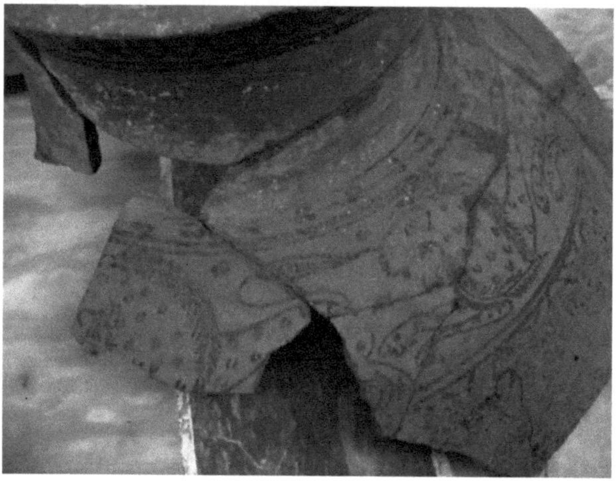

Fig. 5.23 Pot_III_4

red-flowered money plant produces long-stemmed flowers, which seems to be the case here.

* * *

Even though the exact location from where the pots were recovered is not known, this type of potsherd from the Bajaur region has however already been published, first by Rahman (1993, 1994) then by Brancaccio (2010) for some of which the place of discovery is known. The list of sites provided by Rahman (1993: 214) from which similar sherds have been recovered suggests that this type of pottery tradition was

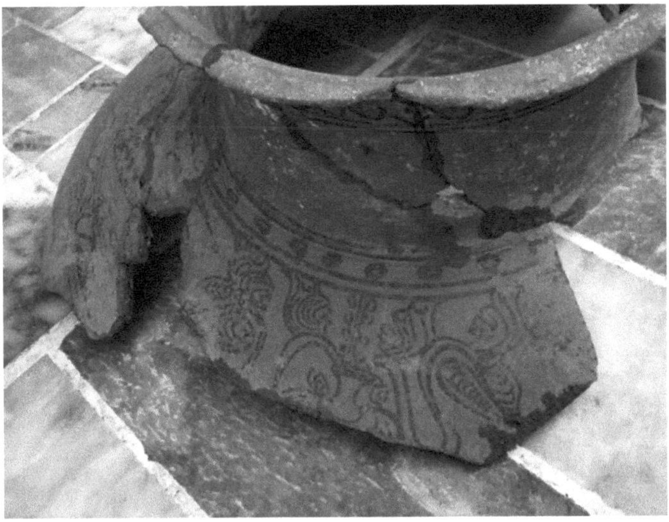

Fig. 5.24 Pot_III_5

not confined to a single site but was used over a wide area, even beyond the region of Bajaur since similar pottery have also been recovered from Mes Aynak site in Afghanistan (Noori et al. 2017). The list provided by Rahman shows that at present the majority of the Bajaur-Mohmand sherds have been found at Serai site in Bajaur.

Regarding the origin and iconography of the human figures, they can be divided into two groups. Those painted on Pot_I and the other group depicted on Pot_II. In these two groups, the facial features, hairstyle and clothing of the characters are not of the same type. Those in the first group have a small round face with a small mouth, nose and eyes. The coiffure is very similar to that of the Buddha's hairstyle where he is depicted with curly hair and an *uṣṇīṣa*. If there was not a single piece of cloth, each character can wear *uttarīya* for the upper garment and a *paridhāna* for the lower dress. They are adorned with ornaments for the neck and ears. The figures in the second group are probably having long hair with a long tuft at the level of the skull; the bun is comparable to the hairstyle of TC figurines (Figs. 5.1, 5.2, 5.3, and 5.4), which was found with the pots and has other similar features like the broad face, the pointed chubby nose and the large almond-shaped eyes. A similar hairstyle and other alike features can also be seen in the Alchon figures which are added to a bronze bowl recovered from Kashmir Smast (Nasim Khan 2006: 80, Figs. 76, 77). The painted one probably wears a long dress and carries a scarf which runs behind his back and of which both ends pass in his arm, one around his right and the other around his left arm. The figures do not appear to be adorned with jewels or they may be wearing open torques like those worn by the men in the Yakatoot painting (Nasim Khan 2015: Fig. 1; Nasim Khan 2016). Despite these dissimilarities between the two groups, their iconography still suggests that both may be of indigenous descent and are not of foreign origin but their indirect connection with Central Asia or beyond cannot be ignored. The figures in the first group are probably both male and female while gender of the second group is difficult to determine; they are most likely male characters.

As far the flora depicted on the Pot_I and Pot_II is concerned, similar vegetation has also been attested on alike pottery from Bajaur (Brancaccio 2010) and is identified with the ephedra or soma plant. The identification of the soma plant in Gandhāra art has become an absolute obsession for some scholars and any alike vegetation they observe in this art is tempted to be related to the soma plant. All of these researchers could be right or wrong in one way or another, since logic and authentic proof has not yet been sought. Based on the shape of the plant mentioned in ancient literature, everyone shoots in the hope of having the merit of being the first to identify this mysterious plant. But the events recounted in ancient literature are not always easy to understand in their cultural context, especially for those who do not belong to the same cultural milieu.

Ephedra plant has several different species while only some of them are known in the region. Ephedra generally grows on dry, rocky, sandy slopes at high altitudes, especially on snow-covered massifs termed "cold desert". In Swat and Dir regions it usually grows at high altitude like Mankiyal Serai, Mataltan, Kalam in Swat and for this reason the plant is locally called "Asmāni Boṭē" (Ephedra gerardiana). It is also known by the name of *Somāni* most probably short form of *Asmāni.* The most interesting feature of *Asmāni Botē*, which literally means "sky plant" is that when the stem is pressed its juice smells like pine sap. Locally, it is consumed as a medicinal plant for the treatment of different human and animal diseases. The name of the plant varies from region to region but it never grows on shorelines or next to ponds and rivers.

In some areas of the region, two of its varieties are identified and distinguished from each other by the structure of the plant body. The Pashto term for one of these is *Ghaṭ Aumān* (thick *Aumān*) and the other is *Narē* A*umān* (thin *Aumān*). On their uses as medicinal plants, a recent study shows that the juice, powder, paste and poultice, made from the stem of Ephedra intermedia Schrenk & CAMey (Ghat Omān or Aumān) are used for the treatment of disorders respiratory infections, colds, retained placenta, anaplasmosis and pneumonia in animals such as buffaloes, cows, donkeys, camels, sheep and goats. While the juice, powder, paste and poultice, made from the stem of Ephedra major subsp. procera (C.A.Meyer). Bornm (Narai Omān or Narē Aumān) is used for the treatment of colds, bloating and urinary disorders in animals such as buffaloes, cows, donkeys, camels, sheep and goats (Abidin et al. 2021: Table 1). The term *Hum* or *Hom* quoted by Brancaccio (2010: 333) may be derived from Asmāni < Somāni < Omāni/Aumāni < Omān < Hum or Om.

There are other several similar medicinal plants, which grow on the snow-covered massifs, such *Kwanjē* (Dryopteris juxtaposita), *Baba Ghwakhē* and *Laḍora* (Diplazium esculentum); they are generally eaten raw. The last one is also mixed with curd and is a favourite dish of the autochthones. The other medicinal and edible plant which grows in the hilly area of Bajaur, Dir and Swat is *caralluma tuberculata* locally known as *Pamankē* or *Pamangē* or *Pamaney* etc. It is a leafless perennial erect herb with a maximum height of one meter, but this height is rare. Its stem is fleshy

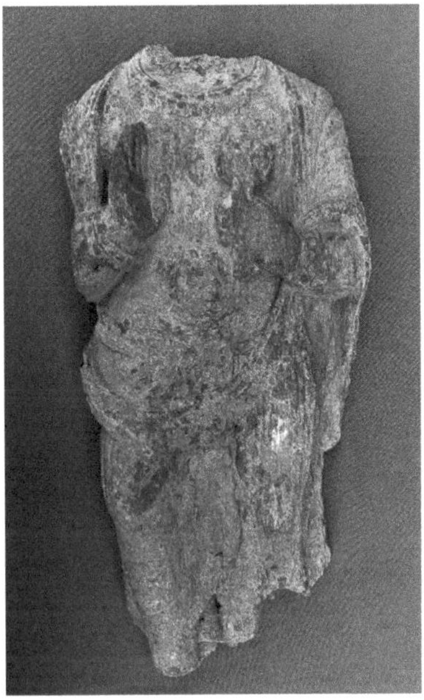

Fig. 5.25 Bodhisattva carrying a lotus flower

and angular with soft spines in the notches. As for the flora represented on the first two pots, presented here, it may have nothing to do with ephedra or the soma plant, but as the presence of geese and fish suggests, it is a vegetation that generally grows in ponds or marshy land or in the lowlands. Most probably, the flora represents lotus flowers.

The lotus motif is generally considered to represent abundance, fertility and nature and is frequently depicted in Gandhāran Buddhist art (Fig. 5.25). Ancient art from Egypt also displays lotuses carried by both men and women in paintings and sculpted art (Figs. 5.26 and 5.27) or some images are emerging from the flower or another cases the flowers are harvested by individuals from ponds. It is used in both secular and religious contexts. The Egyptian deity Nefertum is identified with the god of perfume and is usually depicted with a lotus flower. In a painting of a scene from the tomb of Djehouty, Thebes, Djehouty is depicted smelling a lotus blossom, and his mother, who holds and carries lotus flowers, receives offerings (Fig. 5.27).

Another important painting from Egypt that may be more interesting for our Bajaur pottery imagery research is a fragment of a polychrome funerary painting, such as Nebamun fishing in the swamps (Fig. 5.28). He holds a stick in his left hand and three birds in the other which is depicted with a bouquet of flowers hanging over his arm. Behind stands his wife and is depicted with lotuses in her right hands and some decorated at her head. Her daughter is seated below and collects the lotus flowers. In his forehead, he shows his cat-catching birds. Further to the left there is

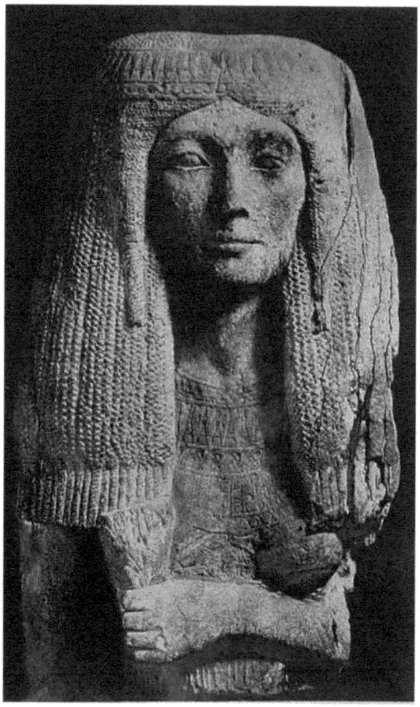

Fig. 5.26 Sculpture shown holding probably a lotus flower

a thicket of long-stemmed papyrus[5] and a frightened bird. Fish are depicted below the waterline.

At this stage of the research, I dare not seek any direct historical or cultural relationship between the images carried by the pottery from Bajaur and the images depicted in the Egyptian paintings, but the aim here is to show that the ancient paintings of Egypt also display similar flowers which are already identified as lotus flowers. Erika Schmitt, who contributed significantly to Gandhāra art, finds no relation between the lotuses from these distant regions. She says,

> Mediterrane Lotusformen des ägyptischen Typs fanden sich in der G.K. nicht. Die Motive satnden den indischen Formen näher, allerdings im Sinne von frei erfunden Rosetten, die nur nominell als Lotus identifiziert werden. Inwieweit die Rosetten der Volkskunst der Himalayagebietes von den Kulturträgern auch als Lotus bezeichnet werden, entzieht sich meiner Kenntnis. (Schmitt 1971: 288)

However, to conclude from the above, the whole scenario depicted on Pot_I may represent certain community achievements. The presence of aquatic plants and animals, such as lotus, blue iris, catfish, shows that the act could occur in a waterway or in a pond. The event appears to be related to flower-picking, fish-catching, and bird-trapping ceremonies. Due to the use of pottery in a wide area, such an event may not be an ordinary one or of a certain individual nature, but they may be relevant either for some kind of special community secular gatherings, or they may have a

[5] The plant is identified as a papyrus but it appears to be a flowering plant and the flowers are similar to those held by Djehoutys in Fig. 5.26. Papyrus is primarily a foliage plant with bracts showing clusters of flowers in the axil.

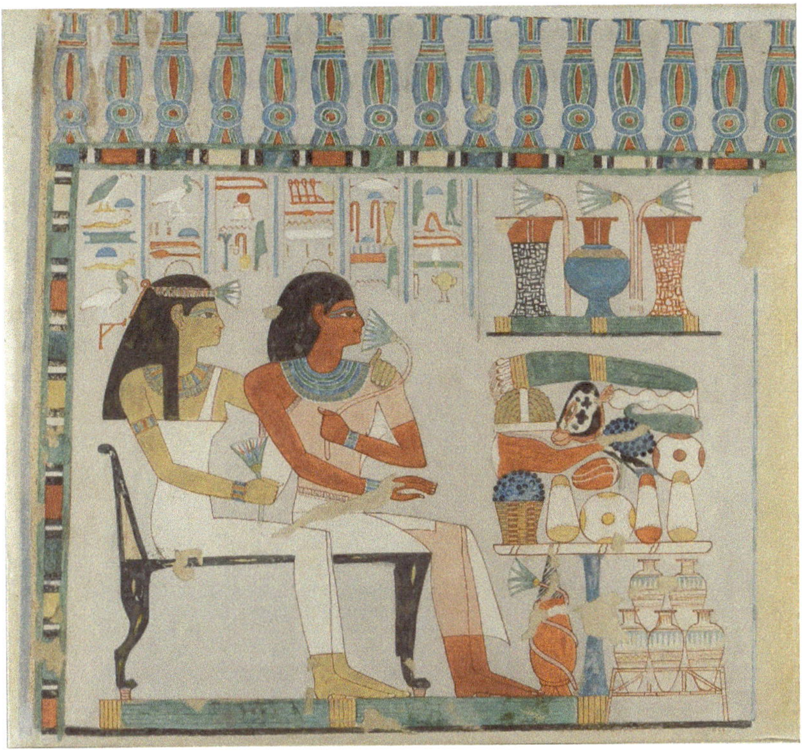

Fig. 5.27 Djehuty and his Mother Receiving Offerings, Tomb of Djehuty, circa 1427–1400 B.C (Ref. Wikimedia commons). Metropolitan Art Museum, Accession No. 15.5.8

religious origin or they may even carry both the secular and religious context, such as the spring festival of Kalash, the Chilam Joshi or the harvest festivals of the Kalashi.[6] Their iconography and other elements like the tuft of hair and clothing suggest that the human figures depicted on Pot_I have characteristics of Indian origin.

The images on Pot_II also carry similar flowers as on Pot_I and can be presented with the same concept. However, the hairstyle of the figures, here, is very strange and their facial features are both Indian and Central Asian in makeup, more particularly they are comparable to the Alchon busts.

The decorations on Pot_III are wildlife and floral designs and are difficult to place them in any particular cultural context; they could be both Indian and Central Asian. The lions and the form of flora painted on Pot_III are already attested in the Buddhist art of Gandhāra and there is a very good reason to believe that there would have been an indigenous idea behind this scene. Concerning the environment where the scene takes place on Pot_III, the presence of the fish suggests that, as in the two previous cases, this scene also takes place in a wetland.

[6] On these festivals see Siiger (1974: 87–92) and Palwal (1974: 93–94).

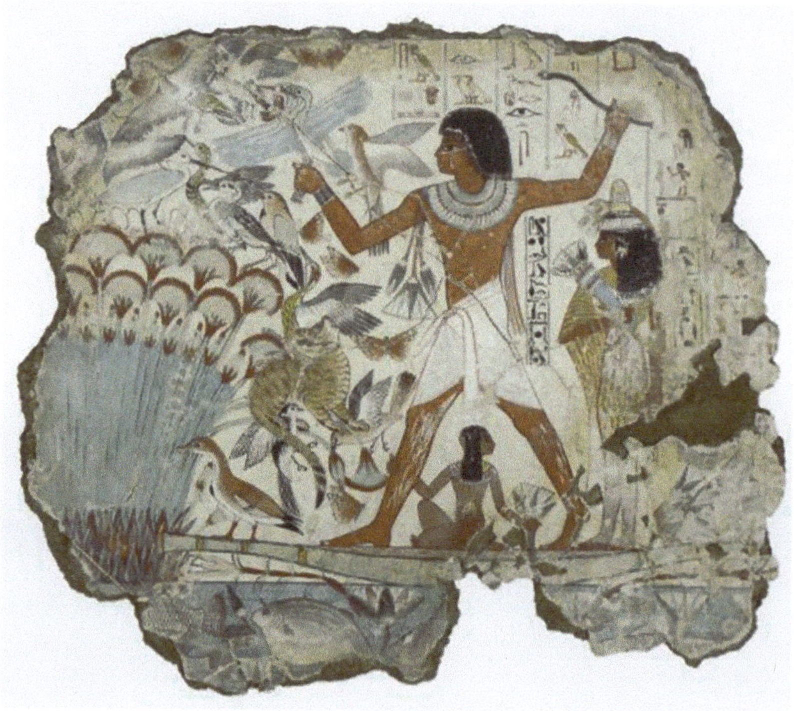

Fig. 5.28 Nebamun Hunting Fowl in the Mars—1390–1350 BC (Ref. Wikimedia commons). British Museum Accession No. 37977

If we put all the designs on the pots together and consider studying them in their entirety, the whole shows an interesting similarity between the subjects of the Bajaur pottery and the Egyptian paintings in the British Museum. Is it just a happy coincidence or there was a cultural link between the two despite the long distance and time span between them? Anyway, time and space have little meaning when it comes to the dissemination of cultural elements from one territory to another since this diffusion is not linked to any treaty and does not require any document. If elements of the Indus Valley Civilization were able to reach the Nile, Euphrates and Tigris or vice versa, Gandhāra must also have received or copied elements from countries of the ancient Nile. A frieze in the Lahore Museum shows similar flora growing in a water pond. The frieze was found in Sikri site and is number 2114/GR-379 (Fig. 5.29).

Date

In the absence of any epigraphic and numismatic evidence, the date of the pottery mainly depends on their laboratory examinations. The date proposed for pottery published by Pia Brancaccio is somewhere between the second and seventh centuries AD (Brancaccion 2010: 329, note 2). The iconographic study may also suggest a

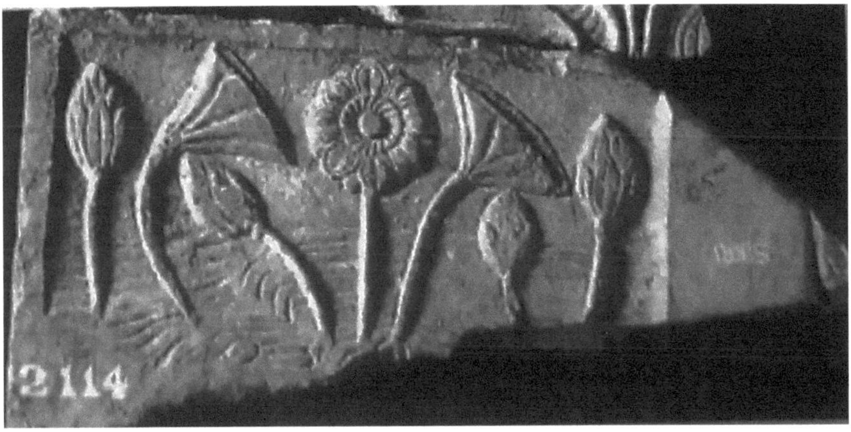

Fig. 5.29 Stone panel in the Lahore Museum

date later than the first century AD. For example, the characters of the second group represented on Pot_II have an elongated chubby face with a large pointed nose and long almond-shaped eyes—raised to the sky, and with long, almost straight eyebrows. These features remind me of the figures in the frescoes discovered at Yakatoot in Peshawar; on a paleographic background, these paintings are dated to the fourth/fifth century AD (see Nasim Khan 2015: Figs. 1–3; 2016, Figs. 3–5). The Yaktoot paintings also show almost similar faces with a chubby profile, large pointed noses and long almond-shaped eyes, and wearing a torque which opens from the front. Their eyes are also raised to the sky. Overall, the Yakatoot frescoes belong to the Gandhāran School of Buddhist paintings, the style of art that may have existed between the second and sixth centuries AD (Nasim Khan 2015: 51). Additionally, a bronze bowl from Kashmir Smast (see Nasim Khan 2006: 83, figs. 78, 79; 2018: 329, figs. 12.5, 12.6) bears Alchon busts with almost alike hairstyle as those depicted on Pot_II; the bowl is dated to the fourth–fifth century AD (Nasim Khan 2018: 329). Based on these similarities, the date of Bajaur pottery may be more precisely between the fourth and sixth centuries or may belong to the Huns who ruled the area from c.350–657.[7]

[7] On Huns, see Nasim Khan et al. (2008: 31–42).

Chapter 6
Skill and Techniques

The artists in the past have used different pigments and has tried to demarcate with colours the different parts of the body prominently. To create a basic palette, initially and probably five colours, i.e. yellow, red, brown, white and black, were used with a mixture of earth, burnt charcoal, chalk and animal fat around 40,000 years ago. But with the passage of time the relentless revelation has occurred in colour combinations and this theme remained more complex.

The use of pigments for body decoration and for applying human expressions and ideas to a variety of mediums has a long history. Minerals, plants and fruits have been used as dyes since prehistoric times. In that primitive age, pigments were also extracted from plants and fruits and were used for aesthetic purposes, communication and to quench religious thirst. In this respect, different colours have been used in this expressive art and other purposes.

In the prehistoric period[1] of rock art in Pakistan, the most prominent pigments which have been used are red, black and white. These colours were applied inside and generously to the rough surface of the cave to represent human figures, hand and foot prints, animal drawings, hunting and combat scenes, flora and fauna, geometric patterns as well as abstract designs. With the domestication of animals and the agricultural activities in the Neolithic period, the development of pottery also followed the development of agriculture. The household objects from Baluchistan were decorated with a variety of themes from simple line designs to geometrical paintings, birds and animal designs and other multi-coloured patterns. The three main colours used for household objects, toys or objects of worship are yellow, red, black and white. With the introduction of a new type of polychrome pottery in around 3500–3000 BC, square and triangular geometric patterns were also becoming part of the decoration. The *pipal* tree leaf design seems appeared for the first time at Mehergarh,

[1] The question of date for such drawings remains open. I am not quite sure about the date of that art designated as prehistoric art paintings. I presume they are not so early in date but in the absence of any scientific analyses, it would be too risky to opt for this option.

M. Nasim Khan, *Gandhāran School of Buddhist Paintings*,
https://doi.org/10.1007/978-981-96-9310-8_6

Baluchistan, in the third millennium BC. A wild donkey or horse is also introduced to depict on pottery from Mehergarh and dated to the second millennium BC or earlier.

With the rise of the Indus civilization around 3000 BC, a variety of designs are painted on the pottery. Among these are animal drawings, multi-coloured patterns and Togau designs, geometric patterns mostly painted in red. Among the animals' drawings are the brown-painted ibexes. In the first half of the third millennium BC, the pottery painted in grey was abundant and decorated with geometrical reasons and fish and animals' drawings painted in black. Other typical motifs are the *pipal* trees, gazelles and hump bulls which are usually painted black. There are examples of birds alternating with humped bulls, attached to *pipal* trees, with different designs painted on their bodies. Images of horned deities (??) were sometimes painted on pots like those from Rahman Dheri archaeological site (Durrani 1988: Fig. LVI, 1–8)[2].

The tradition of expression with paintings continued into the historic period and is applied in both cave shelters and wall paintings. So far, there is no substantial scientific study to analyse the cave paintings in the region, whether they belong to the historical or prehistoric period. Like rock carvings, the criterion for dating rock paintings is mainly based on their style. But such criteria can sometimes be a bad guide since a particular style has been perpetuated over the centuries. None of the pigments in the rock shelter paints have been analysed for their composition. The same goes for the murals of Gandhara. Prior to the discovery of the Paṭvano Gaṭai paintings (Nasim Khan 2000), almost no one knew about some of the region's stunning wall paintings, but they have yet to be scientifically analysed with respect to their material and pigments. The nature of the paintings from the historical period depicts both sacred and secular subjects. The most common of the pigments used in these paintings are the orange, red, chocolate, black and white, and blue is found primarily in paintings from the Buddhist period. The paintings from the Buddhist period are more elaborate and are mostly found inside the Buddhist settlements and rock shelters. The colours, used on the rough surface inside the caves, are mostly red or brown and rarely black and white (see supra). Frescoes have been used both in rock shelters and as murals inside religious built structures and secular buildings such as Aziz Ḍheri (Nasim Khan 2010) and Yakatoo (Nasim Khan 2015).

In the medieval period of Pakistan, paintings remained a central theme in the aesthetic beauty and could be seen in both secular and religious buildings, applied to household objects, became part of textile designing, body decoration, illustrations of books, etc. Despite being considered as an important element in the daily life of the people little cab said about the source and combination of colours used in these paintings. The only scientific analysis concerning paintings from the Sikh period and the Hindu period buildings are the studies of paintings at Katas Raj, located in the Jehlum region of Pakistan (see Naveed Khan 2017: 72–78; Rauf 2021: 57–63). Their analysis showed that the combination of colours is based on earths or earth colours and that the basic composition of earths was usually clay, silica, manganese dioxide, alumina and iron and that these pigments are characterized on the basis of different

[2] I believe these are simple animal drawings like others depicted on pottery from Rehman Dheri. Polychrome decoration is commonly used on pottery from the same site (see Durrani et al. 1991).

earths or clays materials such as umber, sienna and ochre. Analysis of the pictorial layer of the Berragi Haveli frescoes, in Katas Raj, confirmed that the artists used kaolin (white earth or also called Chinese clay) and lime for the white, red ochre for the red, yellow ochre for yellow, lapilazuli for blue and Glauconite or Terre-Verte, a ferrous silicate compound, for the green colour. The colours used in the Havelis of the Sikh period at the Katas Raj complex in Jehlum, Pakistan are as follows: yellow ochre, red ochre, burnt or dark red, carbon, dark-brown lime and calcium sulphate, green earth, Lapislazuli. The study made by the two young scholars on the pigments used in the Sikh Havelis and the Hindu temples of Katas Raj can serve as a model and introduce such a study into the analysis of the Buddhist paintings of Gandhāra to know their composition.

Conclusion

The discovery of paintings from the Buddhist period in Gandhāra is of great importance to the historian of Buddhism and Buddhist art in Gandhāra. This emerging field of study has revealed at least four different aspects, mainly related to Buddhist architecture, art and iconography. Firstly, and most importantly, we had been convinced, for lack of evidence, that the absence of frescoes in Gandhāra was probably due to the unfavourable and humid environment of the Gandhāra region, and that Gandhāra artists probably lacked the skills to execute this type of art. But these discoveries have proved the contrary, and we must now conduct our investigations with greater care and caution when studying a Gandhāra Buddhist site. Indeed, it is highly likely that other paintings of this type will be discovered in this region. Secondly, current examples of the existence of paintings in Buddhist settlements prove that, if not all, most Gandhāra Buddhist monasteries were endowed with such art, but during illegal or official excavations, they were destroyed or remained unnoticed, or even ignored, due to their rare and fragile nature, as was the case at Aziz Ḍheri. Thirdly, the presence of some early period paintings suggests that this art has coexisted with stone, stucco and other media since the birth of Gandhāran Buddhist art. Fourthly, and most importantly, these paintings suggest an approximate date and place of origin for the first image of the Buddha, which still remains an enigma. We can assume that the first image of the Buddha was produced in Gandhāra during the first century BC. The paintings at Kala Tassa show two images of the Buddha that could belong to the first century AD or even earlier. The material study of the paintings would also confirm their date.

Unfortunately, the analysis of the colours used in paintings from the Buddhist period in Gandhāra has not yet been studied, but the pigments need to be scientifically analysed to know the exact colour scheme, which would help to understand the source and origin of the materials used in the colour combination. The only study to date in this field is the analysis of paintings dating from the late Sikh and Hindu periods at Katas Raj, located in the Jehlum region of Pakistan, which shows that the colour combination is based on earth or earth colours. One of these examples confirms that the artists used kaolin (white earth or also known as Chinese clay) and lime for white, red ochre for red, yellow ochre for yellow, lap lazuli for blue and glauconite

M. Nasim Khan, *Gandhāran School of Buddhist Paintings*,
https://doi.org/10.1007/978-981-96-9310-8

or Terre-Verte, a ferrous silicate compound, for green. In other examples, the colours are yellow ochre, red ochre, burnt or dark red, carbon, dark brown lime and calcium sulphate, green earth, lapis lazuli (see Chap. 5).

The theme of Gandhāra paintings can be religious or secular, or both, as in the case of the Kala Tassa paintings, which feature both stūpa designs and hunting scenes. The two categories of paintings are, simple line drawings on the rough surfaces of rock shelters and frescoes found inside built structures as well as inside rock shelters. The first group of them represents both secular and sacred themes. The profane drawings are figurative representations and inscriptions written in Kharoṣṭhī and Brāhmī. Figurative drawings are individual human and animal figures or depicted in scenes of hunting, combat, etc. Sacred drawings include Kharoṣṭhī and Brāhmī inscriptions, Buddha and Bodhisattva images, stūpa designs, devotees and at least one example of the Jātaka stories, namely the Titriya Jātaka. All the frescoes or murals are Buddhist in nature and are depicted in a Buddhist context. There are images of the Buddha and bodhisattvas, the Mara family, celestial figures, flora and fauna (?), symbols, floral and geometric patterns.

In terms of date, the four most important sites are the Kala Tassa paintings, dated to the first century AD, the Parlai Ḍab rock paintings, dated to the first century BC and fourth/fifth century AD, the Aziz Ḍheri paintings, dated to the second/third century AD and the Yakatoo paintings, dated to the third/fifth century AD. The date of the Gandhāran paintings is highly variable, but to generalize what we've discovered so far, the terminus post-quem would be the first century BC and the terminus ante quem the fourth/fifth century AD or later.

Bibliography

Abidin, S.Z.U., et al (2021). Ethnoveterinary botanical survey of medicinal plants used in Pashto, Punjabi and Saraiki communities of Southwest Pakistan. *Veterinary Medicine and Science (Vet Med Sci.)* 2021,7: 2068–2085. https://doi.org/10.1002/vms3.582

Agnew, N and Marcia Reed (2016). Introduction. The Dunhuang Cave Temple at Mogao. *Cave Temples of Dunhuang. Buddhist Art on China's Silk Road.* Edited by Neville Agnew, Marcia Reed and Tevvy Ball: 1–15. Published by Getty Conservation Institute Los Angeles.

Ali, I. and Rahman, L. (2005). Survey and Exploration in Bajaur-Mohmand Region, Pakistan. *Frontier Archaeology*, Volume III (2005): 55–90. Publication of the Directorate of Archaeology and Museums, Government of Khyber Pakhtunkhwa. Peshawar.

Andrews, F.H. (1948). *Wall Paintings from Ancient Shrines in Central Asia*, recovered by Sir Aurel Stein, Described by Fred H. Andrews. London.

Aṣṭādhyāyī of Pāṇini. Translated by Vasu Srisa Chandra (1891). Dehli.

Azarpay, Guitty (1981). *Sogdian Painting* – The Pictorial Epic in Oriental Art. London.

Banerjea, J.N. (1936). Vidyadhāra. *Journal of the Indian Society of Oriental Art*, Volume 4, Nos. 1&2: 52–56. Archaeological Survey of India.

Barger, E. & Wright, P. (1941). Excavations in Swat and Explorations in the Oxus Territories of Afghanistan. *Asian Arts and Archaeology,* series No. 1. PP. 5–270. India.

Becatti, Giovanni (1968). *The Art of Ancient Greek and Rome.* London.

Blänsdorf, C. et al. (2009). The Polychromy of the Giant Buddha Statue in Bāmiyān. *The Giant Buddha of Bāmiyān. Safeguarding the Remains*, edited by Michael Petzet: 237–264. Berlin.

Boreux, C. (1926). *L'Art Égyptien.* Bibliothèque de l'Histoire de l'Art. Paris

Brancaccio, Pia (2010). The Pottery from Bajaur: A Window into the Late Gandharan Tradition. *Coins, Art and Chronology II.* The First Millennium C.E. in the Indo-Iranian Borderlands. Edition, Michael Alram – Deborah Klimburg-Salter – Minoru Inaba – Matthias Pfisterer. : 329–340. Wien.

Brentjes, von B. (1981). Archäologie Afghanistans. *Das Altertum*, Heft 3, Band 27: 133–146. Akademie-Verlag Berlin.

Bussagli, Mario (1979). *Central Asian Paintings.* New York

Bussagli, Mario. (1978). *Treasures of Asia.* Central Asian Paintings. From Afghanistan to Sinkiang. Translated from Italian by Lothian Small.

Callieri, Pierfrancesco (1997). *Seals and Sealings from the North-West of the Indian Subcontinent and Afghanistan* (4th Century BC – 11th Century AD). Publication of Institutu Universititario Orientale Instituto Italiano.

Dani, A.H. (1968–1969). Buddhist Rock Engravings in Dir. *Ancient Pakistan*, Volume IV: 251–257. Bulletin of the Department of Archaeology, University of Peshawar. Peshawar.

Dani, A.H. (1983). *Human Records on Karakorum Highway.* Centre for the Study of the Civilizations of Central Asia, Quaid-i-Azam University. Islamabad.

M. Nasim Khan, *Gandhāran School of Buddhist Paintings*,
https://doi.org/10.1007/978-981-96-9310-8

Dani, A.H. (1995). *Human Records on Karakorum Highway*. Mr. Books Publishers, Book Sellers, Islamabad.

Dupree, Nancy Hatch. (1974). *The National Museum of Afghanistan* – An Illustrated Guide. Published by the Afghan Air Authority and the Afghan Tourist Organization, Kabul.

Durrani, F.A. (1988). Excavations in the Gomal Valley. Rehman Dheri Excavation Report No.1. *Ancient Pakistan,* volume VI. Research Bulletin of the Department of Archaeology, University of Peshawar. Peshawar.

Durrani, F.A. Ali, I., Erdosy, G. (1991). Further Excavation at Rehman Dheri. *Ancient Pakistan*, volume VII: 61–115. Research Bulletin of the Department of Archaeology, University of Peshawar. Peshawar.

Durrani, F.A., Taj Ali and Rehman, I. (1997). Excavation at Gor Khuttree. A Preliminary Note. *Āthāriyyāt (Archaeology)* 1:185–212. Peshawar.

Faccena, D. (1980). *Butkara I (Swāt, Pakistan)* 1956–1962, volume 3, Part 3, Text, IsMEO-Rome.

Faccena, D. and M. Taddei (1962). *Sculptures from the Sacred Area of Butkara I*, 2 volumes. IseMEO-Rome.

Faccena, D. Butkara I (Swāt, Pakistan) 1956–1962, Part 5.1,2. Text and Plates. IsMEO-Rome.

Fan, Jishi (2017). *Dunhuang. A pearl on the Silk Road-A Treasure Trove of Buddhist Culture.* English translation by WANG Pingxian.

Fazal Sher (1993). Architectural Remains of Gango Dher (Aziz Ḍheri), *PUTAJ* 1993–1994: 18–25. Peshawar.

Filigenzi, Anna. (2010). Post Gandharan/non Gandharan: An Archaeological Inquiry into a Still Nameless Period. *Coins, Art and Chronology II*. The First Millennium C.E. in the Indo-Iranian Borderlands. Edited by Alram, M. et al.: 38–406. Wien.

Fussman, G. (1989). Gāndhārī écrite, gāndhārī parlée. *Dialects dans les literatures indo-aryennes*, edited by Colette Caillat, Paris. Publication de l'Institute de civilizations indienne, fasc. 55: 433–501. Paris.

Fussman, G. (1994). *Upāya-Kauśalya. L'implanation du boudhisme au Gandhara.* Bouddhisme et Cultures locales. Quelques cas de réciproques adaptations: 17.51. Publication d'École Françasie d'Extrême-Orient, Paris.

Fussman, G. (2011). *Catalogue des Inscriptions sur Poteries. Monuments Bouddhiques de Termez – Termez Buddhist Monuments I*. Publications de l'Institut de Civilization Indienne. Paris.

Fussman, G. and König, D. (1997). *Die Felsbildstation Shatial.* Materialien zur Archaologie der Nordgebiete Pakistans (MANP), volume 2. Mainz.

Ghose, Madhuvanti. (2003). Masque d'Homme. *De l'Indus àl'Oxus*. Archéologie de l'Asie Centrale. Catalogue de l'Exposition. Edited by Bopearachchi, Osmund et al.: 319. Lattes.

Haesner, Chhaya (1999). Paradise Scenes in Central Asian Art: Autochthonous or modelled after Gandhara Art? Coins, Art and Archaeology. Essays on the pre-Islamic History of the Indo-Iranian Borderlands. Alram, M. and Klimberg-Salter, Deoborah, E. (eds). 423–452. Wien

Haewon, Kim, Jo Yeontae, Cheon Juhyun, Park Seungwon (2013). New Research on Central Asian Paintings in the National Museum of Korea. *Archives of Asian Art*, Volume 63, Number 2, 2013: 165–178.

Hansen, V. (2012). *The Silk Road. New History.* Oxford.

Hultzsch, E. (1925). *The Inscriptions of Asoka*, Corpus Inscriptionum Indicarum, Volume 1. Oxford.

Humbach, Helmut (1976). Zwei iranische Namen in indischer Überlieferung. *Die Sprache* 22, 1: 36–39. Wiesbaden.

Ingholt, H. (1957). *Gandharan Art in Pakistan.* New York: Pantheon Books

Jettmar, K. and Thewalt, V. (1991). *Between Gandhāra and the Silk Roads.* Rock-carvings along the Karakorum Highway, Lok Virsa Pakistan. Islamabad.

Kakar, F.D. (1992). The Antiquity of Human Settlement in Quetta Valley. *Pakistan Archaeology*, 27: 1. Islamabad.

Kakar, F.D. (2000). *Cultural Heritage. Balochistan Conservation Strategy.* Background Paper. IUC. The World Conservation Union, Pakistan

Kakar, F.D. (2003). Art of Rock-Shelters of Advanced Palaeolithic Man in Balochistan, Pakistan. Early settlement in Quetta Valley. *South Asian Archaeology*: 312–325.

Kakar, F.D. (2005). Discovery of Upper Palaeolithic Rock Art in Balochistan, Pakistan. *South Asian Archaeology 2003*, edited by Ute Franke-Vogt & Hans-Joachim Weisshaar: 21–25. Aachen

Kakar, F.D. and Khan, M.B. (2008). *Preliminary Report of Archaeological Excavation at Jinnan Wali Ḍheri – Taxila (4th– 8th Century AD). Buddhist Monastic Complex*. Published by the Ministry of Culture, Department of Archaeology and Museums, Government of Pakistan.

Kalhoro, Zulfiqar Ali. (2014). The Discovery of Rock Paintings in Sindh. *Journal of the Pakistan Historical Society*, Volume LXII, No. 3. Karachi.

Khan Khattak, M.H. (1997). *Buner*. The Forgotten Part of Ancient Uddiyana. Karachi.

Khan, B. et al (2003). *Swabi and its Cultural Heritage* (Archaeological Survey and Documentation of Cultural Wealth). Department of Archaeology and Museums, Government of Pakistan.

Khan, F.A. (1969). *Architecture and art treasures in Pakistan*: Prehistoric, protohistoric, Buddhist, and Hindu periods Hardcover – January 1, 1969. Elite Publisher.

Khan, G.R. (2015). *A Catalogue of Sculptures from Butkara III (Swat)*, Khyber Pakhtunkhwa, in the SSAQ Museum of Archaeology and Ethnology, University of Peshwar, volume I. Publication of the Department of Archaeology, University of Peshawar. Peshawar.

Khan, M. A. and Mamood-ul-Hassan (2004). Discovery of Mural Paintings from Jinan Wali Dheri, Taxila Valley. *Journal of Asian Civilizations*, volume XXVII, No.1 (July): 14–23/27. Islamabad.

Khan, M.A. and Mahmood-ul-Hassan (2008). A New Discovery in the Taxila Valley Archaeological Excavations at the Buddhist Monastery of Jinan Wali Dheri. Gandhara. *The Buddhist Heritage of Pakistan. Legends, Monasteries, and Paradise*. Exhibition Catalogue: 302–307. Mainz

Khan, M.A. and Mahmood-ul-Hassan (2011). Archaeological Excavation at Jinnan Wali Ḍheri, Taxila Valley, Pakistan. *Proceedings of International Workshop on Gandharan Cultural Heritage held from 1–3 December in Islamabad*: 29–72. Published by the Taxila Institute of Asian Civilizations, Quaid-i-Azam University, Islamabad. Islamabad.

Khan, S.N. (1995). Report on the Archaeological Survey of Swabi District. *Ancient Pakistan*, volume XI: 75–174. Research Bulletin of the Department of Archaeology, University of Peshawar. Peshawar.

Khan, S.N. (2002). Preliminary Report on Aziz Ḍheri Excavation (First season 1993). *Journal of Asian Civilizations*, volume XXV, No.2, December 2002: 22–45. Islamabad.

Khan, Z.Y. (2017). Recent Discoveries of Painted Rock Shelters in Buner, Khyber Pakhtunkhwa, Pakistan. *Gandharan Studies*, volume 11: 79–96. Published by the Ancient and Medieval Gandhara Research Group. Peshawar.

Kingrani, Aziz (?).Tharia cave paintings in valley of Pallimas, Balochistan, Pakistan. https://www.academia.edu/14070626/

Kintaert, Thomas (2005). The Use of Primary Colours in the Nāṭyaśāstra. Sāmarasya. *Studies in Indian Arts, Philosophy and Interreligious Dialogue - in Honour of Bettina Bäumer*. S. Das, E. Fürlinger (eds.): 245–273. New Delhi.

König, D. 1999. *Die Felsbildstation Hodur*. Materialien zur Archaologie der Nordgebiete Pakistans (MANP), volume 3. Mainz.

Konow, Sten. (1929). Corpus Inscriptionum Indicarum, Volume II, Part 1. Kharoshthi Inscriptions. Oxford.

Lavin, K, Ali, I, Erdosy, G. (1994–1995). Terracotta Human Figurines. *Ancient Pakistan*, volume 10 (special issue), Excavations in the Gomal Valley, Rehman Dheri Report No.2: 82–163. Research Bulletin of the Department of Archaeology, University of Peshawar. Peshawar.

Legge, J. (1998) (Reprint). *A Record of Buddhistic Kingdoms*. Munshiram Manoharlal Publishers Pvt. Ltd. Delhi.

Lerer, A.Judith and Sims-Williams, Nicholas. (2011). *Seals, Sealings and Tokens from Bactria to Gandhara* (4th to 8th Century CE). Wien

Lo Muzio, C. (2008). Remarks on the Paintings from the Buddhist Monastery of Fayaz Tepe (Southern Uzbekistan). *Bulletin of the Asia Institute*, volume 22: 189–206. Michigan.

Lo Muzio, C. (2011/2014). The Legacy of Gandhāra in Central Asian Paintings. In the Shadow of the Golden Age, Art and Identity in Asia from Gandhāra to the Modern Age, *Studies in Asian Art and Culture (SAAC),* volume 1, edited by Hegeward, Julia A.B: 115–136.

Macdonell, A.A. (1909). *A History of Sanskrit Literature.* London

Mahmud, M.K. (1981). The Origin of Fresco Painting in the Province of the Punjab and Its Development During the Mughal Period. Proceedings of the Hijra Celebration Symposium of Islamic Art, Calligraphy, Architecture and Archaeology (March 1–6, 1981, volume II: 529–541.

Marshall, S.J. (1951). *Taxila.* In three volumes. Cambridge University Press.

Marshall, S.J. (1960). The Buddhist Art of Gandhara. Cambridge.

Maxwell, R.E (1882). *Report on Buddhist Researches at Chargul,* by 10th Company Sappers and Miners, from 19th to 21st April 1882, Under Command of Lieutenant C. Maxwell, R.E.

Muhammad, Waqar, Gul, M.M., Ullah, M. and Ghayyur, S. (2018). Excavation at the Buddhist Site of Jinnan Wali Ḍheri – Taxila. A Preliminary Report. *Gandhāran Studies,* vol. 12: 95–104. Published by the Centre for Gandhāran and Buddhist Studies. Peshawar.

Naeem Qazi, M. (1993). Ornamental Motifs found in the architecture at the Buddhist Site of Aziz Ḍheri (Gangho Dher) District Swabi, NWFP, Pakistan. *Pakistan,* No. 27 & 28, Spring & August 1993: 73–78. Peshawar.

Nasim Khan, M. (1994). Rock-Carvings and Inscriptions at Helor Das. *Antiquities of Northern Pakistan* III: 201–211. Mainz.

Nasim Khan, M. (1995). *Thor Nord, Helor Dast Ouest, Helor Das l'Est.* Publication de Trois Sites Archeologique Dans l'Haute Vallée de l'Indus. Ph.D. Thesis submitted to the Universitée de la Sorbonne Nouvellle, Paris III, France.

Nasim Khan, M. (1998). Fauna in the Rock-Carving site of Thor North (Northern Areas of Pakistan). *Ancient Pakistan,* volume XII: 169–176, Research Bulletin of the Department of Archaeology, University of Peshawar. Peshawar.

Nasim Khan, M. (1998a). Rock Art in Pakistan. *The Glory that was Pakistan.* 50 Years of Archaeological Research in Pakistan, 45–48. Peshawar.

Nasim Khan, M. (2000). Buddhist Paintings in Gandhara. Peshawar.

Nasim Khan, M. (2000a). Rock-Carvings at Kinro-Kor: A Prehistoric Site of the Northern Areas of Pakistan. *Lahore Museum Bulletin,* XIII (2), July–December 2000, 1–7. Lahore.

Nasim Khan, M. (2006). *Treasures from Kashmir Smast.* The Earliest Śaiva Monastic Establishment. Peshawar.

Nasim Khan, M. (2007). The Coins Collection in the Royal Asiatic Society. *James Tod's Rajasthan,* edited by Giles Tillotson 80–85. MARG Publication, India.

Nasim Khan, M. (2009). *Kharoṣṭhī Manuscripts from Gandhāra,* second edition. Peshawar

Nasim Khan, M. (2009a). Painted Inscriptions from Kashmir-Smast - Study and Analysis. *Gandhāran Studies,* 3, 127–159, Journal of the Ancient and Medieval Gandhāra Research Group. Peshawar.

Nasim Khan, M. (2010). *The Sacred and the Secular.* Investigating the Unique Stūpa and Settlement site of Aziz Ḍheri, Peshawar Valley, NWFP, Pakistan. In three volumes. Peshawar.

Nasim Khan, M. (2010a). Wima Takto – One or Two. Archaeological and Numismatic Evidence from Gandhara. *Gandhāran Studies,* 4, 11–30. Published by the Ancient and Medieval Gandhāra Research Group. Peshawar.

Nasim Khan, M. (2011). Terracotta Heads from Ancient Gandhara. *Ancient Pakistan,* volume 22: 99–110, Research Bulletin of Archaeology of the Department of Archaeology and Social Anthropology, University of Peshawar. Peshawar.

Nasim Khan, M (2014). The Sacred and the Secular. Excavation at the Buddhist site of Aziz Ḍheri (Preliminary Results of the Field Campaign 2011/2012). *Collection of Papers of 2014 International Symposium on Dazu Studies and the 70th Anniversary Celebrating the First Investigation into Dazu Rock Carvings*: 55–72. Published by the Academy of Dazu Rock carvings, Chongqing, China.

Nasim Khan, M. (2015). Gandhāran Buddhist Paintings and Sculptures. Antiquities from Yakatoot – Peshawar, *Gandhāran Studies*, volume 9: 37–86, Journal of the Ancient and Medieval Gandhāra Research Group. Peshawar.

Nasim Khan, M. (2016). Fresco Paintings from Yakatoot (Peshawar), Gandharan. *Journal of the International Research Institute for Advanced Buddology*, Soka University, volume XIX: 47–56. Publication of the Centre for Advanced Buddhology, Soka University. Tokyo.

Nasim Khan, M. (2018). *Kashmir Smast. The Earliest Seat of Hindu Learning*. In two volumes. Published by the Centre for Gandhāran and Buddhist Studies. Peshawar.

Nasim Khan, M. (2018a). Studying Buddhist sculptures in Context (II). The Case of the Buddhist site of But Kara III, Swat, Gandhara. Study dedicated to Prof. Abdur Rahman. *Gandhāran Studies*, volume 12: 1–94. Published by the Centre for Gandharan and Buddhist Studies. Peshawar.

Nasim Khan, M. (2022). Calamity of Gandhāran Archaeology. Excavation at the Buddhist site of Pataka in the Kabal area of Swat, Pakistan. Dedicated to the Memory of Mr. Asad Ali. https://doi.org/10.13140/RG.2.2.19838.87363

Nasim Khan, M. (2022a). Studying Buddhist Sculptures in Context (IV): The Case of Stūpa No. 7 at Aziz Ḍheri (Gandhāra) and the Concept of Ten Directions of the Universe. Published in *Śāntamatiḥ Manuscripts for Life* — Essays in Memory of Seishi KARASHIMA, *Bibliotheca Philologica et Philosophica Buddhica* XV: 263-275. Publication of the International Research Institute for Advanced Buddhology, Soka University. Tokyo.

Nasim Khan, M. (2023). *Buddhist Period Painted Vessels from Bajaur, Gandhāra*. https://doi.org/10.13140/RG.2.2.15237.01764

Nasim Khan, M. (2024). Gandhāran Buddhism. Stūpa Worship - From Communal to Household Rituals. *Journal of the Institute of Oriental Philosophy, volume 33*: 237–250. Published by Soka University. Tokyo.

Nasim Khan, M., Errington, E. and Cribb, J. (2008). *Coins from Kashmir Smast – New Numismatic Evidence*. Peshawar.

National Cultural Relics Bureau 2003. Peking

Naveed Khan, M. (2017). *Study and Analysis of Fresco Paintings of the Hindu Period Temples at Katas Raj, District Chakwal, Punjab*. M.Phil Thesis submitted to the Department of Archaeology, University of Peshawar.

Nazir Khan, A. (1998). Chaghdo Rock Paintings. *Journal of Asian Civilizations* (Formerly Journal of Central Asia), volume XXI, No. 1, July 1998: 100–104. Islamabad.

Nazir Khan, A., A. Nasir, L.M. Olivieri 7 M. Vitali (1995). The Recent Discovery of Rock Paintings in Swat. A Preliminary Note. *East and West*, Volume 45: 333–353. IsMEO-Rome.

Nishikawa, K. (1994). *Ranigat*. A Buddhist Site in Gandhara, Pakistan, Surveyed 1983–1992. In two volumes. Report of the Kyoto University Scientific Expedition to Gandhara, Edited by Prof. Koji Nishikawar. Kyoto University Press.

Noori, N.A., Olivieri, L.M. and Iori, L. (2019). Fashion Ware in Mes Aynak, Logar: Chronology and comparison (with an Appendix on a single specimen of tulip-bowl from Site MA-100), *Afghanistan*, volume 2.1: 91–114.

Olivieri, L.M. (1998). The Rock-Carvings of Gogdara I (Swat). Documentation and Preliminary Analysis. *East and West*, Volume 48: 57–91. IsIAO-Rome.

Palwal, A. R. (1974). The Harvesting Festivals of the Kalash in the Birir Valley. *Cultures of the Hindukush*. Selected Papers from the Hindu-Kush Cultural Conference held ta Moesgard 1970, edited by Karl Jettmar, Franz Steiner Verlag, Wiesbaden: 93–94.

Pfisterer, Matthias. (2013). *Hunnen in Indien*. Die Münzen der Kidariten und Alchan aus dem Bernischen Historischen Museum und der Sammlung Jean-Pierre Righetti. Wien.

Porada, Edith (1965). *Ancient Iran*. London.

Rahman, A. (1968–1969). Excavation at Damkot. *Ancient Pakistan*, Volume IV: 103–250, Research Bulletin of the Department of Archaeology, University of Peshawar. Peshawar.

Rahman, L. (1993): Thin Sectioned Red Ware Bowels, The So Called Fashion Ware. *Ancient Pakistan*, volume VIII: 209–216, Research Bulletin of the Department of Archaeology, University of Peshawar. Peshawar.

Rahman, L. (1994). Pottery Collection from Jrando Kamar. *Lahore Museum Bulletin*, Volume VII, Centenary issue: 73–76. Lahore.

Rauf, S. (2021). *Documentation and Analysis of Fresco Paintings of the Sikh Period Havelis at Katas Raj, District Chakwal, Punjab.* M.Phil Thesis submitted to the Department of Archaeology, University of Peshawar.

Rehman, S. (1996). The Archaeological Exploration in Buner. *Archaeological Reconnaissance in Gandhara*, pp. 1–79. Publication of the Federal Department of Archaeology and Museums, Government of Pakistan.

Rockhill, W. (1884). *The life of the Buddha and the early history of his order*.

Sadakane, Keiji (1992). The Genesis of Buddhist Paintings in Ancient India and its Early Development –With Special Reference to the Relationship with the Buddhist Communities to Paintings in Early Time. *Aesthetics*, Number 5 (1992): 90–103. Published by the Japanese Society for Aesthetics.

Salomon, R. (1996). *Ancient Buddhist Scrolls from Gandhara.* Seatle: University of Washington.

Samad, A. & Khan, Z. H. (2016). Archaeological Survey of District Buner: Preliminary Report. *Frontier Archaeology*, Volume 6: 1–74. Peshawar.

Samad, A. et al (2021). *Abba Sahib Cheena.* Archaeological Excavation 2020–2021. Preliminary Report. Published by the Directorate of Archaeology and Museums Government of Khyber Pakhtunkhwa, Peshawar.

Sardar, B. (2005). *Buddhist Rock Carvings in the Swat Valley.* National Fund for Cultural Heritage, Ministry of Cultures, sports and Youth Affairs, Government of Pakistan. Islamabad.

Sardar, B. (2016). Painted Rock Shelter in Murghazar Sub Valley of Swat. *Journal of Social Sciences and Humanities:* Volume 24, Number 1, Spring 2016: 125–141. Islamabad.

Sarianidi, V. (1985). *Bactrian Gold*. From the Excavations of the Tillya-Tepe Necropolis in Northern Afghanistan. Translated from the Russian Shkarovsky-Raffé Arthur. Aurora Art Publishers. Leningrad.

Schmitt, E. (1971). *Ornament in der Gandharakunst und rezenten Volkskusnt im Hindukush und Karakorum*, Dissetationsreihe des Südasiens-Instituts der Universität Heidelberg. In Kommission bei Otto Harrassowitz, Wiesbaden.

Siiger, Halfdan (1974). The Joshi of the Kalash. Main Traits of the Spring Festival ta Balanguru in 1948. *Cultures of the Hindukush.* Selected Papers from the Hindu-Kush Cultural Conference held ta Moesgard 1970, edited by Karl Jettmar, Franz Steiner Verlag, Wiesbaden: 87–92.

Singh, Madanjeet. (1965). *The Cave Paintings of Ajanta.* Thames and Hudson. London

Stein, A. (1929). *On Alexander's Track to the Indus. Personal Narrative of Explorations on the North-West Frontier of India.* London.

Stein, A. (1930). An Archaeological Tour in Upper Swat and Adjacent Hill Tracts. *Memoirs of the Archaeological Survey of India,* No.42. Calcutta.

Suleman Khan (2018). A Preliminary note on Fresh Archaeological Excavation at Jinnan Wali Ḍheri, Taxila Valley, Pakistan. *Gandhāran Studies*, Volume 12: 27–36. Publication of the Centre for Gandhāran and Buddhist Studies. Peshawar.

Tanabe, Katsumi. (2007). *Gandhara Art from the Hirayama Collection.* Kodansha.

Taniguchi, Yoko and Cotte, Marin (2022). *The Wall Paintings of Bamiyan, Afghanistan. Technology and Materials.* Archetype Publications Ltd. UK

Tanveer, T. (2006). Recently Discovered Buddhist Paintings From Taxila (Pakistan): A Stylistic Analysis. *Ancient Pakistan*, Volume 17: 19–28. Research Bulletin of the Department of Archaeology, University of Peshawar. Peshawar.

Tissot, Francine (2003). Le Bouddhisme en Afghanistan. *De l'Indus à. Archéologie de l'Asie Centrale.* Catalogue de l-Exposition. Édité par Osmund Bopearachchi et al., pp. 281–286. Lattes

Tucci, G. (1958). Preliminary Report on an archaeological survey in Swat: 279–328. *East and West*, Volume 9. IsMEO, Roma.

Vassal, V. (2021 or 2022). La fleur de lotus ou Nelumbo nucifera dans les mosaïques grécoromaines Greko-Romen Mozaiklerinde Lotus Çiçeği veya Nelumbo Nucifera. JMR 14, 2021 341–353. https://doi.org/10.26658/jmr.1014577

Vialou, D. (1998). *L'art des grottes*, editions Scala, Paris.
Watter, T. (1904–1905). *On Yan Chwang's Travels in India* (in 2 volumes Bound in 1). Royal Asiatic Society London, UK. Reprinted in 2004. Dehli
Wheeler, S.M. (1960). *The Cambridge History of India. Supplementary volume – The Indus Valley Civilization*. Cambridge.
Williams, P. (1989). *Mahayana Buddhism*. The Doctrinal Foundations. London
Yunusova, N.Z. (1997). Tajik Skull Cap. *Journal of central Asia*, volume XX, No.1. July 1997: 1–27. Biannual Journal of International Association of the Study of the Cultures of Central Asia.
Zar Ḍheri Archaeological Excavation of an Ancient Buddhist Site in Pakistan. Tokyo National Museum Archaeological Mission to Pakistan.
Zin, Monika. (2013a). The Identification of Kizil Paintings VI. *Indo-Asiatische Zeitschrift. Mitteilungen der Gesellschaft für indo-asiatische Kunst*, 17. 2013: 5–15.
Zin, Monika. (2013b). "Buddhist Narrative Depictions in Gandhāra, Gandhāra and Kucha – Similarities and Differences that Favour a Theory about a Lost 'Gandhāran School of Paintings'". *Buddhism and Art in Gandhāra and Kucha. Buddhist Culture Along the Silk Road: Gandhāra, Kucha, and Turfan, Section I*. The Comprehensive Data Collection of Gandhāran Art and its Integrated Study Grants-in-aid for Scientific Research (A) 20242003, Japan Society for the Promotion of Science. Edited by MIYAJI Akira: 35–66. Ryukoku University.
Zwalf, W. (1996). *A Catalogue of the Gandhāra Sculpture in the British Museum*. In two volumes. Cambridge University Press.

Index

M. Nasim Khan, *Gandhāran School of Buddhist Paintings*,
https://doi.org/10.1007/978-981-96-9310-8